MODERN SCANDINAVIAN POETRY

THE PANORAMA OF POETRY 1900 – 1975
in Kalâtdlit-nunat (Greenland), Iceland, The Faroe Islands,
Denmark, Saame Poetry, Norway,
Sweden, and Finland

English versions
by
Martin Allwood, Wystan Hugh Auden, Paul Britten Austin,
Frederic Fleisher, Thord Fredenholm, Robin Fulton,
Keth Laycock, Robert Lyng, and others

Introductions
by
Kristinn Jóhannesson, Inge Knutsson, Kai Laitinen,
Finn Stein Larsen, Helmer Lång, Israel Ruong,
and Eilif Straume

GENERAL EDITOR
Martin Allwood

A NEW DIRECTIONS BOOK

Cover vignette by Igor Jańczuk

Library of Congress Cataloging in Publication Data
Main entry under title:

MODERN SCANDINAVIAN POETRY
(A New Directions Book)
   Bibliography: p.
   1. Scandinavian poetry — 20th century — Translations into English.
2. English poetry — Translations from Scandinavian languages.
I. Allwood, Martin Samuel, 1916 —

PT 7093.M6 1982   839'.5   81— 38320

ISBN 0—8112—0818—4   AACR2

Copyright © 1982 by Martin Allwood

Composed in Sweden and printed in Italy
First published clothbound by New Directions in 1982.
Published simultaneously in Canada by George J. McLeod, Ltd., Toronto

New Directions Books are published for James Laughlin by New Directions Publishing Corporation, 80 Eighth Avenue, New York 10011.

This book has been published in collaboration with the Anglo-American Center, 565 00 Mullsjö, Sweden. The publication would not have been possible without grants from the following institutions:

Nordiska Kulturfonden

Svenska Institutet

Ministeriet for Kulturelle Anliggender, København

Det Kgl. Utenriksdepartement, Oslo

Undervisningsministeriet, Helsingfors

*

The manuscript for this volume was closed in November, 1977. When relevant information beyond this date could be included without too great changes, it was included. — British orthography has been preserved in original British translations, American orthography in American translations.

*

A Note
on the names of the Scandinavian countries.

The native names of the Scandinavian countries are:
Iceland — *Island;* The Faroe Islands — *Føroyar;* Denmark — *Danmark;* Norway — *Norge;* Sweden — *Sverige;* Finland — *Finland* or *Suomi* (the country is bilingual).
After the completion of the manuscript for this book a spelling reform has changed the name of Greenland (in Danish *Grønland)* from *Kalâtdlit-nunat* to *Kalaallit Nunaat.*
The Scandinavians usually refer to their part of the world as *Norc n* (The North). The word *Skandinavien* (Scandinavia) is, however, also used.

*

For various reasons, a few poets who were invited to contribute to this anthology declined to participate:

Per Lange, Denmark
Artur Lundkvist, Sweden
Maria Wine, Sweden
Ragnar Jändel's heirs, Sweden
Ruben Nilson's heirs, Sweden

ASSISTANT EDITORS AND ADVISORS

Kalâtdlit-nunat (Greenland)

The General Editor takes responsibility for the poems included.

The Faroe Islands

The General Editor wishes to express his sincere gratitude to William Heinesen and Inge Knutsson for their collaboration on this section of the book.

Iceland

Magnús Arnason gave me much help with the Icelandic part of ''20th Century Scandinavian Poetry'' (1950), the forerunner of the present anthology. Many of his views were still valid in 1977, when the manuscript of this volume was closed. Robin Fulton and Halldór Pálsson at one point helped me. Alan Boucher kindly let me profit by his experience. But in the later phases of the work I have been mainly assisted by Inge Knutsson and Sigurdur A. Magnússon. I owe a very special debt of gratitude to Sigurdur, whose energetic labors made it easy for me to conclude the work on Iceland.

Denmark

Work on the Danish part of the anthology was not at all times easy. I want to thank Bent Irve for his kind and highly competent contribution to a solution of the Danish problems. When Bent was unable to continue as Danish advisor, Erik Stinus generously stepped in to complete the work.

Other Danish friends who have contributed good advice are Uffe Harder and Jørgen Sonne.

Saame Poetry

Within the geographical area of this anthology, the Saame (Lapp) people live in the northernmost parts of Norway, Sweden, and Finland. Unfortunately, it was not possible to make a systematic presentation of Saame poetry in the 20th century; we can only show a few samples. Israel Ruong, the learned expert on Saame culture, helped me to find my way. Bo Lundmark's Swedish translations inspired me to attempt the English versions.

Norway

Thanks to the generous and competent assistance of my principal Norwegian advisor, Øistein Parmann, work on the Norwegian part of the anthology never ran into serious difficulties. We also received valuable ideas from Asbjørn Aarnes and Åse-Marie Nesse, and I thank them both cordially for their assistance.

Sweden

During the entire work on the Swedish section of the anthology I have had the benefit and pleasure of the learned and sensitive advice of Helmer Lång, one of the foremost knowers of Swedish literature today. Robert Lyng also gave me valuable advice on Sweden and other sections of the book.

Finland

Because of my ignorance of the Finnish language I was in special need of help and advice as regards the Finno-Finnish section. I was fortunate in receiving most competent aid from Tuomas Anhava and Kai Laitinen. I also want to direct a special word of thanks to Ulla Mäkinen and Tove Skutnabb-Kangas for their patient and never-tiring help with the Finnish part of the book. Philip Binham pitched in, and many of the authors themselves helped to improve the English versions.

In the Swedish-language section I am greatly indebted to Erika Lyly, Thomas Warburton, and Lars Huldén for advice and criticism.

The secretaries of the two Finnish authors' associations, Pirkko Pesola and Kerstin Nyquist, helped me throughout the work.

The General Editor

THE TRANSLATORS

Some 90 translators have collaborated to make this anthology possible. It was the General Editor's aim to present not only samples of the best Scandinavian poetry, but also the best translators. Since it was often impossible to find a translator for a particular poet, too great a share of the translations often fell to the chief translator.

I have collaborated for almost fifty years with Keth Laycock in the task of translating Scandinavian poetry into English, and making the best in English and American poetry known in Sweden — a lifetime of friendship in the service of mutual literary comprehension.

Among the translators special mention must be made of Robert Lyng, who not only collaborated with the chief translator in the poems signed R.L., but also carefully checked a considerable number of the other translations.

I also wish to mention Ulla Mäkinen, Tove Skutnabb-Kangas, Richard Impola, and Philip Binham, without whose patient labor and ever-ready assistance the Finno-Finnish section could not have been completed.

Inge Knutsson generously made his brilliant Swedish translations of the poetry of the Faroe Islands available as a starting-point for the English versions, thereby making this interesting section possible.

Finally I wish to mention with a veteran translator's deep respect Helen Asbury, Thord Fredenholm, and Paul Britten Austin for their superb and singable renderings of the extremely difficult songs of e.g. Birger Sjöberg, Evert Taube, E.A. Karlfeldt, and Nils Ferlin.

All the English translations in this book were submitted to the authors or their legal heirs for criticism and approval prior to publication. Changes were often made at the suggestion of the author, and in some cases entirely new poems were substituted. The editors wish to thank all the authors and their representatives for their collaboration.

For financial reasons, the final version of the book had to be somewhat abbreviated The editors regret this necessary omission of a few poems.

The introductory essays were translated into English by the General Editor.

The General Editor

THE TRANSLATORS

M.A.	Martin Allwood, Great Britain and Sweden
C.A.	Carl Anderson, U.S.A.
N.J.A	Nils J. Anderson, U.S.A.
M.A.A.	Magnús A.Arnason, Iceland
H.A.	Helen Asbury, U.S.A.
W.H.A.	Wystan Hugh Auden, Great Britain and U.S.A.
J.A.	Joseph Auslander, U.S.A.
P.B.A.	Paul Britten Austin, Great Britain
G.B.	Gerry Balding, Tasmania
Gab.B.	Gabrielle Barfoot, Northern Ireland
R.B.	Ronald Bates, U.S.A.
P.B.	Philip Binham, Great Britain and Finland
P.Bj.	Páll Bjarnason, U.S.A.
A.B.	Alan Boucher, U.S.A.
E.B.	Emil Boyson, Norway
M.B.	Mia Berner, Norway and Sweden
(B.C.)	Bo Carpelan, Finland
N.C.	Nadia Christensen, U.S.A.
R.C.	Roger Connah, Great Britain
G.D.	Glenn Doyle, U.S.A.
G.Dz.	Grazyna Dziersko, Poland
L.E.	Lennart Edberg, Sweden
C.E.	Cate Ewing, U.S.A.
P.F.	Peter Farmer, Great Britain
M.F.	Mike Fedullo, U.S.A.
F.F.	Frederic Fleisher, U.S.A. and Sweden
L.F.	Lars Forssell, Sweden
T.F.	Thord Fredenholm, U.S.A.
R.F.	Robin Fulton, Great Britain

G.M.G.	G.M. Gathorne-Hardy, Great Britain
K.H.	Kerstin Hane-Forssell, Sweden
H.P.H.	Harold P. Hanson, U.S.A.
E.H.	Einar Haugen, U.S.A.
P.H.	Piet Hein, Denmark
R.S.H.	Robert Silliman Hillyer, U.S.A.
J.H.	John Hollander, U.S.A.
A.H.	Anselm Hollo, Finland and U.S.A.
B.H.	.Birgitta Hylin, Sweden
R̄.I.	Richard Impola, U.S.A.
S.J.	Skuli Johnson, U.S.A.
C.J.	Crosby Jones, Great Britain
G.K.	Grant Keener, U.S.A.
R.P.K.	Robert Prescott Keigwin, Great Britain
C.K.	Carl King, U.S.A.
W.K.	Watson Kirkconnell, Canada
(I.K.)	Inge Knutsson, Sweden
K.K.	Knut Kolsrud, Norway
B.K.-A.	Binnie Kristal-Andersson, U.S.A. and Sweden
F.L.	Fred Lane, Great Britain
K.L.	Keth Laycock, Great Britain
Ri.L.	Rika Lesser, U.S.A.
C.D.L.	C.D.Locock, Great Britain
(B.L.)	Bo Lundmark, Sweden
R.L.	Robert Lyng, U.S.A. and Holland
V.M.	Verne Moberg, U.S.A.
K.M.	Knud Mogensen, Denmark
L.A.M.	Louis A. Muinzer, Great Britain
(U.M.)	Ulla Mäkinen, Finland and Sweden
C.N.	Carl Nesjar, Norway and U.S.A.
N.O.	Nancy Ogle, U.S.A.
K.O.	Karl Olson, U.S.A.
H.P.	Hermann Pálsson, Iceland and Great Britain
F.R.	Forest Redding, U.S.A.
C.R.	Charles Richards, Great Britain and Sweden
M.R.	Muriel Rukeyser, U.S.A.
(I.R.)	Israel Ruong, Sweden
Y.S.	Yvonne Luttrop Sandstroem, U.S.A.
H.D.S.	Helen D. Sarvig, U.S.A. and Denmark
C.S.	Caroline Schleef, U.S.A.
(S.v.S.)	Solveig von Schoultz, Finland
S.S.	Stephen Schwartz, U.S.A.
G.S.	G. Singh, India and Great Britain

L.S.	Leif Sjöberg, Sweden and U.S.A.
(T.S.K.)	Tove Skutnabb-Kangas, Finland
B.S.	Bernard Spivack, U.S.A.
J.S.	John Stone, Great Britain
C.W.S.	Charles Wharton Stork, U.S.A.
N.B.S.	Nils-Börje Stormbom, Finland.
B.Sw.	Birgit Swenson, U.S.A.
M.Sw.	May Swenson, U.S.A.
C.E.T.	Cid Erik Tallqvist, Finland
(W.Th.)	W. Thalbitzer, Denmark
A.T.	Anthony Thompson, Great Britain
K.T.	Ken Tindall, U.S.A.
J.T.	Jerry Turpin, U.S.A.
R.B.V.	Richard Beckman Vowles, U.S.A.
E.W.	Erik Wahlgren, U.S.A.
H.W.	Helge Westermann, Denmark and U.S.A.
I.W.A.	Inga Wilhelmsen Allwood, Norway and Sweden

CONTENTS

KALATDLIT-NUNAT (GREENLAND)

ICELAND

14

THE FAROE ISLANDS

17

NORWAY

FINLAND — SUOMI

In the Swedish language

27

29

SUGGESTIONS FOR FURTHER READING

KALATDLIT— NUNAT

(GREENLAND)

HENRIK LUND (INDALERAQ) (1875 — 1948)

Nunarput — Our country

O, ancient our country! O, beacon of ice!
With glittering snowlocks round your forehead,
our faithful old mother, who bore us in your arms
and promised us the prey from mighty waters.

Like wild, wayward children we grew on your earth,
grew up close to you here in your mountains.
Our name is Kalatdlit, engravéd in our lore,
a worthy name before your hoary features.

While yet we were nourished by riches from you
we longed to make progress in the new world.
Renewing the bonds that connect us with the past
now onward we will move toward distant futures!

Ye aged, great nations, stretch forward your hand,
now slowly we wish to follow after.
We yearn to be using our language and thought
in books and writing and the works of culture.

Impossible now to be resting in peace —
Kalatdlit, arise, and meet the new world!
As free men we henceforward claim our sacred right.
Begin to have new faith in Greenland's power!

(W.Th.) M.A.

VILLADS VILLADSEN (1916 —)

Aviâja and his family

*When the husband had been killed, his wife decided to follow him with
his children — down to the place where no hunger is felt. She does this*

*out of despair because the family has lost its breadwinner. Before she
and her children leapt into the water she said to her children:*

"My beloved children, my jewels!
Today is the very last day
that we are among the living on this earth,
the last day that we suffer from hunger!
The time of our starving is past,
we will soon be on our way down there.
Come now, we are going down to Father,
let's leap into the water!"
— — —
All moved to the edge of the rock
to throw themselves into the water.
They leapt into the waves
one after the other, — the oldest first.
One could just catch a glimpse of the children's hair in the waves.
Then they were gone again.
The dead ones, when the ocean swallowed them —
they were never seen again.

Two of the children were seized with panic,
they did not want to move.
They burst into tears, they wanted to escape,
they were afraid of the huge waves.
The mother took her frightened children into her arms
and spoke lovingly to them — for the last time —
and helped them to leap into the water.

The woman looked a little frightened,
like a dog from whom you have taken the young.
She went up to the house
as if she were looking for something.
Shortly afterwards she went down again
and stood on a precipitous cliff.
Then she sat down with her back to the sea.

Her rich hair blew out
when the wind touched it.
The waves surged up against the face of the cliff
as if they would reach for her hair.
The woman looked as if she were asleep.
To her the lapping of the waves was like an incantation.
She smiled. What could she have seen?
No one knows.

She let herself fall backwards deliberately
as if she were just dreaming.
Now her soul went down,
back to her ancestors.
Life was extinguished in the mother and the children

but in reality it merely moved to another place.
Life flares up again ever more powerfully
down there where no one feels hunger.

M.A.

ARKALUK LYNGE

This is our country
(Tourist publicity)

Is there anything to brag about?
Look how majestic and beautiful the landscape is,
look at the ice-capped mountains,
look at the tupilakkas,
look at the Greenlanders,
smiling human beings
(turn your face away) with their hands in their pockets,
look at the children
the cute little tots
(don't look at) their ragged clothes.

Is there anything to brag about?
Look at the houses
they look like little models
or play houses
but they are real homes

Friday (forget it)
beer in one hand
in the other a child
— a crying child.
Look at our country
with Danes
to look up to.
They walk on the planks
on the cement
— whom do they help?
Look at the inland ice of our country
melting in whiskey.

Our country is really great

M.A.

MALIK

restlessness

restless
I'm going out even if it's pouring with rain

because I can't stand being in here
I'm going out into the rain

away from
these big houses
and these strange people
the rain
won't stop me

if I were a necromancer I would have flown away
I would have moved
I would have been spirited away

ájái ja ái ájâ â
ájái ja ái ájâ â
ája iarra ájâ â
ája iarra ájâ â

surely you can understand
that I'm restless

I'm going out into the rain

M.A.

ICELAND

ICELAND

At the beginning of the 20th century Iceland was still a part of the Danish national state, and Icelandic society for the most part showed the same features as during the previous centuries. Icelandic society was a society of farmers and fishermen, primitive, and with few centers of population. At the turn of the century about 20% of the inhabitants were found in towns.

The struggle for independence of the Icelandic nation was mirrored in its literature. The poets wrote about their native country, and its past, and, hopefully, future greatness. From the very first Icelandic poetry was cast in strict forms. Alliteration and final rhymes were a heritage from Edda poetry and Skaldic verse, and gradually poetry was enriched with new types of poetic form which, on the whole, were a continuation of the old Nordic rules. This Icelandic dependence on form is alive even today, but many authors have cleared a path of their own out of this undergrowth of formal rules — regarded by some readers (and writers) as impenetrable — and begun to write in free verse.

The 20th century arrived as a slow dawn. In 1904 a certain degree of self-government was granted to Iceland, with an Icelandic Prime Minister living at Reykjavík (the first person to occupy this post was the eminent poet Hannes Hafstein, one of the pioneers of realism in Iceland) and in the wake of this change followed certain improvements in the labor market, and in the cultural life of the island. Iceland got her own university in 1911, and an Icelandic cargo shipping company was formed in 1914. These two events may symbolize the increased degree of independence. One transfers academic training to the country, the other gives to the Icelanders control of commercial transportation. Iceland had been without ocean plying ships since the 13th century, a fact of capital importance to an island nation. The most important event, however, occurs in 1918, when Iceland becomes an independent country in personal union with Denmark.

One of the poets at this early dawn is *Sigurdur Sigurdsson* (debut in 1906), a neo-Romantic who united the 19th century with the new day. Without relaxing his demands for strict observance of the formal rules he moves poetry closer to the simple spoken language. The debut of *Örn Arnarson* (pseudonym for Magnús Stefánson) was not until 1924, but he is also a symbol of the morning atmosphere that prevailed among

41

the Icelandic people. Much of his poetry deals with the life and fate of the fisherman.

At the beginning of Icelandic independence — which coincides with the end of World War I — new poets appear with great personal openness, popular simplicity, and a freer poetic form. One of them, *David Stefánsson* (debut in 1919) took his point of departure in the earlier folk poetry, and wrote of the nostalgia of youth and its difficult emotions. *Tómas Gudmundsson* (debut 1925) is the first poet to sing of the ebullient beauty of the young capital, Reykjavík. *Jóhannes úr Kötlum* (debut 1926) is at first a fiery romantic soul with ardent patriotic poetry. His production embraces everything from classical, formally bound poetry to the free verse of the post-war period.

In the 1930s the depression came to Iceland and taught the people a new truth. Romantic poets like Jóhannes úr Kötlum abandon dreaming for socialist verse with a critique of society, but Tómas Gudmundsson locks his doors and lives on in the dream of the beautiful world. *Halldór Laxness* is at this time moving in the direction of the socialist novel, but in 1930 publishes a volume of poetry which puzzled many readers with its burlesque and futuristic content. *Steinn Steinarr* (pseudonym for Adalsteinn Kristmundsson, debut 1934) continues in the same direction and becomes one of the prophets of modernism in poetry with his volume Tíminn og vatnid (Time and water) 1948. But the poet who completely breaks with the mass of formal rules is *Jón úr Vör* (debut 1937) with the epoch-making work Thorpid (The fishing village) 1946, a cycle of poems which deals with the lives and destinies of the people in a small, genuine fishing village in West Iceland.

The growing understanding of the connection between the problems of Iceland and the larger international problems — which had come in the 1930s — now becomes an important factor in Icelandic poetry. *Gudmundur Bödvarsson* (debut 1936) is a good example of this. And beside an impressive poetic production, and his full-time work as a farmer, he also succeeded in giving the Icelanders a translation of Dante.

Snorri Hjartarson (debut 1944) strikes his own path, and attempts to unite the old tradition of writing with the new formlessness. His past experiences as a painter left deep traces in his imagery and in the composition of his poems.

Kristján frá Djúpalœk (debut 1943), known among other things for his popular and rather humorous poetry in the style of the popular hit, has gradually become more and more interested in mysticism. He adheres to traditional poetic forms.

In the early 1940s Iceland is drawn into world politics. The country is occupied by the British in 1940, becomes an independent republic in 1944, enters NATO in 1949. The social structure changes rapidly, the towns grow, and new social patterns are formed. By 1950 more than 70% of the population live in built-up areas. The "big world" has suddenly moved into Iceland. The cold war, and the question of the presence of American defense forces at Keflavík color much of the post-war cultural debate. The writers are often classified as "right" or "left".

Stefán Hördur Grímsson (debut 1946), *Hannes Sigfússon* (debut 1949), *Einar Bragi* (debut 1950), *Sigfús Dadason* (debut 1951), and *Jón Oskar* (debut 1953) all belong to the so-called "atomic poets" writing in free verse; politically they represent various degrees of leftism. *Jóhann*

Hjalmarsson (debut 1956) and *Matthías Johannessen* (debut 1958) are among the younger poets of this generation who belong to the "right", i.e. represent the non-socialists. The poetry of Jóhann Hjalmarsson sometimes contains surrealistic traits, and Matthías Johannessen works with bold and often disconnected images and thoughts. He also continues Tómas Gudmundsson's songs in praise of the capital.

Sigurdui A. Magnússon (debut 1958) is an extremely active cultural worker with leanings toward the patriotic-radical side. He has, among other things, translated modern Greek literature into Icelandic.

As distinct from these poets, who all work largely without rhymes and alliteration, *Hannes Pétursson* (debut 1955) uses these poetic elements in a highly personal way, which brings Snorri Hjartarson to mind. *Thorsteinn frá Hamri* (debut 1958), on the other hand, finds materials for his poetry in folk tales. In his verse he often draws complicated images, using the classical elements of poetry in his own manner.

The youngest generation of Icelandic poets is here represented by *Nína Björk Arnadóttir* (debut 1965), and *Thurídur Gudmundsdóttir* (debut 1969). Both have entirely abandoned the old tradition of form and write free verse with short, introverted scenes rich in imagery.

This short introduction can obviously not give a detailed picture of Icelandic poetry in this century. For that much more space would be needed, and more poets. Nor has any attempt been made to evaluate the authors, or to discuss their mutual relations. The aim of this collection is to awaken the reader's interest, and thereby to open the door for more extensive reading.

Kristinn Jóhannesson
Göteborg
Sweden

SIGURDUR SIGURDSSON (1879 — 1939)

Christmas Eve

Children's eve — with royal lights and Christmas tree.
A peaceful snooze in church on mother's knee.
No Christmas cat! But a little cart to draw,
and a little rubber bird to squeeze at: Aw, aw, aw!

Children's eve — that all too soon must take to flight.
For after play and laughter comes "Good-night!"
Mama brings a piece of bread that heals all sorrow,
and the child sleeps, slice in hand, until tomorrow.

Grown-ups' eve — but varied store the years have brought.
Old memories come beating in on waves of thought.
Old folks' eve — from stooping heads frost melts away,
and haloed light shines over little children's play.

W.K.

MAGNUS STEFANSSON (ÖRN ARNARSON) (1884 — 1942)

Chickens

In a chicken coop some chickens
resided neat and trim.
The cock was their head and master,
and the hens believed in him.

They lived in congenial spirit
according to chicken law,
till presently one of the old hens
developed a serious flaw.

She'd hop to the heap of rubbish
above the rest of the flock
and stretch her neck with great effort
trying to be a cock.

The cock then swore in silence —
but what can he do, poor bloke,
if a hen-house suffragette
demands her right to croak?

M.A.A.

The journey

Starting forth on Fate's long journey,
fired with hope, the eager lad.
Brand new shoes and some provisions
served his needs and made him glad.
But some wonder-wine of courage
was the best thing that he had.

Having reached life's hilly stages,
hemmed about with sleet and snow,
on a drift the swain now seated,
says in accents weak abd low:
"Lunch kit empty, outworn shoes;
and the road gets worse, I know."

"Barefoot and without provisions
it is hard to trudge the snow.
Yet were anything in the bottle
I'd bestir myself and go.
Heaven is now my hope and stay.
Hast Thou not, O Lord, I pray
a drop to fill that flask of mine?
I feel I'm through without the wine."

— Utter silence everywhere!
Is there prohibition there?

P.Bj.

The hussy

Your flaming fires of youth and beauty
when once burnt out, you can't renew.
Faded cheeks and frozen heartstrings
and feet rheumatic wait for you.

Although you buy the red of roses
to rouge your cheeks, it does no good.

No man will ever turn towards you
nor ever trust your maidenhood.

Discard this vain and stupid tinsel!
Youth has never known rebirth.
Your soul becomes the whore of Satan,
your sinful flesh but clay and earth.

M.A.A.

DAVID STEFANSSON (1895 — 1964)

The shadow

Like God's own heart
I'm pure tonight,
fair as his wishes all
and free as His might.

All men would I gladden,
for all I would smart:
I'm the shade of the love in
a woman's heart.

S.J.

JOHANNES úr KÖTLUM (1899 — 1972)

Prayer

The bombs are falling, breaking children's heads.
The old fall, burning without moan or sound.
Your brother's bride is shattered into bits,
your mother's breast becomes an open wound.

Where are they now, our blissful odes to the sun,
sympathy, wit, and dignity of the White?
Must I see him a villainous troll again,
must I gaze in silence upon his blight?

Where can one flee when all is terror and fright
— nothing to hope for except blood and tears —
while the faint music of a singer's lyre
drowns in the sickly yells of lies and fears?

Flower of field, and beast that we have tamed,
mysterious moor and sun-bathed fell and mart:
listen now, while the man of weapons dies,
to your friend's speech, the tired call of the heart.

Nature, the cradle of all and grave of all:
rejuvenate and save my soul from strife,
give me again my joy, my hope, my song,
give me again my faith in human life.

M.A.A.

TOMAS GUDMUNDSSON (1901 —)

The harbor

The flags of all the foreign nations
and ships here keep their tryst,
the proud wave-riders who beat the ocean
and conquered storm and mist.
With open arms the harbor receives them
and gives them shelter and lee;
for ships are the guests of every harbor,
their home the infinite sea.

The blood in your veins here surges most briskly,
O city, rising, young!
From here the jubilant noise and bustle
upon your streets are flung:
the speeding lorries, the clattering wagons,
the ships all hooting loud,
the odour of tar, the asphalt, the sunshine,
the swarming busy crowd.

And ships are coming and ships are hooting
and ships all go their way.
The youth with eyes of yearning and dreaming
after them stares all day.
He hears the songs of distant harbors,
his soul begins to roam:
Russia, Asia, England, China,
Africa, Spain and Rome —

Above the traffic of pier and harbour,
high above ships and boats
in sphinx-like mystery, mosque demeanour
the mighty coal crane gloats.
It shovels coals, it shovels coals
from early morning to night,
its voice across town and bridge carries
a message new and bright.

It penetrates the din of traffic,
it glides through the lorries' throng.
Wondering, the coal-heavers listen
to the mighty coal-crane's song.

Some incident struck a sudden glimmer
in eyes that are cold and tired.
— The *Long Splice* is coming, rounding the headland.
The *Bothnia* leaves tonight.

M.A.A.

HALLDOR LAXNESS (1902 —)

She was all that you loved

She was all that you loved and cherished,
all that you yearned for and dreamed.
You sang her in verse all your wisdom,
you taught her all you esteemed.

I found in your heart's coverts hidden
the budding of truth and sight,
the emblem of all that is highest
in earthly life and light.

And guiltless we lived them together,
those truths that the world unite:
from drama of pleasures inconstant
to saintly sins of delight.

M.A.A.

GUDMUNDUR BÖDVARSSON (1904 — 1974)

Brother

Flakes over grave and cairn
driving inland,
solitary wooden crosses
shaking with age.
I bade the boisterous wind
lower its voice a little.
— You were the quietest of men,
my brother and friend.

It there became clear
to me in the graveyard left,
tracing an old acquaintance
in mind's dark crook and cranny,
how loving and kind
was the wordless reticent gift,
never remarked
and never mentioned by any.

49

How feeble our tardy thanks
sink in the silence
recited like an excuse
to a vanished friend.
How far we stand from that hour
when parting once
we pressed a stiffened hand
at the end.

A.B.

SNORRI HJARTARSON (1906 —)

The roads are waiting deserted

The roads are waiting deserted in the forest
for your light feet
the wind is waiting quietly in the dark
for your blonde locks
the brook is waiting silently
for your hot lips
the grass is waiting wet with dew
and the birds are silent in the trees

our eyes meet

between us fly black thrushes
with the glitter of the sun on their wings

(I.K.) M.A.

The days have come

The days have come
of which you say: they do not please me

The sunshine the grass
the song in the trees grow pale

Rain darkens the day
and mist enshrouds the road to the inn

No one travels with you
and you eat your bread and wine alone

In your bed you hear
the footsteps of sleep approach and fade

What little you possess
can be taken away: it was given for nothing

For nothing for nothing mutters the night
and the Pleiades behind the clouds

Pray to the angel and to the seven stars:
Strike, O strike my dull eyes with light!

                    (I.K.) M.A. R.L.

STEINN STEINARR (1908 — 1958)

            Children at play

In laughing sunshine
            I sat and gazed
at sunburnt faces and naked feet.

My mind bore the shadows
of nights full of sleet;
my hand was heavy and cold.

Once there was a man
            in an unknown land.

A handful of sand.

And all is told.

                    M.A.A.

            Marble

This Hellenic splendour,
this Roman glory
is the dust
upon my surface.

                    M.A.A.

            Verdun

It happened here one bright and sunny May day
the mighty secret which no man has guessed,
and ever since by grief and anguish stricken
wanders my soul, and searches without rest.

Comes spring again with scent of snow-white flowers
and sparkling radiance round dale and fell.
My soul alone through haunts of past scenes wanders.
O seek with me! For it was I who fell.
                    M.A.A.

                                            51

Sea

I have wandered along sun-warmed beaches.
And the roar from strange seas
mingled with the murmur of my blood.

I have left havens in every land
and flowed in the wake of every tide.

And at the bottom of the immeasurable depth
    I've buried my will my awareness
and I no longer know
    if the sea is myself
or myself the sea.

H.P.   R.F.

A poem about Christ

It was evening.
We were sitting in the garden,
two urchins.
And we were watching the sun
disappear
behind the mountains
in the far distance.
It's so strange, you feel,
when you are young,
for the sun to disappear
from the sky
beyond distant mountains
— just as if a stranger's hand
had snatched away
your toys.

And we
who did not see the evening
from the safety of the sun-white day
sat speechless and wondering
facing a black wall
we couldn't climb over
— the night.
And we were sitting in the garden
two urchins.
It was then
you told me your secret
the great secret
no one before
had an inkling of.
It was so beautiful
and mysterious,
the most beautiful secret in the world.

and we sat whispering
to each other
amazing
winged words
about the sun
that would shine high in the sky
bigger and brighter
than ever before,
and about men
who would be so good to the children.
''Everyone will be so good then,''
you said,
''as good
as the flowers.
And never again shall we need
to fear the dark
for when the world has been redeemed
there will be no more night.''
We were sitting in the garden,
two urchins,
one evening
two thousand years ago.

                                        H.P. R.F.

White horse in the moonlight

        White,
        white like the wing
        of my first dream
        is his mane.

        Like a long, long journey
        on a flax-pale steed
        is man's life.

        And with long slender hands
        the shadow of death clings
        to his mane.

                            H.P. R.F.

                The staircase

        This staircase is just like
        all other staircases
        in other houses.
        It leads down into the cellar
        and up into the top floor,
        so humble and courteous

towards everyone
who walks on it.
And here it has been
since the house was built,
for half a century or even longer,
it has heard and seen everything
that has happened in this house
summer and winter
spring and autumn.
As quiet and serious
as it is today
it has always been,
whether children or old people
trod its steps,
whether the occupants
were celebrating their wedding
or being carried to the grave.
So strange is this staircase,
so incomprehensible
in its simplicity,
like life itself,
like the reality
behind the reality.

H.P. R.F.

KRISTJAN frá DJUPALÆK (1916 —)

To the memory of a poet

As water trickles through a roof that leaks
and drips upon the floor without design,
like the sad tracks of birds in muddy creeks,
or wisps that winds of autumn catch and spin,

thus was your life, my brother, bearings gone
lost in a world that shed few guiding beams.
Was all my dreadful warfare fought in vain?
you ask despairing — and the answer comes:

To possess a dream in the day's confusion
and yearn for song in silent forest places,
to catch between the clouds a glimpse of sun
with grief at heart — for a poet this suffices.

A.B.

JON úr VÖR (1917 —)

The bird is faithful

The stones are still not dry
and yet the bird has started singing.

54

Hoar-flowers in bloom
and the sun absorbed
in a new love-affair
with the satellites.

But the bird is faithful,
sets to with fresh hope,
sits on another stone
as wet as the one before.
It doesn't weary of singing
the sun will return.

A.B.

Rest your wing

Rest your wing in my poem
little bird on the long flight
from morning till evening.

Lean, star, upon a flower in my garden
for an instant on your journey
through time and space.

Like a blade of grass in the sand by death's ocean
grow the roots of him who does not move.
No one asks from where he comes.

S.A.M.

STEFAN HÖRDUR GRIMSSON (1920 —)

In the evening

In the evening when the sun bleeds
into the edges of the mountains
and the dim-green shadow falls to rest
at the foot of the hill
and the blue bay
turns into red wine
a little girl comes out saying:
who wants me for his own?

S.A.M.

Dance on the sand

I lingered all night on the beach
where men with horns ran back and forth
playing with red metal

and women with twisted cleft hoofs
swayed their hips in a powerful dance
while the moon's sneer fell on their breasts.

I stood aside and the night passed.
I watched the play of the horned ones
and I watched the dance of the women
who trampled on the white flowers of the sand.

I stood aside wiping my forehead,
wiping my forehead to examine
whether I had grown horns.

Finally when morning appeared in the east
like a ruddy schoolboy
I saw where the Lord almighty came across the bay
riding on a bumpy businessman
and spurring him on with his feet.

Then I removed my hat
for I am a Lord-fearing man.

                                                    S.A.M.

JON OSKAR (1921 —)

Search

I have watched the children talk through the moon's fingers
while I was walking up by the wild crane's bill
in search of the beauty of the single path.
It was in the night of pairing.
And I have seen the children dip their bread in the clear skies
of the moonlit night, and see:
they drank from the glasses of autumn
with the ardour of thirsty mouths
while I was walking up by the wild crane's bill
and I have seen them drink their life from the glasses of autumn
when I searched the single paths of the earth
for the night's promise
in the night of pairing.
And I have seen their bare thighs
slip from the moon's fingers
to meet like white doves
that rub necks together
while I was walking up by the wild crane's bill
that breathed a thirst of life to my nostrils
so that I lay crazed in the grass
in the night of pairing
when I walked the single paths of the earth
in search of beauty.

                                                    A.B.

EINAR BRAGI (1921 —)

Fiery steeds

Fiery steeds
(with brave harps of song
in their chests
and stray wagtails fluttering
over the heart's breakers)
gallop off on sharpshod hooves
over glittering ice expanses —
the shell-thin bridge
between the vaults of life and death.

(I.K.) M.A.

Fame

Slowly

the noose is tightened
round the slender neck

and the moor-bird
raises its voice
in anguish

then the world's din
subsides for a while

people listen
in surprise to the song
and set new

snares.

(I.K.) M.A.

HANNES SIGFUSSON (1922 —)

Africa

Their arms plowed profits for them from the nut-brown fields
in Africa: mounds were formed
and blood trickled in their tracks

Muttering priests walked stooping
scattering pious words of God
in the ugly wounds

And then the wind pulled the harrow of the skies
from morning till night: the piercing claws of the rain
nailed every living nerve
and shattered every objection

But their harvest was a surprise:
from the wide fields grew
no Christian humility,
no white cotton

but fully armed men
united peoples

resilient as steel
in the tempest

(I.K.) M.A.

180 thousand

Individuals

One hundred eighty thousand

One drop every third hour

Glittering they drop deep
down to a depth of forty fathoms
drinking the shimmer of mother-of-pearl
and the secrets of the deep-sea currents.

Little stellar systems are formed
like whirlpools in the deep

Sea-anemones and spittles

Discordant cog-wheels in a clock

Time pulls them apart
They reject each other
like fire and water

(I.K.)   M.A.

SIGFUS DADASON (1928 —)

Take a gun in your hand

Take a gun in your hand
take a gun in each hand.

Stretch your arms
and fire
right out into the air.

Fire without thinking
or hesitation
— there's sure to be someone in the line of fire.

The witnesses to this murder
were — after all —
absent or are gone.

The judge will at most
regard the guns
the murder
and the witnesses to the murder
as symbols in a work of art.

(I.K.) M.A. R.L.

The great joy

The great joy: not knowing when you took my hand
if you took my hand
— or if our hands were only hands —
when we were talking with each other; not knowing if we were talking
with each other
— or if our words were only words.

And the greatest joy was when the time came when we knew that our
hands and words were alive and perfect and not just hands and words.

(I.K.) M.A. R.L.

The roads of my country

The roads of my country
are remarkable roads.
To those that travel them
they might seem more down to earth than most others.
Those who walk them
wade the mire of complete self-love.
It would doubtless be more logical
to walk them barefoot.

Such roads — I have heard —
also exist in Siberia:
Yakutskaya Tadzikstan
and Kirgizskaya.

For my part I have trodden none such
save in my own country
at least I cannot remember doing so
I am sorry to say.
To tell the truth I think it more than likely
that roads of this kind may also be found in New Zealand
and moreover it seems to me clear
that very similar roads
must cross the land of Chile.

A.B.

SIGURDUR A. MAGNUSSON (1928 —)

Solzhenitsyn

Pierced by the winter cold
he stands eagle-faced
in the snow-misted cone of a street-lamp
listening to the echo
of a million-voiced chorus
from the abysmal night
hovering over the Gulag Archipelago

His perception keen
as a bird's
sense of direction

Crowds avoid him
like a leper

His truth
gnaws the Establishment pillars

His conscience
a whole generation's affliction
is fatally contagious

S.A.M. M.F.

MATTHIAS JOHANNESSEN (1930 —)

The city laughed

Remember the moment when you stood by the lake
and stared at your face
and in your eyes the blue sky was mirrored
deep and thirsty as the laugh of the girl
who came to you with flashing teeth,
and recalled the tern that dived for stickleback.

Then night came
and when the last wave had borne
your shadows to the shore
rose a new day.

Remember, when the city spoke to you
and you understood the laughter of the street
and the gaiety of crowds dancing
to the snarl of trombones and squeal of fiddles
penetrating your soul
like the slender fingers
of a girl at the bar:
you laughed and sang
and did not see when the dark stole into your faces
and night passed gentle hands
over red lips.

And the city laughed in your hearts.

Remember, when a stranger entered your house
and sought your youth, culled flowers from warm lips
and gave instead the laughter of a child
brimming your ears like surf on the blue cliffs
or wind in a green dell.
Later you felt that none could escape the city
he has inhaled
like the scent of a young woman
and before long new eyes watched you,
two hands touched
two words ...

and the night kissed a withered autumn flower.

Remember, when youth abandoned you
running lightfoot into the city
and left you standing there with empty eyes
and a shiny pate reminding of the journey
into age and darkness:
the night caressed a wan cheek
and brow that once burned from thirsty lips
the night passed an icy hand
over the leaves of trees, to make them fall
to the deep red autumn earth,
and before long the trees stood lonely
by the black metalled streets,
ancient trees with bare livid branches
— cold stiffened fingers
pointing a question at those who passed

while the city laughed.

A.B.

HANNES PETURSSON (1931 —)

Dawn

Again morning vaults
young and rosy
over the nation's city.
With headlines grown silent
yesterday's newspapers
are dying in the corners of the homes
and no cabs with sleepy eyes
are looking for passengers any more.
The banks are brooding
over loan applications and bills.
The old tower clock strikes
and the many-fingered hand
of the harbor closes like a claw
round merchant ships and boats.

The quiet forms a great circle
round a lonely bird's voice.

(I.K.) M.A. R.L.

From Bright nights

The May night comes —
lighting its fires in the north,
one fire after another in the sky,
but in the city twilight falls.
The streets become silent, stop
thinking aloud — and stare
with yellow lamp eyes.

All
the houses close around themselves
full of talk and kisses.

In the background mountains
with burning skies on their shoulders.

(I.K.) M.A.

Departure

O conceit
Thought I was learning
song bird speech
thought I was taking into my possession
rock softness

water hardness
Thought I was disappearing
to listen to the herbs of my country growing,
to see the silence of the mountains.

I'm still sitting here by the window
looking for wisdom in the daily papers.

(I.K.) M.A.

Copernicus

In the evening, beneath lighted moon and stars,
they come home from the fields; and the breeze
carries fading echoes of chimes, while drooping and silent
they walk along past a weathered crucifix
with their ancestors' old and worn-out tools on their shoulders,
but pleased that everything is so firmly fixed:
look, there moon and winds, here road and growth.

They don't know that he who often greets them every day
cut this earth from a mouldering root and threw it
like a pebble far into darkness and void.

S.A.M.

Talking to a tree in leaf

I'll not be a poet until I find that you
are part of my blood, I've become you:
a leaf-green harp in the hands of darkness and light,
heaven and earth, become a living bridge
uniting sun and chilly earth in one;
become a potent instrument in life's hands,
a harp of living strings — just like you.

S.A.M.

THORSTEINN frá HAMRI (1938 —)

The visitor

I nudge you my friend
    if I could make you realize
    now there's no time to be wasted
    for he is on his way
You must consult your convenience
    and drink your coffee right up
    (even quietly if it is on the hot side)
    and don't hesitate to smoke one more pipe

and think: what can the fellow want?
I advise you moreover to take a look at the paper
 and yet with the utmost circumspection remembering the one
  that approaches
 and you can safely fold it up
 and stick it in one of your pockets
 think: should I now be obliged to rack my brains —
for it would be better for you to prepare for what's coming
Knock the ash firmly from your pipe
 and if it's your custom
 say God reward you for the coffee
 and then I think it's wisest for you to be going
 even say to yourself: should I now be asked to show judgment —
 it might be healthy for you
And should you happen to have the childish habit
 of fidgetting on the floor after mealtimes
 you must leave it behind you
 and yet a fraction towards he door
 and don't forget your hat
For now the time has come:
 yet don't be afraid my friend
 he only makes simple and fair demands — —

A.B.

Settlement

Beyond the tree line
rise the naked peaks

there
outside of history and law

the lost man breaks his way

and looks about him on the rock
without doubts and without sorrows
without guilt

Here I belong

(I.K.) M.A.

Assistance

The papers and the radio give us news
of the genocide
and now it is everyone's duty to participate:

so we tear out our hearts,
hang them on our chests

like awarded honors
and take a good long walk

before we go to sleep
on our mistakes
and turn over completely
to the dream of life.

(I.K.) M.A. R.L.

In the field

When I was younger
I stood alone in my field
looking across the river
at the black bank —
soon it would slide into the water,
and I silently feared it.

The times change
and man too
but I always see this black bank in my mind's eye;

and now
I ask that we
a few farmers together
do something:

one can make a new bed for the river —

(I.K.) M.A. R.L.

Staying out-of-doors

We who stay out-of-doors
acquire a kind of mountaineer's sense

which is considered foolish
by some people
kept and preserved by the spirit

but which gives us endurance
when time is so short
that there is hardly enough time:

consciousness of a world
which has made up its mind to stay

(I.K.) M.A.

JOHANN HJALMARSSON (1939 —)

From the circus

Suddenly out of the floor
sprang the head of the conjuror
the eyes of those present on his neck
but before an unscalable rock
and humming-birds vibrated in closed cages
and the lions roared with vexation
the head walked across the floor
clay-handed on feet of jet
and began to vomit acrobats
Persian horses
and ringmasters with whips
top-boots and imperials
and the performance spread to the street
till the city was possessed by jugglery
the horses reared on the housetops
the acrobats displayed their skill
on the masts of ships
the ringmasters marshalling their troupe in five directions
and all wore the masks of imps
the whiplashes cracked
and fierce cries echoed throughout the streets
until the head
sank into the earth
as quickly as it had come
but the audience still went on
bleating like lambs
and the band played
a Country Sunday.

A.B.

THURIDUR GUDMUNDSDOTTIR (1939 —)

Child

The child plays with silence
building a house of sunbeams
and straws
that lean over the stone

The straws
stiff, resilient,
yellow straws in the bright mind of the child
resting fingers on silence

Building a house of sunbeams
and straws
that lean over the stone

Resting fingers on silence
until it crumbles

A.B.

NINA BJÖRK ARNADOTTIR (1949 —)

We fall asleep again

Was there weeping in the night?
Did we hear whispering at the window?

Was it just a dream
and our gloomy thought
or the fall of the rain
that talked with the twilight?

No, someone is weeping outside
as one weeps that has a harboured grief.

But we fall asleep again
laugh or enjoy each other
and deaden the thought
that God weeps in the night.

A.B.

THE FAROE ISLANDS

THE FAROE ISLANDS

Like Iceland, the Faroe Islands were colonized by Norwegian emigrants in the middle of the ninth century A.D. Later the islands became a part of the Danish realm, albeit with a certain amount of self-rule after 1948.

Gradually a native Faroese language developed; the oldest written memorials of this language date back to the 14th century. Then there is a vacuum, but about 1800 the islanders began to record their medieval ballads, which had been preserved in the oral tradition, and which are still a living feature of Faroese cultural life.

The ballads were partly composed on the Faroe Islands, and have been very important to the survival of the Faroese language through the centuries. Modern Faroese poetry came into being about a hundred years ago, and it found linguistic models in the old ballads.

Faroese literature is, however, mainly a creation of the 20th century. The first novel came in 1909, and the first volume of poetry, written by J.H.O. Djurhuus (1881 — 1948), which is not without a certain distinction, came in 1914.

There are today some 50 000 persons whose mother tongue is the Faroese language, and they have access to a considerable literature. There are significant prose writers on the islands, but the dominant genre, both quantitatively and qualitatively, is poetry.

The great name in Faroe literature is *William Heinesen* (debut 1921), who occupies a rather special position since he writes in Danish. His novels and short stories have placed the Faroe Islands on the map of world literature. His first four books were, however, volumes of poetry. One may characterize his lyrical work by saying that — just like his prose — it shows the same well balanced proportions between specifically Faroe and more general material, which makes it so easily acceptable to an international public.

An age-mate of William Heinesen is *Christian Matras* (debut 1926), who has made an important contribution to philology, i.a. as a compiler of a dictionary. In his poetry he unites exact nature descriptions with symbolism, which expands the portraits of his native background into generally valid comments on man, and his life and circumstances. This is the significance of Matras and Heinesen to the younger generation, and this gives Faroese poetry for the first time a dimension which can make it interesting to others than the Faroe people themselves.

The Faroe Islands possess a magnificent, dramatic landscape with high mountains and deep valleys, where the grass has a special brilliance as it stands green against a background of brown, black, and blue mountain sides. Round the islands extends the infinite ocean, from which the people derive most of their livelihood. From the sky shines the eternal, life-giving sun.

It is not unnatural that the Faroe poets should devote much energy to describing and praising nature. *Karsten Hoydal* (b. 1912, debut 1946) writes almost scientifically exact poetry with light and water as the dominant features. Unfortunately his best poems are rather large compositions, too large to be included here.

In the younger poet *Steinbjørn Jacobsen* (debut 1966) one finds the same feeling for the magnificence of nature and its infinite creation of life. Otherwise this poet is one of the few Faroe writers who have succeeded in combining a political commitment with artistic ambitions.

Nature may also, in the traditional symbolist manner, be made to harmonize with moods and thoughts. This is often the case in the poetry of *Regin Dahl* (debut 1936). He writes a kind of decadent verse, melodic and singable, which sensitively registers nostalgia, sadness and regret.

There are very few women in Faroe literature. The major woman poet is undoubtedly *Gudrid Helmsdal-Nielsen* (debut 1963). Her nature descriptions contain fine shades and employ very expressive metaphors, but have gradually developed toward greater and greater terseness.

One of the recent poets deserves special mention: *Hedin M. Klein* (debut 1969). His work displays greater linguistic and metaphoric complexity than that of any of his contemporaries.

Only a few persons have been able to devote themselves to full-time literary work. Most of the Faroe literature has been created in spare moments, evenings and holidays, or on ferry trips between the eighteen islands. Publishing is not very advanced; usually the authors themselves have to pay for printing and distribution. But in spite of adverse material conditions, Faroese writing possesses an impressive breadth and depth. It is composed in one of the world's smallest languages, but reveals to us aspects of life which are unique. It is one of the many voices in life's great, blended choir.

Inge Knutsson
Knislinge
Sweden

CHRISTIAN MATRAS (1900 —)

Snow light shone on the ground

Snow light shone on the ground
We were skating on the tarn ice like a cluster of flies
when night fell.
Then a gigantic rock emerged from the evening
quiet and strong
and heaven crowned with stars
a head on the white earth.

(I.K.) M.A.

WILLIAM HEINESEN (1900 —)

Temple storm

Against a background of glittering splinters
overturned tables
broken glass
opened cages
bouncing coins
fleeing sheep and oxen
swarms of frightened pigeons
furious merchants
bankers and priests
and soldiers with drawn swords

In the midst of all the clamor:
the man with a whip
the son of man
with wrathful eyes

73

and strong young teeth
in his savagely distorted mouth

M.A.

Darkness speaks to the flowering bush

I am darkness.
Do you feel my cheek against yours?
Do you feel my black mouth against your red one?

I am darkness and you scare me.
You are night and eternity —
I feel your chill breath.
You are death.
You want me to wither.
But I want to live and blossom.

I am darkness.
I love you.
I want to wither.
Blossom and wither.
Wither and rise again in your flowers.
Wither and rise again and again.

I am Night. Death. Eternity.
I love you.
I would pine away if you did not exist
and were waiting for me here
with the frightened torches of your mortal flowers.
With your living brothers and sisters
of hot, red kisses
deep in my solitary, black heart.

M.A.

A thousand masts in rain

What a wonderful city of this world!
They are enlarging the departure ramp down at the ferry
and it's all clogged up with scaffolds.

One gulps down a mouthful of bitter aquavit
before crossing to the island of Cythera.

Then out into the forest of scaffolds.
Then out onto the water
with a little thrill in your chest.

Enchanting rain and mist.
Enchanting workday,
slush and slosh and mud.

74

How good and true it all is.
How marvelous the trivial things
when the background is happy expectation!

M.A.

Winter lights its fires on our mountains

Winter lights its fires on our mountains.
Now the quiet, opal-grey days are here,
and the magic early twilight
with the red knife-point of the new moon at the horizon,
the squall days
with the polychrome quarry skies of their dawns
and the grey, stormy days when the ocean blossoms.
Now the playful northern lights return
and the majestic constellations
and the roads with wildly sparkling ice crystals.

And now you too are here
my dead friends,
you whom I miss always and deeply,
warming your hands at my winter fire.
Look, your favorite dishes and drinks are on the table
and the music you loved
fills the living-room.
There your voices too come to life
your happy laughter,
your exclamations of surprise
when the lights of the majestic Andromeda haze, millions of years old,
appear in the lens of the telescope at the open window
allowing a precious drop of eternity
to flow to our mortal eyes.

M.A.

Writing on a frozen window-pane

I am death.
I bring you enigmatic gifts —
crystals and scintillating stars.

You cannot read the writing on your window pane.
Scornful triumph
or secret consolation?
Or nothing but a strange, exalted game
beyond all sense and meaning?

See how luxuriantly my herbs grow!
Do you recognize the pattern of life
on my silent white canvas?

Defiantly swelling bulb in the earth!
Budding tang mid storm and breakers!
Your longing and your hope!
Indomitable rose of your heart!

M.A. R.L.

REGIN DAHL (1918 —)

Girl in a window

And the joy was as poor as a discotheque night
with electric guitars and sickening, stale air
and the whole way home just desolate and cold
with coarse and cheap retorts.

And the joy was as vulgar as a doorway fuck
done with your eyes tightly shut
where no touch was beautiful and fresh,
just revolting like laying a ghost.

But once we walked hand in hand in our valley
and no one could separate us
and a kiss at the kitchen door as a last goodbye
was a wonder and consolation.

(B.H.) M.A.

Windy summer

Windy summer, cloudstacks gliding
in the sunset like heavily laden ships
and north of the mountains
the green fire.

Windy summer, westerly wind
combing the grain and the crowns of the trees —
up there under blue mountains
they're waiting, waiting —

Wide is the world, no one knows
the road and the time —
in flaming fires are forged
sword blades and destinies.

Wide is the world, no one knows
the guest or the day —
the rising night wind
plucks at the roof's turf.

(I.K.) M.A.

NAPOLEON DJURHUUS (1928 — 1971)

Jealousy

In my heart she's dancing now
till twelve o'clock and more.
The trembling strings of my heart
are her dancing-floor.

She's dancing with her love,
dancing until she's warm.
Round his manly neck
she puts her lovely arm.

For now is the month of spring.
The dance of love it is
sweet — and my dearest love,
now you are only his.

But all the steps that you dance
till twelve o'clock and more
hurt so much in my heart
for it is your dancing-floor.

(B.H.) M.A.

STEINBJØRN JACOBSEN (1937 —)

Sheep

On the rocky ledge
in the high shore mist
sheep are walking
the gorge is the path's end.

Muttering seaweed
a bleating left behind up there
the ocean rising and sinking
and the sun an eternal fire

(I.K.) M.A.

GUDRID HELMSDAL-NIELSEN (1941 —)

Thaw night

And the rain came.
The drop that broke
the shell of ice.
The heavens breathed,

the heavens which had been held
in the tight embrace of the cold.

Tonight winter lies
on its death-bed;
it draws its breath heavily,
sighing —
like a huge animal
which has placed itself
round the world.

(I.K.) M.A.

HEDIN M. KLEIN (1950 —)

Voice from life

Life is hard, devastating,
joy always false.
Most of us always lose —
in the long run all.
        Planed planks, cool metal
frail smiles.
        By and by one learns
to die betimes.
        This:
before everything begins
all is at an end.
        Before one dies
one is supposed to swoon away
emptying out slowly:
out through eyes, ears, mouth:
        ulcers, heart failures, poisoned fish,
        cobwebs, dermatitis
        for ever and ever —
Oh no!

(I.K.) M.A.

DENMARK

DENMARK

Two books from the 1850s may serve as introductions to the Danish poetry of our century. One of them is Walt Whitman's "Leaves of Grass", the other Charles Baudelaire's "Les Fleurs du Mal". Whitman registers and catalogs with indiscriminate enthusiasm all the wonders, great and small, of the new world. He identifies wholeheartedly with the vigorously expanding American nation, glorying in its multitudinous, varied, even contradictory manifestations. The author of "Les Fleurs du Mal", on the other hand, turns inward to his own self in a mood of boredom and revulsion at his own corrupt epoch. With his exquisite, refined sense of form he creates his own, subjective world of symbols for which he feels a nostalgia that can find no goal in the real world. In these two books, the expansive, life-worshipping man of action confronts the fragmentized, introverted man of reflection and vision.

The two great poets *Johannes V. Jensen* (1873 — 1950) and *Sophus Claussen* (1865 — 1931), who open the Danish section, were both influenced by the two monumental figures of modern poetry mentioned above. The prose lyrics of Johannes V. Jensen's volume "Poems 1906" cannot be imagined without Walt Whitman as the central source of inspiration. True, the youthful verse of Johannes V. Jensen shows a fruitful, violent, and indignant revolt against symbolism, and one can still hear it in "The red tree" in the "raucous croak from my melancholy marsh heart.". But one certainly also feels a nostalgia for a dramatically active and intense life of reality. The power, and the condensed, close feeling of reality in the lyrical descriptions of Johannes V. Jensen's environment often arise in the attempt at investigating a reality with qualities that can lull to rest his longing for the infinite. In his mature work he is more and more successful in this attempt. The lively, indignant *parlando* of his youth is succeeded by well-controlled, monumental compositions in the style of rock engravings (e.g. "The earth and light").

Claussen's love for the poetry of Baudelaire is well-documented. His congenial translations of this poet are among the most important creative interpretations of foreign poetry in our language. But there are also striking similarities in the attitudes of the two poets. In his youth Claussen suffered erotic defeats and insufficient critical appreciation which made him reject the social and cultural life of his contemporaries in Denmark, substituting a visionary world of imagination. In the powerful poem "Imperia" he projects his own frustration into a cosmic experience, with the Queen of the Earth as his mouthpiece. These two poems by Jensen and Claussen, related in their motifs, illustrate nicely the scope, as well as the radical ideological nature of the differences present in the poetry of the turn of the century.

Let us make a rapid survey of the Whitman line and the Baudelaire line in 20th century Danish poetry.

In company with Jensen we may place the cosmic poet and worshipper of our biological drives, *Thøger Larsen* (1825 — 1928). Here, too, we must place *Emil Bønnelycke* (1893 — 1953) — our only whole-hearted futurist — with his anthems to modern technology and dynamic big city life. In his poetry from the Twenties and Thirties *Otto Gelsted* (1888 — 1968) is constantly engaged in a battle with the dark and chaotic aspects of life, and professes a philosophy with a strong humanist faith in the meaningfulness of thinking, teaching, and reforming in the service of progress. His deep humanist commitment becomes the common hallmark of a series of poetical works with very different outward appearences: in the poetry of *gustaf munch-petersen* (1912 — 1938) and his lyrical search for the forgotten, simple, and primitive man from the "lowest country"; in *Jens August Schade's* (1903 — 1978) constant, sublime ecstasies at the marvelous manifoldness of erotic love (his only really independent follower is *Jørgen Nash* (1920 —). In this group belong also *Piet Hein's* (1905 —) poetry with its evolutionary inspiration, as well as *Ove Abildgaard's* (1916 —) spirited and sensuous verses. Finally, one also discovers a striking affinity with Johannes V. Jensen's intrepretation of existence in the "confrontation poets" of the Sixties.

A description of the Baudelaire line in the lyrical poetry of this century will be somewhat more complicated. Here we may begin with Tom Kristensen (1893 — 1974). Superficially one may regard his early verse as expressionistic, if by expressionism we are to understand the modern world of the big city used as a vehicle of self-expression. However, his poetry never really remains satisfied with such a concrete inventory of the world around him. Actually, this world is nothing but fuel for his subjective phantasms. There is a clear affinity here with the symbolists on which Tom Kristensen worked for his Master's Degree. He wants to communicate feelings and attitudes, not things, and he is especially fascinated by extreme mental states: intoxication, exaltation, narcotization, inspiration, anxiety, and profound dreams. He works all this into shape in his attempt at creating for himself an artistic and human identity. Later in his development one may discern a tendency to move toward deeper, more irrational layers of consciousness. This process gives rise to courageous and penetrating analyses of states of nihilism and disillusionment and their preconditions. His youthful exuberançe and colorfulness fade away — only tears, grey and silver remain, the climate becomes autumnal, the tone and voice sad and low-pitched. The moods of disillusionment and nihilism expressed in Tom Kristensen's poetry come into being at this time as similar experiences in Europe at large. In the midst of the modern industrailized world T.S.Eliot investigates the topography of The Waste Land. In his Cantos, the scholar Ezra Pound pays a visit to Hades, and in the Duino Elegies Rilke arms his soul and mind for the struggle against big city life, superficial and void of content.

The experience of emptiness and a lowered zest for life is the stated or unspoken precondition of much of the Danish lyrical poetry of theis century. It was possible to arrive at this attitude in many different ways: by a commitment to the preachings of nihilist writers, by a realization of the social disintegration and insecure values in the wake of two world wars, and by a feeling of utter confusion at the contradictions of the contemporary world. And these experiences could, indeed, be handled in many different ways. Precisely this circumstance may indicate an important boundary between on the one hand a number of poets who write who write between 1920 and 1960, and on the other hand a group of authors who publish their work after the latter date. One may describe the former as late symbolists, and the latter as confrontation poets, to use a term introduced by the main literary critic of the Sixties, Torben Broström.

The late symbolists comprise two generations: that of Tom Kristensen (together with *Per Lange* and *Paul La Cour* (1902 — 1956), and, two decades later, the group round the literary magazine Heretica: *Thorkild Bjørnvig* (1918 —), *Ole Wivel* (1921 —), *Ole Sarvig* (1921 —), and *Frank Jæger* (1926 — 1977).

The poetry of confrontation begins with *Erik Knudsen* (1922 —), and has its intellectual center in *Klaus Rifbjerg* (1931 —). Here belong poets like *Per Højholt* (1928 —), *Jørgen Sonne* (1925 —), *Robert Corydon* (1924 —), *Jørgen Gustava Brandt* (1929 —), *Ivan Malinovski* (1926 —), *Jess Ørnsbo* (1932 —), *Benny Andersen* (1929 —), *Poul Borum*, and *Inger Christensen (1935 —)*.

How can we differentiate between the two groups of poets? As has already been stated — their manner of handling the the condition of catastrophe and the feeling of crisis. The late symbolists create a vault of resplendent poetry as an act of reconciliation above the waste land. The poetic image becomes a divine image, and poetry a doctrine of salvation. "The poem becomes more powerful the more untraceable the relation it expresses. In the image the disparate elements are joined together in simplicity," Paul La Cour writes in his "Fragments of a diary". The poetic product becomes a small world of its own, a substitute reality — or an exorcism of reality. Its architect becomes a creator in the true sense of the word. He oscillates between the pathos of a visionary and doubt about his calling.

The confrontation poet places himself at the center of an explosion which he looks at directly and registers in raw collages. But he also tries to come to terms with humble and broken things, an attitude which Jørgen Gustava Brandt has successfully described as "taking temporary lodgings." Confrontation means accepting the crisis as a permanent condition. It is an encounter with things, people, and situations unhampered by previous commitments — not an encounter with such metaphysical super-concepts as "das Ding an sich", man, myth, or the sublime and starry moments of mankind. One discovers that the potsherds of existence do not necessarily have to be entrusted to the hands of an archeologist. The sherd may be a meaningful thing in itself. "Reality is smart enough", as Rifbjerg says in "Camouflage".

Let us take a closer look at some of the main figures in this double constellation of late symbolists and confrontation poets.

The poetry of Paul La Cour is wholly enveloped in a gigantic metaphor

83

of plant growth with organic connections between all the individual parts of the plant — nature, man, the poet and his work. The foremost offshoot — the blossom of the plant, as it were — has a tendency to isolate itself from the rest of the organism. This is poetry, about which La Cour has written brilliant and profound things in the most read Danish poetics of this century, "Fragments of a diary."

In Per Lange's classic, lucid world of ideas the orphic poet is at his most exalted level. He knows the glory of inspiration, but also its price.

The conditions of crisis and catastrophe were felt and registered by two poets of the Forties in an especially moving way. As the freedom fighter's constantly present danger of being killed in action. Morten Nielsen found a completely original expression for this existential theme: death as an ever-present, constituent part of the most intense joy of being alive. *Halfdan Rasmussen's* (1915 —) first volumes contain themes from concentration camps, liquidation of stool-pigeons, atom bomb experiments, and Nazi tyranny. Anger at the brutality of dictatorship has followed him as a central theme throughout his literary work, but he can also strike happier notes in his incredibly brilliant collections of "Nonsense verses."

At the centre of the group round the culturally advanced periodical "Heretica" was Thorkild Bjørnvig. From the very beginning death, love, art, and nature were his motifs. Death was an enemy, but also a phenomenon which must be given a legitimate standing in the consciousness of adult Europeans, and not just repressed. Love as a personally experienced life-force with a thousand faces. Art with its Janus mask: it is Bjørnvig's indubitable alter ego, but it is also a traitor robbing life of its power. And finally nature: an infinitely lavish resource in Bjørnvig's world, as long as we do not torture it to death. In his latest collections Bjørnvig has abandoned his high literary style, and speaks directly and in universally valid terms about things that are close to his heart (e.g. "The dolphin" about global pollution.)

Ole Sarvig's complete lyrical tetralogy is a personal and coherent phenomenal world whose core is the story of the mystical religions about the life-cycle of the seed of grain through hibernation, death, germination and growth. He has been very successful in making these ideas express something essential to his expectant contemporaries.

Ole Wivel's poetry from the Forties also concentrates on the motif of change and transformation, usually with a longing for deliverance ("The fish").Wivel became a sensitive and independent introducer of Eliot's polyphonic technique. In his later poetry he takes a stand with regard to many of the political problems of the post-war world.

Frank Jæger describes with musicality and rich imagination the situation of the crisis-conscious poet all the way from the experience of innocent roguery ("Virtuous poems") to the frightening realization of absolute nothingness (his latest volume "Idylia").

And now to the confrontation poets of the Sixties. One may establish a common denominator in this poetry by saying that it stands in opposition to the cult-conscious adventist lyrics of "Heretica". The confrontation ·s concerned both with exposing the phenomenon, and at the same time describing it in its total fullness. To expose the phenomenon means freeing it from a moldy layer of earlier sentimentality or pathos. To restore its artistic fullness is to see it afresh, as if it had never been seen before, to see it from many new concrete and intellectual angles. To all the poets of this generation poetry very literally becomes a process of perception.

Erik Knudsen must be regarded as the portal figure of the poetry of confrontation. The central aim of his earliest poetry is to expose phony sentimentality and false estheticism to a lyrical analysis. There is a constant dialectic in his poetry between the two poles of his mind, symbolically indicated by the flower — whatsoever is closed, static, self-evident and idyllic; and the sword — whatever is open, dynamic, active and struggling. And this conflict works forcefully and with great inventiveness through the forms of the antithesis. The mottled personality galleries of history (The night of St. Bartholomew), the elegant landscape idyll and literary cliches yield to a bitter awakening to artistic and human commitment. However, Knudsen's satirical unmasking of illusion and corruption takes place with no easy capitulation to harmony and utopia. His unmistakeable (socialist) commitment does not impair the quality of his verse.

In several books of poetry Rifbjerg engages in a search for the forgotten and repressed past in order to come to grips with himself and reality here and now. To achieve this aim he makes use of many devices — utterly simple descriptions, a kind of catalog style, suggestive dreamlike streams of consciousness, and well-staged and pointed sequences of images. In his most recent lyrical development he successfully introduces large contemporary social, political, and cultural themes in his poetry ("Scenes from daily life").

Per Højholt concentrates on the problems of the text itself with a strange mixture of simplicity and exclusivity. His work contains a blend of racy jokes, courageous experimentation, and penetrating philosophical analysis. And quite apart from its obvious, brilliant qualities, his poetry has also proved capable of interesting professional philosophers. His "Turbo" is the most important contribution from this generation.

Jørgen Sonne writes two kinds of poems — furious, and cool. In the furious ones (e.g."Other eyes, another world") there are violent thrusts and leaps. Everything is whirling, pushing and gliding. In the cool poems of reflection (as in "Adrift") a peacock's tail of reflections and associations is gathered elegantly and lucidly round a clearly presented object.

The lyrical production of Jørgen Gustava Brandt is so extensive that it cannot yet be conveniently summarized. But the author of this preface wishes to refer enthusiastically to the two poems presented here, which both represent central experiences in Brandt's universe. "Deeper into it" is an encounter with the sentimental view of the past. "The man with a guitar" deals with a convalescence which gave rebirth to reality, and turned it into poetic material for Brandt.

The poetry of Ivan Malinovski operates with various degrees of accessibility. His first collection of existential, erotic and biological motifs appeared in heavily armed modernistic form. Later collections — presented in quite simple language — are conceived as political weapons against capitalism, and more than that — they are good poetry.

The imagistic brutality of Jess Ørnsbo, which one is tempted to call a modern baroque, strikes especially hard at social and religious taboos. He himself has given a brief description of his own poetical method: poetry as a switchblade knife.

Benny Andersen's strength is his ability to describe the irritation we all feel at quite concrete circumstances around us. However, we always understand that the failure to adjust to the environment is symptomatic of a far more serious problem of alienation. Benny Andersen's linguistic weapon is grotesque verbal humor. In "Svante's songs", which are close to the great Nordic art song tradition, he gives a highly comic form to a central modernistic theme: the passing, modest, "small" happiness of existence in the midst of a crisis.

In the wake of Per Højholt a type of poetry develops at the end of the Sixties which has been called "the third phase of modernism" (the first being that of the "Heretica" group, and the second that of the poetry of confrontation). It has many facets. The "metapoetic" fascination of the writing itself finds its foremost expression in the main work of Inger Christensen, the poetic cycle "It", a whirling lyrical process which begins with an intensive preoccupation with the process of creation, goes on to the construction of a total view of civilization, and ends in pure nothingness. Another aspect of the poetic activities of this period is the so-called "systemic" poetry which was created on concrete patterns and modules (Per Kirkeby and Kirsten Bjørnkjær are good examples). Finally, concretism is introduced from a background among certain German authors, as well as computer-lyrical experiments (Vagn Steen and Jørgen Nielsen are all-round representatives of this interest).

It is not easy to say in what direction the poetry of today is headed, but one may perhaps recognize two tendencies. One can be exemplified by the group round Charlotte Strandgård, who very early found her style in poems of social reportage and controversy (relations between couples, drug addiction, alcoholism, sex roles). The other points toward a new surrealism, where more or less concrete centemporary experiences appear in a linguistic garb of wild and violent fantasy, as in the poems of Peter Poulsen and Sten Kaalø.

Finn Stein Larsen
Riisskov
Denmark

SOPHUS CLAUSSEN (1865 — 1931)

Dreams

All the songs about dreams have a sweet-scented birth.
— Dreams are the devil's own angels on earth.

That the devil the better may scorn, they entice —
singing of joy to reveal a vice.

Joy turns to frenzy, and frenzy to screaming,
burnt out in hell flames of treacherous dreaming.

M.A.

With those who are waiting

None must be forced, there must be no entreating:
man and the sun must be free in their meeting.

We sounded our horns and we moved our drums,
and now we are waiting, but the day never comes.

Perhaps you were ready to dance with the sun —
and lo! what the darkness of mankind has done!

Humanity's darkness, and God's, entrenched —
all my newly born senses drying unquenched.

While *they* are still sighing to worthless lyres
our hearts and kidneys burn with new fires,

and our nerves, where the ebb and the flow is denied,
although all their Gods have been crucified.

Imagine: to speak, but the language is strange to you!
Think: you would shine, but the night was taboo.

We're living a life that is lost in the shade
on credit from a future that is yet to be made.

M.A.

Imperia

I am Imperia, Queen of the massive globe,
strong as the cold which sleeps in the mountain's womb,
dark and relentless as if I were dead in the tomb.

Glory I long for. I know no mildness.
I am the untilled waste, the barren earth
which gives us stones for bread and cannot give birth.

No one can wake me except my lover,
the Fire, my Lord, in whose service I faithfully dwell
unto the nethermost circle of burning hell.

All is in vain, but the tremor we feel.
All that grows and thrives on my skin like mold —
all I shake off when the earthquake's God I behold.

Under the turf that is turned by the plow
rests my iron core untouchable and free.
Each man with a barren heart has something of me.

The spring grain that gives us our nourishing flour
runs blue with coal and iron from the veins of my heart.
If the land is unhappy, *mine* is the unhappy part.

Each man who is out of tune, with no tone
after the songs they have sung in choirs and flocks,
each man who is out of tune is a rock of my rocks.

Cold to the antics and noise of the living
a deep primeval music I always list.
Strike them with lightnings and earthquakes and bid them desist!

I am Imperia, Queen of the massive globe,
strong as the cold which sleeps in the mountain's womb,
dark and relentless as if I were dead in the tomb.

Poisonous craters, smoke-filled depths,
holes that are stinking of sulfur and metal black
open their yawning abyss when I mount my attack.

I sank the castles of kings in the ocean,
I turned the poor man's happy day to tears,
I am immeasurably rich for millions of years.

Come to my heart which fear ne'er tamed.
The door is wide open. Impetuous, I wait for my lover.
Black is his flesh. Our bliss will be widely famed.

M.A. R.L.

JOHANNES V. JENSEN (1873 –˙ 1950)

The red tree

The boiling kettle of the tropical night
foams over at daybreak ...
Rain, rain from the zenith!

The sun comes up through a cloudburst,
and out of the rain-tortured dawn
leaps a sole flash of lightning
with an uncanny power of illumination —
long drops, perpendicular rungs of water
stand motionless as if made of glass.

But behind this glittering trellis of rain
a blossoming tree spreads out
its high red canopy —
as fiery an apparition
there in the lightning and the red of dawn
as a hot volcano of blood
from the heart of the earth.

And after the terrific crash
that followed the lightning
all things grew deep and still,
while the dawn spreads
and the rain hisses.

Now spring and autumn meet
at the lightning flash and under the dazzling rain
in the red-blooming gardens of Singapore.

For now the tree stands there dripping green,
aflame with blossoms,
and the rain that threshes its crown
sweeps with warm watery hands
the withered flowers and leaves
in a limping autumnal waltz
down toward its roots,
while bright gleaming sprouts and buds
everywhere open their eyes
in the crown that reeks with the moisture.

The tree uplifts itself glowing
above its own fallen leaves
like an undying bonfire
snowing down ashes
yet with a thousand new spires of flame.

Ho!
Through the drunken deluge-throb of the rain
and the red tree's heavy rustling
I hear as it were the tramp of time,
the whinny of horses, incitement of drums,
galloping, whizzing of arrows.
Fresh tones of trumpets! Hosts are exulting!
Thalatta! The sun at Austerlitz!

All things go on victorious, and die.
Why do I sit here alone with the rough shard
of my brooding sluggish heart?
Who has snuffed out the lightning flash of my fate?

C.W.S.

The wandering girl

Who are you then, wild girl,
wandering by on the highway,
pushing your way in the wind
in the red westerly sunshine?

It is late; are you trying to keep
a tryst with the swift-winged tempest?
He is a flyer! you find
him never until he has fallen.

The amorous wind presses
your thin dress to your knees.
The wind lingeringly outlines
your young wandering waist.

Why do you breast the tempest?
Why bend against the wind?
It will lift you; strive no longer …
The storm! yea, that is I!

R.S.H.

The earth and light

Have you ever tried to imagine the earth,
tellus mater,

early one morning when dawn
like a golden-haired goddess
rises from the east?
Have you been able to figure
how this ball
turns into the light
with its European side
while China and California
sink into the shade,
half the world waking up
and the other half going to bed?

Have you grasped
how this freely suspended
gigantic body
turns round itself
in outer space
clear and blue
dressed in oceans
and multi-colored by five continents,
rivers flowing like veins
through the dense forests,
and with glittering ice
like a dead man's eye
at each pole?

Have you realized
the age of the earth?
Have you any idea
how old life is on earth?
Have you translated the cipher code
of the fossils into life,
and felt a gust of wind
from the tepid gardens
where the trilobite lived?
Have you registered
the sound of life
from the flying lizard
as it keeled over
on its skinny wing
in the twilight
like a phantom
against the sunset glow
in the youth of the earth?

A well of bottomless
millions of years

and transformation of created beings
to peer down into
— such are the ages of the earth.
A powerful row
of concrete miracles
is the world,
a fountain of joy,
the source of our thought.
The greatest of miracles
hangs over your head,
a fireplace in heaven,
the sun.

Thus it is:
the sun is shining
and you see it
unless you are a mole.

The finest gift is to *see*.
The only thing that lasts
is to *know*.

The shooting star,
a fiery writing in the sky
signs your contract
with existence:
the earth's ore
and the meteor
from the distant universe
have the same origin.
There are many forms
but of one world only.
The earth is real
under your feet
and above your crown
it can be grasped with your hands.

That was your childhood hope:
that you would see Lake Constance
and Gibraltar,
and the Cape of Good Hope
if you were lucky,
and the penguins
at the south pole
and the bird of paradise
in New Guinea.

Did it fall to your lot
to see the flying fish
in the sunny seas
under the monsoon?

Did you see the Southern Cross

like a diamond brooch
on the other side of the threshold
of the white man's world?

Did you see the skies of Magellan
south of the south —
the glimmer of other universes
beyond the universe?

Did you see the *sack of coal,*
the starless,
black hole
above the Pacific,
a well out from this world,
and out into nothingness?
Ugh!
Better be cosy
here at home under the Pleiades!

Well lighted
is the world.
Sources of light
well forth from the planets.

Go and stand in your courtyard,
have the sky above you,
then you are at the center
of space and time.

Your pulse beats
with all creatures
that have a heart.
You came into being
as a part of the earth,
a minimal percentage
of the earth's iron
is in your cells.

Your blood is as salt
as the Pacific Ocean.

Fresh rain —
if you have tasted it
you have tasted the sky.

What make is that car
over there?

And man, look —
here comes a woman!

M.A.

THØGER LARSEN (1875 — 1928)

Sunshine in a room

O, peaceful sunshine rests
on tables, floor, and wall.
A wordless dream bewitched
my little room and hall.

O, see the orchid's leaves
through heaven's open door.
I feel that I'm awake
down on the ocean floor.

The grass and branches sway,
the wind does gently sough.
Of all the times it is
sometime or other now.

Down here beneath the weight
of the air's stupendous sea
the dream comes through the pane
to die its death with me.

Omniscience under a seal
to me its secret gave:
a friendly guest in the now
calls on a furnished grave.

And in the corner stands
the dear old arm chair.
Sir Isaac Newton sits
in a patch of sunshine there.

Close by my little window
is a marvelous blue.
I see the selfsame sunshine
that Isaac Newton knew.

The light's enormous silence
has confused me so —
the lifeless room is dreaming
and all my flowers grow.

I myself am dreaming,
a seed in the goddess' womb.
The world is but a vision
seen in a blissful tomb.

The backs of worthy books
stand there in faded gold
and call us with a voice
two hundred years old.

O, wondrous, precious sunshine —
my soul can grasp you here!
O, may this hour dwell
with me a thousand years!

                         M.A.

OTTO GELSTED (1888 — 1968)

     April 9th

At dawn the dark birds flew
with scream of motor-screw,
squadrons that swept across the city's brow.
We saw them go, and seeing,
knew to our innermost being
that we must taste the bread of bondage now.

A morn of cloudless blue.
The sun, so sorely due,
shining at length, but as on sightless eyes.
Cramped in her captive chain
lay Denmark, dumb with pain,
in deepest need and unknown agonies.

But on that fateful day
when bleeding there you lay
and all about was gloom and mortal fear,
we saw you then and, seeing,
knew to our innermost being
that never did we hold our land so dear.

                         R.P.K.

     The hammer of the Lord

Your soul must glow on the anvil of the Lord.
Rejoice, the Almighty is sharpening his sword.

Every spark that the iron yields
lights a flower in his sombre fields.

Let it blaze, let the hammer-blows ring —
starry flowers from the anvil spring!

O may he see that his work succeeds!
Beauty adorns his terrible deeds.

Each time the iron with pain will shout —
greater the glory that he hammers out.

                                                    95

Hail! to every fire of pain,
Hail! every hammer's smarting whine.

You must be tempered in a hotter forge
till you are as hard as the hammer of the Lord.

M.A. R.L.

ALLAN BOCK (1890 —)

Already as a boy

Already as a boy
said smart Mr. Normann
I felt clearly
that it doesn't matter
what one is really like
— but what one says and does
and *is* together with people.

So I've been as careful
as a young girl
about my reputation —
I always thought:
what are they thinking of me,
before I spoke.

That's why I'm a respected
man today
with a dossier
— well, like a young girl.

And no one knows
what I'm really like,
not even I myself.
Whatever became of me?

M.A. R.L.

HANS HARTVIG SEEDORFF (1892 —)

Sailor's drinking song

All's well with the compass!
Pour brandy in bumpers
and stick in some candy and stir with a spoon!
Though few, we've a quorum
for quaffing our jorum,
and hey, cockalorum! we're bound for Rangoon.
Trala-la-la-la! etc.

At dawn we'll up anchor!
We sailormen hanker
for lasses to love, from the Pole to the Line ...
But there was a maiden
I met her in Aden,
whose love was — lor' lumme! — like brimstone and wine.

She was slim like a lily
yet black as vanilly,
and so was her family, black as herself.
But all things have finis:
A plague on her slyness!
She gave me the go-by for loony O'Jelf.

Still, why begin snarling
when you have a darling
who's blue-eyed and gentle, nor'west o' Dundee?
Pour brandy in bumpers!
For *she* is the compass
to lead us back home through the foam of the sea.

If pay went like lava
on hussies in Java
her looks of reproach are then hard to evade;
in sackcloth and ashes
with tears on our lashes,
we croon the accordion's soft serenade.

But then on the morrow
we're sick of our sorrow —
and hope for another shore-going typhoon.
And if we're seen weighing,
take solace, we're saying:
''We love you, Dundee ... but are bound for Rangoon''

R.P.K.

TOM KRISTENSEN (1893 — 1974)

Reborn

For Marija Kumacova

Out of the darkness and depth beyond measure,
back of the glittering lanterns of Riga,
out of the wellspring of birth deep in Russia
runs your great river, almighty and languid,
Duna, O Duna, my river, my mother.

Moonlit the night like a girl who is blushing,
twilight as brown as the breasts of my loved one.
Dazzled by drops from my dripping eye-lashes

97

I rub the blindness away from my eyelids
only to see you, swimming companion.

You are my girl, Marija, you naked.
Here in your hands, peasant-toughened and knowing,
hide the caresses that fondle my chin which you
take in your hand. You were raised among horses,
gentle Marija, I feel it, I sense it.

Cooled by the mud and the water your kisses.
Earth, is it river or woman I'm tasting?
You have arisen where birth has its fountain
back of the glittering lanterns of Riga,
way back in Russia, yourself a great mother.
Am I your son or your lover, Marija?

Drops that fall down from your nipples are feeding
milk to the river, O mother of Duna,
Mother Marija of Duna the muddy.
Loving you, meeting you after our bathing,
wet in the bushes, and breathing and laughing!
Loving and bearing and born once again!

Mother and woman, Marija, beloved,
brown as the midnight is brown in the moonlight.
Wolfish the glint in the back of your eyes
under your eye-brows, direct and courageous.
Love, my beloved, O hide me in darkness!

Under the moon flows the sky turning purple,
lush like the juice of a fruit that is bursting,
and in embraces and love and deliverance
vanish my fear and anguish of ageing.
I, who was old, have found birth in the river.

M.A. G.K.

The drunkard

Betrayed, and a traitor,
and harrowed my face —
I've fettered myself
to the post of disgrace.

I've chosen the vice
as free as could be.
I followed my humors.
I was free, I was free.

And brutalized, battered,
too late have I seen:
God wanted me such —
but what did he mean?

M.A.

A purple dot

Today I'm a happy man,
I'm full of crazy joy;
the sky above is big and blue,
my heart's a little toy.
Today I'm wonderfully free
from my reflexion's lot —
I'm just a delirious little nut,
a crazy purple dot.

M.A.

*To my friend, the poet Gustaf Munch-Petersen, who died as a volunteer
in Spain*

Good is the sudden death —
suddenly all can be seen.
Suddenly we know what desperate,
thoughtless youth can mean.
Short and direct your road from
body and thought to the word.
Shorter still your road from
life to the dusty earth.

Words that came from the inner
world that no one may know —
prudence could never inhibit
your poetry's freedom and flow.
The selfsame moment you spoke
the truth was in what you said:
not a thoughtful: I think,
but a desparate: I will, instead.

Here the rest of us plod
in muddy art without flavor,
just an unfortunate debt
sponsored by no one's favor,
dusty phrases and words
written safely at home
while you rest, shot down, shot down,
your life's most passionate poem.

M.A.

NIS PETERSEN (1897 — 1943)

Spring at Mariager Fjord

Two golden butterflies have found each other
and eight fine golden wings bear them away.
A tiny little mouse has found another

and they are tempted sorely but — oh, bother,
this life is all too short and all too gay.

The Virgin worked her silken threads, and thickly
the ends were flying all about her feet.
Two nickers petted in a tree so nickly
that cockoo came and told their fortune quickly —
a nest quite full of little nicklets sweet.

Cowslips and anemones were growing,
and cuckoo's meat was on the earth again
— a hundred million flower girls bestowing
their happy smiles, and gentle kisses throwing
to gay and sweetly smiling flower men.

For it was spring, and all the storming
delights of sunshine had run amok.
And on a grass tuft, green and warming
the blacksmith's lassie, her young breasts forming,
was sewing away on a little smock.

                                        M.A. K.M.

            Do you love man?

        Man came towards me —
        dragging, heavy —
        on the road behind him
        slimy traces
        of lying, of suppurating wounds —
        A voice rang out: Do you love man?
        No! I said — I cannot.
        Love! said the voice.

        Man came —
        closer — creeping —
        slavering with lust —
        with flies and vermin in the wounds of his belly.
        And the voice hammered:
        — Do you love man?
        — No! I said.
        Love! said the voice.

        Closer — ever closer —
        inch by inch —
        the stench growing
        from the thousand diseases of lying —
        and the voice threatened:
        — Do you love man?
        — No — I do not love!
        Love! said the voice.

        Then man rose —

100

and he stretched his hand toward me,
and lo! the nail-prints flowered red —
up to the shoulders his naked arms
were covered with black wounds of sin —
and then smiled:
      God so loved …!
Then the scales fell from my eyes —
and I cried out:
      — Man — I love you!
And my mouth was full of blood,
of human blood.

H.W. M.A.

PAUL LA COUR (1902 — 1956)

Suburb

The red houses are set quite low
burning red against the shadows of the trees,
burning red against the blue roads.

The mighty sky is a battlefield
for red days and blue nights.
The earth mirrors the sky's battlefield.

This last flush of red is the suburb's only warmth
and the chapel with its leprous wall
and the café
and the many freezing children.

M.A. R.L.

The stranger

Peel him off to the man I am, ye powers,
peel him off down to me.
He is tired of borrowing my eyes, my ears, my tongue,
crying with used tears, breathing with my lung
and never sleeping in his own bed,
my hard body.
Melt the lead of my eyes,
break my sides open,
set the stranger free,
he who is much more than I,
and pull, with the cruel arms of birth
a naked boy
out of my blood.

Peel him off to the man I am, ye powers,
set the stranger free.

M.A

101

JENS AUGUST SCHADE (1903 — 1978)

Me

Have you seen my eyes?
They are worth seeing:
there are midsummer nights
like candles in a mirror —
and living women
and playing leaves.

I know of no one
who can see like me.
I amuse myself
by going round looking at myself,

what a mouth I have,
how big and sweet,
how light brown.

                                        M.A.

Inga

I love you like a lemon-yellow ship
sailing across the ocean, shining moon!
Sweet rustling! All powerful Inga Lyngbye,
the power and the wild glory of life
in a little skirt. Are you standing there magnificent
staring out to the sea with your hair
loosened, golden, a round moon
about your head! Are you standing now
with the whispering night wind in your hair
loosened like a mirror of golden billows
under the moon which is rising from the ocean —
rising in mists that envelop you
like your skirt — fluttering a little
under the moon — you walk home
quiet, fresh and naked under your skirt
to your little house in the moonlight
across the earth's darkness which your golden hair
makes bright on the coast of Denmark.

                                        M.A.

Youthful longing

Oh, I'm longing for the fiord
where they catch the cod at night,
and the fisherman's old hat
catches the moon's pale silver light.

Oh, I'm longing for the fiord
and the thousand young and happy
people of the distant North
bathing naked with a girl —

a girl whom they themselves undressed
and whose hungry mouth will cry
with the stark, voluptuous pleasure
that's like pain, by lust possessed.

M.A.

SIGFRED PEDERSEN (1903 — 1967)

Anthem to an inn

Right through the stuffy joint
shines the Dennison crepe,
shines Mr. Ludvigsen's nose.

Dusty the Dennison crepe,
shiny Ludvigsen's nose,
right through the stuffy joint
shines the Dennison crepe.

The Janizary moves,
stomachs up and grins,
wails through his tinny trumpet
noisily improvising
tunes in the foul, thick air,
Sweet little Lou, are you there?

Sweet little Lou, wake up,
here's the aspirin tablet.

Come on, let's go and dance
out on the crazy floor.
All is a teeming chaos,
couples are brushing by
turning like eels in a net,
turning and passing by.

Sweet little Mouse, wake up!
Here's your aspirin tablet,
pick up the streamer and smile,
then you must knit your brow —
look like a queen for a while!

Then sing your native tunes,
sing of the Sailor Black,
sing of the rolling downs,
cheat me of fifteen crowns.

Everything whirling and turning
boiling like whiskey and soda.
Bottles of beer on the table
glitter unreal and harried.
Mouse, are you really married?

Stiffly shines Ludvigsen's nose,
dusty the Dennison crepe.
Shiny Ludvigsen's nose,
shiny the Dennison crepe,
dusty Ludvigsen's collar.

Right through the stuffy joint
shines the Dennison crepe.

                                    M.A.

PIET HEIN (1905 —)

Analysis of omnipotence

I pondered upon
God's omnipotence
and gave up for a problem
so deep and immense.
But I heard two small totters
sift it.
Can God do everything He wants done?
said number One.
That's what He can do,
said number Two.
— Can He also make such a heavy stone
that He cannot lift it?

                                    P.H.

Conversation on the road

   Little cat,
   little cat,
   walking there alone!
   Whose are you?
   Whose are you?
   By golly, I'm my own.

                                    M.A.

   Moral Gruk

   I follow a law
   which is relevant still.

The classic one:
hear, see, and speak no ill.

But wishing no evil
to you and the rest,
one may be permitted
to hope for the best.

P.H. J.H. M.A.

Literary Gruk

I've landed today in a peaceful nook
and dug myself down in a book on a book.
And all is unreal and bookish-stylistic,
and yours truly — yours truly becomes quite artistic
like a product of language and style, and I look
like a man in a book on a book on a book.

M.A. S.S. P.H.

Noble funerals arranged

The Nobel prize
needs a candidate.
Of course, by the hopeful crowd
you're stunned,
but none is sufficiently
well-known and great,
or sufficiently
moribund.
Remember, it's not
a scholarship late —
it is
a funeral benefit fund.

M.A.

Knot bad

My wife is a knitter.
She has quite a knit-fit.
But that seems to fit her
for she is a knit-wit.

P.H.

GUSTAF MUNCH-PETERSEN (1912 — 1938)

thought

everything carnal
is the soul's expression —
the pure soul
makes everything holy —
the feeble soul
gambles innocently
with the fate of others —
there is nothing
impure in the flesh of man —
and all of creation
is also only
the soul's

C.N.

prayer

powers, that rule over heaven and earth
the sun and the storm and the sea,
powers that rule, unseen by the eye,
the ways and the life of man,
powers that rule, unseen by the soul,
horrors and wars, infamy and sin,
powers, in agony I beg —
give me light for my work,
powers, let me not useless die,
mighty ones, burn your stamp
deeply into my wavering mind —

M.A. C.N.

HALFDAN RASMUSSEN (1915 —)

Sardine

Dreamed of escaping once. Was at the bottom
weighed down by five headless brethren
who were preaching every day that a can
was safer for little fish than the Atlantic.

Thought of many strange things. Told
stories and fables to the others.
Sang of the sea, and the Milky Way's
great shoals of fish in heaven.

Tried to wake them up. But all
were sleeping in their fat oil
and were very satisfied with it
and with the whole canned world order.

Dreamed of San Sebastian who would
come from Atlantic morning mists
to liberate all the world's little sardines
with his great golden can opener.

Longed for deep water. Was pressed
into a nice conforming sardine with a spine
by and by resembling that of the others,
soft and flabby like a stillborn lug worm.

Never dream of the ocean any more. Have quietly
accepted this canned church
where I can rest securely between my brethren
while we are waiting for the holy oil.

M.A.

Shoals of fish

Stillness surrounded by fading light.
Rhythm.
Signs which are for ever a code.
Vanishing image.
Hesitant like the music
of released shadows.
Gliding forms
representing nothing.
Patterns on their way to new patterns.
Dream.
Fleeting apprehension
erased by wind and current.

M.A.

OVE ABILDGAARD (1916 —)

Navel

Severed root of my body
centre of my universe
little belly-button.

Since your knot was tied
I am a free-floating balloon.

But who is holding the string
from which I escaped
through myriads of struggling wombs.

If only I could take this hand
and find the way back
like a fish against the current.

That's why I sought you so often
little navel-flower.

But I caught a tail in primeval forests
and only let go when the apes bit me.

Now I roam about among other balloons
with a heavenly yearning in my soul.

Longing for the spring
that runs in the earth
where the earth is dry.

                                        H.W. M.A.

In the bathtub

Like an unborn child in the stomach of the bathtub
I return to the happy dream condition of my origin.
Like an egg under a brooding hen
I lie snugly under the wings of God.

If only I could keep my head down
and bathe my eyes in the motherly fluid
until the shapes of experience are dissolved
and God infuses his spirit into my chromosomes.

Then my rebirth, now
that I will soon rise from my bath,
would open the gateway of my senses
        and I would see God's eyes.

                                        M.A.

TOVE DITLEVSEN (1918 — 1976)

A mother's anguish

A pure, sweet girl is what I most desire,
one who would bear life's riddle in her breast
and in her eyes the sweetness of the night.

Then by her bedside I will kneel and pray
she may be sweet and know no pain or longing,
as gentle as the tender evening light,
born to be a mother and a lover.

But if it is a boy with strong, big hands,
defiant brow, and power in his thought,
then make him one who looks to earth, O God,
and seeks the little joys of earth with patience.

But if my son has eyes of stronger vision,
and if Thou givest him the flame of Art,
then I will carry candles to Thy churches,
then I will kneel before Thy mighty altar
and raise up cross on cross above Thy graves,
because Thou gavest to my fruit Thy eyes.

But if he is one who trembles in the tempest
and falls with salt winds from the east,
a boy who yearns and wishes for the stars —

and if his eyes betray that thirst at birth,
and round his tender lips that emptiness
which gives me fear and anguish most of all —
ah, if Thou brandest him with darkness black
and setst the Cain's mark on his troubled brow,
unhappiest of all that dwell on earth —

an artist born without the holy gift,
then kill him, God, before he sees the light.

                                        M.A.

             The eternal three

     There are two men in the world who
     are crossing the path I see,
     and one is the man I love,
     the other's in love with me.

     And one exists in the nightly dreams
     of my sombre soul ever more,
     the other stands at the door of my heart
     but I will not open the door.

     And one once gave me a vernal breath
     of happiness squandered — alack!
     The other gave me his whole, long life
     and got never an hour back.

And one lives hot in the song of my blood
where love is pure, unbound —
the other is one with the humdrum day
where all our dreams are drowned.

Between these two every woman stands,
in love, beloved, and white —
and once every hundred years it happens
that both in one unite.

M.A. J.H. I.W.A.

The snake in paradise

A lad who was new to the city's ways
was feeling awkward and lonely.
When he met with a girl so kind and sweet
he thought her the "one and only"

They kissed each other often and long
in the park with the boughs to screen them,
and fully agreed that nothing on earth
should ever come in between them.

But destiny dogged the pair one night
as they sat at a cinema play;
it was in the Rialto, "The Vampire" was on,
or "The woman who leads men astray".

The lad was entangled as never till then
by Dietrich's languid seduction,
with eyes all a-fever he follows her art
of leading the male to destruction.

He lets go the hand so fondly slipped
into his when the lights were dimming,
and stares at the drama, lost to all
but the world of his passionate dreaming.

He loves her, that glorious woman up there,
and his tightened heart-strings quiver.
This stupid wench that gapes by his side
is nothing to him whatever.

He gives his sweetheart a sidelong look
and notes that her neck is skinny.
To think he has wasted all this time
going round with such a ninny!

Divine Marlene! Just at the end
she melts in a burst of feeling
and dies with her lover's lips on hers,
her womanly soul revealing.

It's over at last, and the house-lights kill
the moonlight's rapt illusion.
"Only reserved seats now for sale",
announces the play's conclusion.

It's raining outside. In his thin raincoat
our hero is almost freezing.
He puts in a surly word or two
while she babbles on unceasing.

But the street where she lives is gloomy and dark,
and dark are the stairs they are mounting.
Why not turn on the electric switch?
But for tastes there is no accounting.

Better a bird in the hand than ten
on the roof, is a wise decision,
and when she pressed her warm mouth to his,
why — a kiss was worth more than a vision.

                                                  C.W.S.

And it was a night like this

And it was a night like this,
a young night with Nordic skies,
the moon up above was heavy and yellow,
the stars looked distant and wise.

And he was the very first,
but after him — how many came?
I bended my head to his questioning gaze
overcome by the joy and the shame.

And hundreds of young girls' novels
enclosed in my arms, complete:
forgotten the time, forgotten the place,
and sin was all black and sweet.

My heart was expectant and frightened,
the winds died down softly round it,
and each little leaf, and each little grass
trembled the tiniest bit.

But mutely the cold filled the forest,
the winds were soon blowing again:
"Forgotten the time, forgotten the place"
— and she found another young swain.

So I stayed with one or another
as such things have happened before.

111

My heart on the highway was left in the dust.
It's no use to me any more.

It was on a night like this,
and I must have been seventeen —
are the sherds of my crimson love
in the long grass still to be seen?

M.A.

ORLA BUNDGÅRD POVLSEN (1918 —)

The burning sea-lion

The sea-lion is here tonight.
He has settled comfortably
on the fire in the stove.
He turns his pointed
black head
shining wet in the firelight.
He looks at me
with his strange round eyes.
Well, let's sizzle, he says.
A few flames start
from his nervous forelimbs.
His pointed snout appears, without the ball now,
as a clear black silhouette against the fire
which is blazing on his inner side
which is turned to the back wall of the stove.
Yes, indeed, now he's sizzling.

Now there's fire
in his powerful
tail-fin too
which rises slowly
and sends
blue and yellow flames backward.
Then he looks at me one last minute
where I'm sitting out in the room.
"Aren't I clever," he whispers
while he's slowly being consumed by the flames
leaving an awful stench
which settles all over my evening house.

M.A.

THORKILD BJØRNVIG (1918 —)

Here

Here in the dark tower of my manhood
high aloft and with no view,

112

memory's images dissolved in my blood,
which flows with sombre, strong desire —
here where all is icy certainty
and no hope, successful action
and no faith,
separation with no
fragrant dream of reunion —
here where I cannot understand
how I ever got here
I know only one thing: to move slowly
my huge tower, my tower of conquest
in waking nights, grey mornings, in the intervals
between laughter and work, intervals
without expression, exchange, embrace,
the pauses when I notice an otherwise
unnoticeable shiver — to move slowly
forward an impregnable fortress,
unknown, and strong as my destiny.

M.A.

Interruption

A certainty is drumming inside me, pulsating to the tips of my fingers,
a certainty from line to line, word to word,
a controlled rage, placidement and vigilant.

Interruption. But the drums go on, do not abate, run amuck
in ugly cacophonies, rhythms and visions confused,
an idiotic and fantastic piece of work — needing

uninterrupted continuity like e.g. a disease or a journey,
lacks position and alibi, can apparently
always be postponed until tomorrow, the day after tomorrow.

But the secret employer (who or whatever he may be
of whatever sex) is always telling me: No, it's now —
and everything runs on idling noisily,

infernally, just at the moment when I was to have finished
as if one were a wound-up clock, runaway, run down.
The rest is emptiness and desperate guesswork,

irritation, convalescence and oblivion
and the question: Is this so-called work, Art maybe with a capital A,
at all worth the trouble — and with other things neglected?

M.A.

JØRGEN NASH (1920 —)

Whoring song

Oh
just like that
without your sheltering petals,
the key
at the body's ticklish lock —
again our mating time!

For spring is indeed
a newborn vitality,
and your nipples
warm amulets of happiness
telling the world
that nightingales
will never perish.

M.A.

Poem to a brother

There are doors one must not open.
There are rooms one must not enter.
There are things one must not paint.
There are words one must not say.
Have you seen an escape artist at work?
Then you have seen the king of the image-makers.

Life's great artistic event is to break out,
break in,
        get moving,
                say No,
break through.
Every renewal is naturally a crime
against the hardened wood of convention,
against the strait-jacket of artistic ideologies.
One day we must all
explode in duck pond paranoia,
in the persecution mania of the law-breakers,
        in terror and awe,
                in dagger and guitar,
                        in luck and gamble.

You called yourself a sea-eagle.
They said you were fresh as a white-tailed eagle.

M.A.

OLE WIVEL (1921 —)

Weep for Balder

Weep for Balder — for the mistletoe
struck the gentle God who had already
feared for his death in sudden dreams.
Victory is Loke's. Nana, pale, is
laid to slumber by her fair Lord's side —
burning, bound for Hell their funeral ship.

Weep for Orpheus — see Eurydice
with her slender arm across her eyes
and hidden face, descending now to Hades.
Hermes knew it, when the god of song
took from his lip the flute's sweet sound away,
stopping at the last turn of the road,
there where lights from human worlds were seen —
Hermes knew Eurydice was damned.

Weep for Jesus — he who only said:
"Take your bed and go", and who commanded
waves to bear him safely to the boat.
He was powerless like mortal men
when he stood again in Galilee
in their midst, and his disciples would
not believe that it was he who spoke —
would but see his bleeding hands and wounds.

M.A.

The fish

You hide away
in the smooth, sleek shape of fish
and glide without a sound through the water
wandering quietly up and down
on tender fins.
What could you see
with your unspeaking eyes?

It feels at first
as if you were men's enemy —
your empty mouth
will tell us only what is written
in the bubble's shimmering roundness
one second — but to burst.

You only dream
in gentle waters, till one day
the wind shall rise, and billows
thunder toward the coast.

You lie there bloody
in foam and tang — and are our Savior.

                                        M.A.

OLE SARVIG (1921 —)

Beach scene

Deserted beach
where everything is grey
and shiny, oily water with no winds
the empty road to other coasts

Slimy algae choke the bottom
greenish grey and brown,
and there are piles of rotting seaweed
on the beach

Here at life's forgotten place
the clouds stand still
with bowed heads
and black shadow birds
point their sharp beaks
at the barrenness

and their raucous throats
grate on the dry, empty boats of the beach.

                                   M.A. H.D.S.

The copper tree

I am the green copper fire
in the early morning.

I am not the moon, I am not the sun,
I am a living soul,
a lover shining so that you can see me
on every road.

I am copper health,
I am no evil, and no memory
of yesterday is in me.

I *am* on this very day,
this early morning when all are asleep
belongs to me,
and only lovers who see me
gather here under the lustre
of my freshly-blown crown.

                                   M.A. H.D.S.

116

Grey rooms

The day's small
grey rooms,
with no furniture,
no color.

Hopeless to find
what you seek
in these rooms,
in the noise and talk of the street.
There's nothing here at all.

Emptiness, emptiness
shouts at you
as you walk
through the castle
of grey rooms.

Nothing.
Incorporeal nothingness,
shadows.

                    M.A. H.D.S.

MORTEN NIELSEN (1922 — 1944)

The account

You say I am not honest.
I am more honest than you.
I am true to a faithfulness
you slowly have torn in two.

You say I was too inconstant.
It is true, and I had to be.
My hands grew weak because you
gave them nothing to carry.

You struggled hard with another
until you were lonely and white.
And I stood by the side of the scales
— there I was found too light.

And this is the gain you have won,
and this your superior might:
that all is consumed. Yet nothing,
nothing consummate.

                    H.W. M.A.

117

ERIK KNUDSEN (1922 —)

My heart cries

My heart cries in the frozen earth:
birds, wither have you flown?
Moon, come out of your sky.
Wind over dust and earth,
rain on the glowing stone.
I hear them roaring in the night,
the wild beasts —
I notice the pin point stars
on the mountain ridge over my bed.
I once had a flute,
I knew how to use a knife;
I have engraved my name
on rafters and rock
where no other hand could reach.
I sang my song
in mother-of-pearl nights,
and heard it as an echo
in the sea-maiden's mouth —

Echo — a song — my song!
Let go, strangling hands!
Leaden gate, let me out!
Take me back, black wind,
take me away from myself!
I am the pennant, I am the bell,
I must dance or die.

M.A.

The Eve of St. Bartholomew

"While I am writing this, they are killing them all."

Out of open windows rush
men in bloody shirts, naked
women with burning hair.
Their hands point to chalked crosses,
doors are thrown open, and the stairs
thunder with heavy boots. The moon
plays on the river's keyboard;
the dead come closer together, joining
their arms and legs in a fish-like pattern,
beautiful to him who sits in his tower
enjoying the horrible nocturnal scene,
with no brother among the men
who sink under the steel, or see
the street swinging under their feet,

with no sister in the pile
of living flesh which the hangman lights up.

Right in the market-place lies a child,
squealing like a mouse, a little seed
fallen on stony ground. The young mother's cry
cannot paralyze the grip of the hard fists,
cannot halt the horse-legs and wheels
that roll on —

The sun lingers behind the green hills,
behind the crosses of the black windmills,
behind turrets and castle walls.
But from distant cities in a foreign land
streams the sound of joyous churchbells,
hands folded in prayer; and stiff knees
bend to the earth, the pure earth.

M.A.

All men want to be gods

All men want to be gods,
all men want to give back to life
a stronger life —
breed children, build castles, write sonnets.

O joy
of devouring the world
to squirt it out in magnificent arabesques,
O happiness
of cutting your name in the tallest tree.

M.A.

ROBERT CORYDON (1924 —)

Twilight hour

The house lies at the back of the stern dark
garden with a sealed expression.

The bouncing musical notes of the leaves
glide over the chipped plaster walls.

The twilight stretches a web
between the sun's yellow branches

and the cat comes out to enter
the fresh jungle of the night grass.

119

Again we are sitting in the little sanctuary
of the gable room with the window open

and the white scented yarn balls of the elderberry bush
rise above the sharp edge of the sill.

The crown, like the day, is about to fade
in the ether-thin darkness.

Below the window the dense branch
system of the bushes with a

black living bird's throat pouring out
the teeming voices of the forest

from out of the darkness
like a spirited tone cycle.

The tiny, square shadow of the bat
writes its lizard scrawl on the attic ceiling

and the distant monotony of a cuckoo
is hurled through the wet bushes.

The summer night settles in the boiling
little conches of our ears.

Our faces close to each other.
We sit like brother and sister in the dark.

M.A. R.L.

ILJITSCH JOHANNESEN (1925 — 1957)

Evening glow

The sun, a choked Medusa in the sky,
staring wildly with her bloodshot eye

sinks while she is mingling cries of gulls
into her snaky hair of chimney smoke.

Well we know what's now about to be:
look on high what most we want to see.

Staring up from cobblestones and gate
we see a savior who will liberate.

Sunset rider on his glowing horse:
Christ the sun upon his flaming cross.

What the heavens deepest may intend
trees and rocks must surely comprehend.

While the sun was darkened by the blood
all the silent houses understood.

Their naked line which stands there petrifies.
Horror is reflected in their eyes.

And before the sun must finally die
there are strewn from out the russet sky

in the bleeding veins of the sun
lantern squalls of tears from Medusa.

M.A.

JØRGEN SONNE (1925 —)

It's you

It's you, say the eyes.
It's birches, it's sheaves
say the arms.
It's falling rain, skerries in the sea,
say two lips.
It's wings and ashes
says the trembling of the fingers.

It's you, says everything.
It's all, says the silence.

It's seaweed and chanterelle,
resin and wind
say the corners of your nostrils.
It's chalk and meadowland
says the skin of the beech tree
It's fleeing deer
say the clawing knees.

It's snow, it's the surf
says oblivion.

It's the juicy fruit in a fury
says the swelling core.

It's the gateway of the races
says the flash of a deadly sleep.

It's the thunder of the universe
say the heart and the foetus.

M.A.

121

Adrift

Nothing to do, only wait.
Time thins out ...
But we were made for greater pressures.
Like deep-sea fish

forced into higher strata of the ocean
we mount and burst
from our inner, evil pressure.
Waiting is murder.

M.A.

Race

A light grey yellow Burmese girl,
lighter than my café-au-lait.
Straight figure, such slender forearms
and, with her high, wide forehead,
a southern Buddha, behind her big
eyelids and deeply set little black pupils.
She is resting in a blue butterfly chair,
and her finger movements
are those of red shadow play figures.
The arcs of her eyebrows are half invisible.
A straight look ...
at close quarters into, and past,
this thin oiled warrior's face.

M.A.

Other eyes — another world

Ice needles grow through the block
and crackle out lightning.
The crushed points whizz
in the booming prism core,
sun-massif, furnace heaving and bearing.
Whiter, wilder the sting-blown blisters
blast over the borne, the smashed thousand eyes,
the pounding armor, electrified grippers
that surges of hunger impel
from out the smarting magnet of sweetness.

A splintered cosmos dances, glows,
and swells from the bliss of searing
in its prismatic whirl.

Bees swarm round the flowering willow.

K.T. H.D.S.

122

Northwest

The fjord slips between yellow banks:
a muzzle licking hay-green land.

Two schooners with foam-spattered planks
slant horns from the forehead; and

chilliness flows over flanks
of mottled sea —

      a roar of strand
where the westwind giant thunders in
with the light of breakers in its skin.

                      N.C.

LISE SØRENSEN (1926 —)

Girl who is waiting

There is expectancy about me, and I know it — and am sure.
Everything is hushed and waits to hear your steps approaching now,
and a great sealed joy is hidden in the quietly waiting night —
you must break what binds it, for the seal was put on night by you ...

There are dark and tender spaces in the pale green fields around me —
and the night is mute and speechless like a clock that does not run.
Through the birches' airy shadows I can see a fleeting image
of your large and open face, and your jet-black raven hair —

                      M.A.

IVAN MALINOVSKI (1926 —)

Critique of silence

        fallow, tongue-tied, hostile land!
        enzensberger

    The traitor is taciturn
    the receiver, the opportunist.
    He who does not join
    the outcry against the owl
    sides with the owl
    "It is my duty to speak
    I will not be an accomplice"
    said Zola. Even the pig
    speaks its mind
    when it is slaughtered. In Denmark

reigns a traitorous
silence, too great for a country
of its size.

C.K.

Critique of the way of the world

Churches disappear between skyscrapers
castle spires are seen no longer
among industry's chimneys. Rulers
replace rulers. When
will the rulers be replaced?

C.K.

Critique of reason

All over the world there are small rooms
where people mate, stubbornly
in spite of all reason

C.K.

FRANK JÆGER (1926 — 1977)

Handshake for Tony

We, who chose the rain,
we have long and callous fingers
and a great big tuft of hair.
All the green crops of the earth
enter into our lungs
with the air.

We, who chose the night,
we get round and owlish eyes
sowed with sights in weird wise.
And our feet walk warily,
for a thought is pressing hard
on our eyes.

We, who chose the country,
carry some eternal earth
in our pockets and our shoes.
Our teeth are crushing kernels,
take one, take a handful of them
if you choose.

We, who made it life,
one day walk athwart the road
ending in the autumn grass
getting rain and night and country
pressed in tightly to our hearts
as we pass.

                    M.A.

CECIL BØDKER (1927 –)

Grass

We're just grass
on the side of a trench
along time's worn highway
just grass
and maybe a singing flower,
maybe sometimes
nettles.

Over us walks
on cloven foot
the goddess of destiny
with waving udders
musty, maybe –
between the pale red horns
of her teats.

Over us bobs
the goddess's beard while she is eating
a little grass
and a singing flower,
chewing
she walks on the broken necks
of the nettles.

We're just grass
on the side of a trench,
a little dusty grass
along a road
where the years drive by
in the coach
with painted gold crowns.

                    M.A. R.L.

PER HØJHOLT (1928 –)
Traveling to the city

The windows flicker by
the compartment, suddenly dark.

The train roars through a wood.
We are dozing in a cube
of orange and cigar air.

Through the passing foliage
we touch on the abodes of the soul.
Grass floors in steep aquarium lighting,

insect wells. — Brighter now.
The forest dances off.

Stops. Watching how
great weeping birches are moving in the wind
on the meadows below the city.

Mothers passing by on the outskirts
of their children's confidence
wrapped in the incomprehensible.

                                                    M.A.

VAGN STEEN (1928 —)

at this point

at this point in the poem I check myself
will your reading check itself
and will you open your eyes to possibilities

or should I express my hesitation in clear
interrogation marks
            alternatives
                        parentheses
                                    quotation marks

at this point in the poem I hesitate
although the poem itself is acceptable I hold back
at this point

don't think I feel more sure than I do
don't think I feel less sure than I do

note the equilibrium
            the point
                        where they intersect
my certain hesitation / my hesitant certainty
my hesitating reader's certain hesitation
my certain reader's hesitant certainty

at this point in the poem we check ourselves

                                                    M.A.

JØRGEN GUSTAVA BRANDT (1929 —)

Further in

Further into his deep block
(baggage removed, taxi rolled off)
he who went away and thinks he will return home,
changed by the sand of foreign days,
use of heavens, blinded by splinters,
in spite of his distinctive slum fart,
sadly familiar with the place, everything different,
hidden away, shrunk — meeting again the ghosts,
stalwart sentry — man of doors and gateways,
just so things happen, now an indifferent charge
of death, the unlived part of secret,
broken alliances, attic window planners, deeper,
deeper into the old block, into the heart.

Eventually released by the object relation of sorrow,
the cries of the rooms, static echo children,
I, I, things, my dear,
not this any more,
not the feeling of a street province, possibly
what they die of, origin, man,
heart bring me their names.
The find of the museum,
thieves stealing in on thick woolen soles,
worm stomachs, carriers of cotton wool,
removed banisters and gateways
are not the matter, for the case is closed,
the block demolished, miles of years replaced,
and the air has withdrawn from its dregs.

What is gone can not be remembered.
Must not be remembered, will never return.
Writing in the pre-Dionysiac hour,
stillness people with absences, yellow
remains of light, room appointments,
the childhood dependence of age, accelerator
forcing the gateway air, at your choice, on tip-toe,
curly, scrubby metal hair, lustreless
coin eyes, the light, small, quick
steps like aluminum chimes,
the silence of approaches and quiet falls,
the opposite point of view: the deep turned
into a wall, triste chromed slot-machine temptations,
maenad stillness, the back side of the world, lost courage,
the marks and stains of the knocked-about planking,
worn steps, worn doors,
going from inner to innermost, not looking for anything,
(the blue-veiled spring breeze is dancing
through all the passages and backyard abysses ...)
standing in the black square of a vague

worry, romantic, a godless latterday descendant,
my hand on the door-handle, the window-panes staring at me,
there is sorrow here but it is kept secret,
also to the heart, visiting many
in the mouth of night. There one is weak.

Walk in hrough the door, the whole block
holding its breath, doesn't want to die,
consciousness doesn't care, all the same to me,
knowing it but saying nothing, condemned
without unnecessary emotion
to the death of a new day ...

M.A. R.L.

BENNY ANDERSEN (1929 —)

On Terra Firma

The fir tree saps away at the horizon
while the dunes cautiously
peep out behind each other's shoulders.
Low water. Scowling black stones
rise up and lick their mouths
with tongues of seaweed.

Pale and embittered, the lighthouse stares.
at the strutting lower jaws of the ships.
What distant coasts have they tasted —
where is there a lovelier spot than here?

A dried-out sea-anemone
points in all directions.

M.A.

Suck

I have announced my new teeth,
but I shall never have teeth
nor ever had any.
Never bit into a woman.
Never gnawed myself out of prison.
I can't chew life,
it's too coarse,
the fiber's too tough.
Once a long time ago
the nipple of the breast gave me suck
and I sank deeper and deeper
with gentle, imaginary swimming movements.
I'll never get the grip again.

I look up to all teeth
but my own gums
won't hold on to them.
All I can do is suck my way.

M.A.

Sound sleeper

Impossible immoderate morning
when you never get out of bed
it's so big
or you just make the edge
the size of a county
you worm your way
under a low damp eiderdown
a lone lost spermatozoon
not fit enough to make it
got to make a pause
draw breath and take courage
no sweaty panic on the sheet
there are still untried folds to follow
no traffic to watch
one is expected out there on the eiderdown border
with questions, appointments, chutes, neckties
one is expected to wake up
it's one's duty to dig oneself out
once a day
and show up
have a bite
grow a little
wait one's turn
stretch
bend
sign something or dance
commit oneself
learn one's lesson
pick it up
but all this eiderdown
makes me very tired
it moves before me like a glacier
what can be propagated through eiderdown
send a blanket Morse message
to impatient superiors,
and family teacups
educators and creditors on guard:
I am alive but with my strength reduced in advance
start a search
with radar, frog men, a few Great Danes.

M.A. R.L.

The same

I'm walking in order to walk
in order to keep walking
not to reach a goal
I don't believe in goals any more
I'm walking to get back
so actually I'm walking in a circle.
I believe in circles,
in circulation.
And when I get back
I'm still the same.
On the whole I'm glad to be I.
I wasn't always,
but now I've gotten used to it
and would not want to be someone else.
Just imagine what I would miss.
The people I know.
If I were just one of them
I wouldn't know them like I do
maybe I wouldn't like them,
and I certainly wouldn't like myself.
So let me stay the same
only more and more so
both in sorrow and joy —
I want all of it.

M.A.

The memories

Sometimes the memories of those days rise up in me
of course I'm much better off now
back in those days
                    I went to the dentist regularly
my fountain pen was often blotting
once I thought
                    my bike had been stolen
and I was very worried about the future
which, as I can see now,
                    has been quite all-right
and still my heart gets sentimental
                    at the memories of those days
when I was never overwhelmed by memories.

M.A.

UFFE HARDER (1930 —)

Express cable

The face of the door twitches
the brown asphalt floor is sweating
and the walls smell of sulfa
one invisible hand presses another

Billows of fog roll over the tracks
and a cold sweat breaks out on the brow of the locomotive
no more no more the wheels thump over the cross-ties
a wet hand closes the mouth of the sleeper
but he wakes up and throws it in the waste basket

The mannequin has whooping cough and ties a red ribbon round
       her forehead
The walls are masks covered with fins
Tomorrow our fingers will be cold and we will start a new day
and the dogs will chase the hobos who will all die
with the exception of him who knifed the mailman with a nail file
and lets himself be brought to the police station
by two cops with colds

M.A.

Late summer

You don't feel like writing a letter
to the old friend you haven't seen for ten years
and from whom you suddenly heard

you are toying with the thought of going to bed early

with what right do we speak of an epoch of love
when possibly something quite different is approaching

There is a golden hue in the sky

The premonition of autumn is also
a kind of heavy gold dust which covers the bottom of the streets

Something still lush and faintly over-ripe.

M.A. R.L.

From here

From here
we're keeping an eye
on the eczema of violence on the earth

131

on the movements of the armies
and on starvation

on a little of the despair which exists in the world
on a little of its suffering
on a little of the pain that howls in the bodies
in the burnt flesh

We keep an eye on it,
that's all.

M.A.

KLAUS RIFBJERG (1931 —)

Midsummer

The summer night
impossibly urgent
I can't remember
who you are
sitting there a big brown silhouette
in the gutter
some girl or other.

Geyser-heavy lilacs rise from the earth,
snowball trees
arrogantly
underlining the summer
scents,
night bird wings.
Holding the edible dusk
between my teeth
and drying the cold distraction from my brow.

What do you want from me
crouching
in the gutter
in the midst of a perfect reality
filled with oblivion
the season's cash presence
which prevents one from seeing
you as anything but
a second
a third
a big slouching silhouette
of lacrymose reminder and recrimination.

I can't remember you
but I feel the accusation
as if waking from a depressing
nightmare

your shadow a bubble
in the brain
thick night odors
perfume on armpit sweat
and you
or another
a bat crashed
shot and injured
wings tattered, arms
crutches in the sleeve opening.

Would not the madness
shoot through me in waves at the moment of waking
at the sudden recognition, my sister,
at the incestuous relation
to a member of the family of bats?
I recognize you,
remember.
You turn your face away, shadow,
resting your radar tears
on me.

                                        M.A.

                    X-ray plate

    A skeletal moment
    sees through the whole environment
    mortar, cement, plaster, stone
    auf wiedersehen
    only the steely,
    the reinforced, appears.

    Surrounded at last by quintessence,
    concretion.
    Clattering, swaying
    descending insect life.

    Dig your teeth in and avoid
    softness, skin, lymph, sinews
    feel dizzy at the sight of the symmetry
    viewed from within
    a flayed, ribbed whale
    from within
    a burnt-out zeppelin
    from within.

    Swaying above
    is still the adjacent property
    but trying the metallic sound of the wings
    steel blades, the bat

stirring up dust with its horny feet.
Wants to take off.
Wants to be its own
flying play pen.

With the steely taste in your mouth
you watch the skeleton reality
groping and calling
for your hand
so we can experience together
the world's flying constructions,
a city on insect wings.

But you are rattling
your hands
like rumba balls
calypso
and the heart cannot see
can only hear
a quick metronome against a rib.

M.A. R.L.

JESS ØRNSBO (1932 —)

Soap hymn

Christ gazing in wood
sends smiles down from the church windows
is seen caught in fishing nets by disciples illiterates
hatching eggs in his armpits
Christ suspended on the swelling crosses of his lovers
basement representations
rosette anatomy in Gothic cathedrals
distorted by rosefingering Bushmen
betrayed by baroque angels
trumpeting in vulcanized nightshirts
Christ a Jew.

Christ rediscovered at last
in demagnetized clothes closets behind the waterpipe gantlets
and stretched tapestries
blessing
with fingers extended on lamp shades
with six-pointed yellow seals
gills in his side
vinegar-burnt to the last viscera
Christ with barbed wire hair
with gas clear eyes
and tiny broken knuckle-bones.

134

entry into Jerusalem
palm branches and spread carpets
freight cars and dead cans
Treblinka Majdanek Oswiecim
Slowly Christ empties his pockets
·of twine, potatoes
and nails.

Christ objectively analyzed
by a doctor
scabies hanging like iron balls
a simple loaf of bread down his back
Christ stripped of his wooden legs and braiding
his dolls and prostheses
his hair of oblique lino
Christ finally ready to wash feet
Christ naked before his time

And the risen savior
soap — —

                                    M.A. R.L.

ERIK STINUS (1934 —)

The Yogi speaks to Vasco da Gama

When one says I
it's not so easy
to comprehend,
it seems big
like a sore in your mouth
and it is so small,
a splinter from a whole
wanting to be the whole facade.
Try to say non-I.

When one says we
like the heads
of nations do
and members of societies
one is really saying
I, my ego,
which is I
on the strength of we.

When one says violence
one is saying one and we
and inventing they;
violence is my power
to uphold I

at the expense of you;
we call it
equilibrium.
Try to say non-violence.

When one says Krishna
one is saying Christ,
the Pope, Allah, all
the old things;
when one says love
one is speaking a word;
when one says one
one is saying: well, my ego,
you are not alone.

Try to be alone.

M.A. G.D.

Colony

Seven years
heaven threatened us
with its tyranny.

Seven years
without the courage
to turn about
and cry at
the burning villages.

Seven years
the stars waited
that man
should stop
praying.

Seven years
hunger harrowed
the land
and the dead were forgotten
in fear.

Now the voice of thunder
sounds from the depths
of the forest.
A spear
stands quivering
in the earth.

M.A. G.D.

BENT IRVE (1934 –)

Lazarus

No one remembers my death
but everyone recalls my resurrection.

I did not describe a moving line
of descent across the sky
like Icarus,
I just died
a simple, terrestrial death.

Thus closes the book of oblivion
around the lives of most.

It was only given to me to reopen it.

When I stood on the threshold
with smarting eyes
and moldy garments
they had to look me up in the records
to be sure that I
had really died.

My fall
up through time
and the dark earth
was only moving
because of my sudden arrival.

From then on the given pattern
was broken.

From then on it has become harder
to die.

M.A.

The houses

We can never quite
make them ours.
There lives in them
a translucent impenetrability,
a walled-in soul.

Their eyes become downcast
with men's sorrow
and they shine with their joy.

Extinguished toward morning
they surround a desert.
But burning through the evening
they are vessels of hope
breasting the night.

                    M.A. J.T.

        Tracks

    A mite
    for the wordless?
    A letter
    in the mail slot of the silent?

    The night
    is running over
    with poetic bluff
    and my sleeplessness
    leaves no mark
    on this sheet.

    But
    the cars out there:
    clear tracks in the snow.

                    M.A. J.T.

        Model

    Standing
    in his studio
    of passing time.

    In front of me: the painter's back
    the eager hand,
    the moment of description
    from now until doomsday.
    His brush in
    the dust and decay of time.
    His shoulder turned to the room's
    burden of confusion and bric-a-brac.
    Behind this painting toiler
    an observer is born,
    and behind this observer
    other observers,
    rows and rows of them,
    all the way from the model
    in the prow of creation
    in the midst of dust and clutter.

138

We stand in line.
We peep in over the backs
of conceit, false certainty,
in over doubts and more doubts,
shoulder after shoulder,
there in the grey dust
defoliated, looted, worn down,
our model, man himself,
mysteriously erect,
stripped to the bone of his will,
alone in the dust,
frames and rubbish.

M.A. J.T. R.L.

INGER CHRISTENSEN (1935 —)

Like a slate-grey ocean

Like a slate-grey ocean
my flat winter brain is suspended
in space

A fleeing lighthouse swings
my falling eyes
around

what we called land
is the closest stars

M.A.

Whispering grass feet

Whispering grass feet
steal through us,
fir-tree fingers touch each other
when our paths cross,
tough burning resin
glues us together,
summer-thirsty woodpeckers
peck at hard
pericarp hearts.

M.A.

139

From The text / Extensions

The things do as the lovers say / be-
cause the lovers do as the things say

if there's to be a ban on loving / the
lovers will comply with the ban / and call it

something else / when the people in power come
to the place of the crime / they will only see

the dust and the fallen statues / the helpless
hanging and the skull fractures / the whole

illiterate suffering / smiling
all is now buried / the process itself

as such is broken up / all is funny
old ruins and silence / they won't see

the naked demonstrators / gently
embracing the broken marble figures.

M.A.

PER KIRKEBY (1938 —)

The angel child paints

The angel child paints with transparent colors on the window
behind the pane is the air and the distant cypresses
and sunshine and snow
where mother's car gets stuck
and Quiet Road which is mother's road
and the Agricultural College
with the strong horses
look, my daughter
is walking through the light
of the transparent colors on the pane
and from the moon
the greatest danger is so close
here my daughter cries
oh how nice and yellow mother is
said the angel child
and how time flies
the summer flowers wither and one morning
the snow falls grey
where the angel child stands at the pane
and floats away in white robes
in blue transparent light
oh what a dark winter morning

oh little girl
your smile pains me
but look she comes out and says
dear old Daddy Bear
go to paradise with me
as soon as you can
and escape from death
now mother is leaving again
from the snow right into the rainy forest
come and play with the angel child
Daddy Bear cries out
the little child with its heart-rending tears
at the world's overpopulation
which is so bad that people are walking up and down between pots and
     pans here
oh her mother is tempting her
my child put a cloth over your face against the sandstorm
and come down here to the Tuaregs in the golden country
mother whispers seductively
in the open door
and then mother sleeps in a silver room
oh says the angel child when she sees it
see the world in my eyes
and the little child looks up
tell me more oh please tell me more
across the shiny flat
the angel child gives commands
from her tank
and the world is
nothing but transparent light

                                                    M.A.

PETER POULSEN (1940 –)

the old age home at Hald

when I go to the grocery store or the butcher or the post office
I pass by the old age home at Hald
there are six hundred windows facing the road
like strange shriveled flowers on the potted plants
which their deceased wives loved and cared for
I see the heads of six old men
they are watching life's television show
from behind the plants that have been alien to them all their lives
but which have now come so close
I salute them but since I am a stranger
they are too embarrassed to return my salute
maybe if I were to sit down in the window a while
when I return the same way
only the potted plants remain in the window
I try not to salute them but I'm thinking:

I'll bet they've gone in to have coffee
since all six of them are gone
and then I add kind of casually:
yes, I'll bet they're all having coffee now
in all the old age homes in the country

M.A.

KIRSTEN BJØRNKJÆR (1943 —)

When the cat is out

When the cat is out
he crosses
the threshold
to the big world
he wiggles
all his whiskers
sniffing mice

He examines everything in the environment
and risks it out to the periphery
but glances sidelong back at us in the door
he starts several times at a sound
and prays that it'll be a mouse
he is a curious and interested cat

but when he meets a strange cat
his tail goes right up
he looks scared
and makes a beeline back to us
in a matter of seconds

I've been
that way myself
but in another way

M.A.

STEEN KAALØ (1945 —)

now and then we humans are quite peaceful

now and then we humans are quite peaceful
sitting in front of the TV screen on a long Saturday afternoon
buying hot dogs in the Zoo
saying something to each other which is really absolutely nothing
buying an inexpensive chair to put in the living room

giving up smoking
and starting again
undressing to lie down on the bed
moving the morning coffee to the open window
reading all the publicity that enters through the mail slot
forgetting completely
the choice bloodbaths we are otherwise being served twenty-four hours
    of the day
and walking off to the butcher humming
and then on to the dairy
to buy a musical loaf of rye

oh yes
now and then we humans are quite peaceful

M.A.

HENRIK NORDBRANDT (1945 —)

Dream

in my dream
I crossed a long line
there were no people
and you were one of them
in the cutest skirt of the party

it was snowing
it was your skirt's first snow
I said: I love you
and meant: your skirt and the snow
are a picture that wants to be spoken

I meant: your eyes are green
like the words in my mouth
are mirrors before they become words
where the poem appears
when I kiss them with the words

I meant:
the poem is a dream
and outside of it
you and I are
beyond reach

and you left me
in the sweetest poem of the party

M.A.

While we are waiting

late in the autumn the windows and the rotten
cabbage stems in this landscape fall down
while we are waiting and our damp heads
swell in the wind because we are waiting

and the wind has abated and this house
is full of the odor of neglected cemeteries
and the sun, late and paler than the dead between the roots,
lights up the dust in the west room and we are waiting

as if charred and quite blind among the furniture
while the darkness grows more intense, like the heart expanding
in your chest because the wind
has abated and the cabbage stinks and only mice

cover this country with their mad skittering
late in the fall when all is ageing and collapsing
decomposing and very ugly while our heads
are full of the odors of fall because we are waiting

and a woman who has been collecting driftwood for years
wants to return to a house we once saw.
we saw it from the ocean in a storm, the house
was almost blown into the waves

when strong sunlight broke into that country.
it was late and the wind abated
like an icon being cleaned
and he who was to appear is not there.

M.A. J.T.

Letter

If one day we should want to meet
(and I really doubt that we will)
then let us for God's sake choose a place
where neither of us has been before.
Some deserted island in the Aegean,
or a beach somewhere near Alexandria.

Some place where the nocturnal parks
don't immediately make us see ourselves
as ghosts, where people when they see us
don't immediately come to think
of those who have died since we last met,
and where we don't turn up in their gossip.

Then we might spend the night together
drinking, talking about nothing
and maybe row out on the ocean in the moonlight
and if we didn't drown, part just before sunrise
happy before we had sobered up.

Well, if there exists a place like that(which I doubt, as I just said)
a place where even certain late rays of sunshine
and the scent of certain nocturnal trees
do not remind us now and then that we have tried
all this so many times before with no luck.

Or let's give up the idea of meeting.

M.A.

DAN TURELL (1946 —)

An old Disney comic strip

An old Disney comic strip
at the bottom of the subconscious
where saintly Goofy is ski-ing in the mountains
and suddenly notices that someone is grabbing at
the hot dogs that stick out of his rucksack
and turns round
and sees a bear
and says in three consecutive pictures
''A bear''
In the first his face is calm
as if it were quite a cool question
of knowing the difference between a bear and a chaffinch
In the second his face is pensive
as if he were thinking: — ''and what on earth does all this
mean''
And in the third picture he is terror-stricken
and runs away crying madly for help

As a rule I myself
never get beyond the second picture

What on earth does all this mean

M.A.

SAAME POETRY

SAAME POETRY

Among the earliest internationally known poetry from Swedish territory we find Saame (Lapp) yoik poems, reported by the Saame student Olof Sirma, and quoted by Johannes Schefferus in his Lapponia (1673). They left a mark in world literature. In Longfellow's poem "My lost youth" we read:

> ... a verse of a Lapland son
> is haunting my memory still:
> "A boy's will is the wind's will
> and the thoughts of youth are long, long thoughts."

Original Saame poetry is always connected with yoiking (juoigos), the oldest known music in Europe.

In the second half of the 19th century *Anders Fjellner* wrote his space epic "The son of the sun", a remarkable poem which in its own manner anticipates Harry Martinson's "Aniara":

> Now the son of the sun sails out
>
> — — —
>
> East winds push the stately ship,
> send the vessel past the moon,
> past the sun's resplendent disc.
>
> Sun and moon grow smaller now
> than the Pole Star, but the star
> outshines the radiant sun itself,
> shining with a different brilliance,
> blinding with its purple rays.

Among the poems included in this anthology we find the final verse of *Isak Saba's* "Song of the Saame race" which came into being at a time when pressure for Norwegianization was strong. Here, too, the Saame people are sons of the sun.

149

In our own time it is above all *Paulus Utsi* (1918 — 1975) who has given the Saame language a distinct voice, whilst at the same time maintaining its characteristic, low tone. In the introductory poem to his first book the word is whispered into a rock, received by someone, carried forward, and turned into reality.

His first poems were published in the review "Samefolket" (The Saame People) in 1964. His first volume of poetry "Giela Giela" (Snaring The Language) appeared ten years later, in 1974. His second volume "Giela Gielain" (Snaring With Language) appeared in 1980, after his death. Utsi expresses in a direct and forceful way his strong ties with his native country and the northern landscape, and he also describes the destruction of Same Eatnam by outside forces.

In "The new mountain waters" we read that

> Human hands dam up the waters —
> the water rises, pushes the Saame out,
> reindeer food washed by the water,
> cloudberry moors, haying meadows.
> The fish has lost its path.

The Finnmark in Norway and neighboring parts of Finland and Sweden is the most important stronghold of the Saame language and Saame culture. Here belongs *Pedar Jalvi*, who wrote short stories and poems in the beginning of the 20th century. In the 1930s *Aslak Guttorm* published his collection of poems "Gohccán spalli" (The Wakened Mountain Wind), from which the poem about the Saame language has been taken. In the Finnish part of the territory we find *Nils Aslak Valkeapää*, a yoiking artist with i.a. the volume "Lávlo vizar biello-cizas" (Sing, Chirrup, Little Bird). Nowadays the grandiose yoiking poem "The reindeer of Oulavuolie" by *Mattias Andersson*, a southern Saame from Västerbotten in Sweden, is also widely known.

Israel Ruong
Uppsala
Sweden

The Swedish versions of Paulus Utsi's poems were produced in collaboration with his wife, Inger Utsi, and also Elli Sivi Näkkäläjärvi, Per Mikael Utsi, and Israel Ruong. Other translations were made by Bo Lundmark. The English versions were based on the Swedish translations.

NORWAY

ISAK SABA (1875 — 1921)

Sons of the sun

O, powerful sons of the sun!
No enemy can conquer you
as long as you will love your tongue,
remember our ancestral words:
Saameland to the Saame people!

(B.L.) M.A.

COARDDA JOMNNA (JON ELDAR EINEJORD, 1939 —)

The Saame story of the creation

God created man
in his image
but Dáza was not satisfied
and began to recreate the Saame
in his own image

*

It's strange
that Dáza wants the Saame
to be like himself

to the Saame
it's greater to be a man
than a Dáza

*

God gave you a native country
say the Dázas
and teach it too

but from whom did the Dáza God
take the country
to give them?

151

The gáma on the Saame foot
leaves no track behind
in nature

why does Dáza put iron on his heel
when he moves about in the wilderness?

Do not put iron on your heel
when you walk in nature

*

They keep the Saames satisfied
with cookies and pastries
the cunning ones

and they themselves take the reindeer meat

*

Our people
had a country
but our people
had no need for boundaries
they only knew
it was there all around them
in the north

you can make boundaries
round other realms
and boundaries may enclose
the thoughts and minds of those who live there

leave our realm
without boundaries

*

All is not gold
that glitters
say the wise men of this world

and turn the others away from the gold
so they don't have to share it with them
                                        M.A.

Saame — Lapp
Dáza — Non-Lapp
gáma — Lappish footwear

152

SWEDEN

PAULUS UTSI (1918 — 1975)

Wounded generation

There are deep wounds in the root's trunk,
there are forces that are drying it out.
The root felt the blows,
that which lives in the earth
cannot defend itself against blows that hurt.
It feels that something is changing
its wind-twisted life.

But in springtime,
when the snow still covers
the frozen earth in the north,
the shoots, driven by the power of the sun's warmth
begin to force the tips of the branches toward the light
through all that resists.

The wounds of the root
do not heal quickly.
But it is happy
when the wind tests the shoots.
Now its self-confidence rises,
its faith that their life-giving power
will carry the heritage forward.

(I.R.) M.A. F.R.

The calf sucks

The calf sucks milk
pushes the teat with her muzzle
Her tail quivers
when mother licks her
The good milk
makes her big
Her forehead itches
she plays with birch twigs
and chews them

(B.L.) M.A. F.R.

I yearn somewhere

I yearn somewhere, know not where.
When the light breaks I want to see the wide plains.
When dusk falls I ask the stars
who I am and where I am now.

(B.L.) M.A. F.R.

153

Love with pain

Like a crooked birch
by the mountain side
my life was
twisted by the wind.

As the stem of the birch
shines against the bare earth
so I long for the mountains,
the plains, the dwellings.
That is my life,
and I love it.

(I.R.) M.A. F.R.

Home country

The people I met
were strangers
and their language foreign.
Youth, weighed down by auto power,
lives in the spirit of the new age.
I do not know them any more
in their language or their spirit.
Where did the young generation go
who were to move us forward,
who stole their work
which they were building so fervently?
What happened to the dream
I was dreaming
when time had stopped.

(B.L.) M.A. F.R.

*The yoik**

The yoik is the home of the thoughts,
where you bring your thoughts.
That's why it doesn't have so many words
to give out —
free sounds fare
farther than words.

The yoik elevates the mind of man,
flies with his thoughts
above the clouds,
has his thoughts
as his friend
in the beauty of nature.

* Saame song

(B.L.) M.A. F.R.

Holy hill

On the holy hill
chimes the bell
the holy bell.

Far into the sky
sound the chimes,
meet the mountains.

Come, come
to the sound,
the church tent, the holy tent.

listening
singing
holy words.

Outside
runs the stream
uniting the songs,

from the mountains
flows the water
in cascades.

(B.L.) M.A. F.R.

The new mountain waters

Human hands dam up the waters —
the water rises, pushes the Saame out,
reindeer food washed by the water,
cloudberry moors, haying meadows.
The fish has lost its path.

The lake was forced by human hands,
rises under weight and pressure.
Promontories, beaches become islets.
The water washes rock and strand,
the waves wash birch and bushes.

(B.L.) M.A.

The word

Whisper into the rock
someone is listening in a hidden place
receives the word
carries it forward
and makes it come true

(B.L.) M.A. F.R.

155

FINLAND

PEDAR JALVI (1888 — 1916)

I run in the mountains

I run in the mountains, wander on the bare ridges,
I climb the high mountain peak,
I stroll in the forest looking at the rocks,
I sit there pondering things, and remember
my wonderful childhood days.

(B.L.) M.A. F.R.

ASLAK GUTTORM (1907 —)

Saame speech

Saame speech, golden speech —
O, why did you joyless sleep?
Die not, mother tongue of ours,
e'en if foreign words and foreign will
dug their grave for you
ere you ever came to bloom,
ere your bud had opened wide.

M.A. F.R.

NILS-ASLAK VALKEAPÄÄ (1943 —)

I don't know why

I don't know why one tree
is taller than another,
why one day is brighter
than another.

But my heart weeps
for the people
every day.

M.A.

NORWAY

NORWAY

In Norwegian poetry, the portal figure to the 20th century is *Sigbjørn Obstfelder* (1864 — 1900). In his work we find much of what commonly goes under the name of *fin-de-siècle.* He is a stranger on this earth (''I think I have landed on the wrong ball''), but he certainly has other feelings than those of hopeless resignation (''Should a human brain reel? O humanity, light your torches!'').

Vilhelm Krag (1871 — 1932) represents both the regionalism — the local connection that was so important in the Nineties and well into the 20th century — and the new religious tone which is in clear contrast to much in the literature and public debate of the Seventies and Eighties. He sings of ''Sørland, my mother country'', and tells us from his island what his ''soul dimly senses.''

The giant of the Norwegian literature of these years, *Knut Hamsun* (1859 — 1952), publishes his now famous collection of poetry The Wild Choir in 1904. His mighty keyboard includes both nostalgia for the earliest and most obscure origins, as well as the innermost nerve and core of the reality that surrounds him here and now. His ''Island in the archipelago'' gives us this and more. He is the poet of the labyrinthine passages of the mind, the sovereign anti-logic of association, the voice of the blood, and the ''prayer of the bones''. World famous as a prose writer, with a prose that is largely pure poetry, his one volume of poetry has also had a lasting influence on the development of Norwegian poetry.

One of those who were most directly influenced by Hamsun's poetic diction, his oral form, and the rhythm of his lines, is *Herman Wildenvey* (1886 — 1959), who was himself to be a source of renewal to every kind of verse in Norway. With Wildenvey a smile again appears on the stern face of this nation. To the smile in his charming linguistic music was added a humorous note, which was popular in the best sense of he word. But it was a humor which, like the music of Mozart, can always be related to sadness. The ambivalences of life, love, and death stand as lanterns at the entrance to the garden of his poetry. And there is room for philosophical profundity behind his engaging form. The garden whispers ''tear-stained and wet: Ferryman Time, whither goest?''.

Olaf Bull (1883 — 1933) made his debut a few years after Wildenvey. It was in the year 1909. We may indeed call this the royal year in Norwegian poetry. Olaf Bull was perhaps the purest poetic intellect in Norwegian literature. With him thought becomes poetry, and poetry thought. Here we encounter an interplay between passion and reflection, intimacy and distance, cast in language of the finest quality. He seeks to exorcize the depths of death and the grave in order to preserve his beloved in the "eternally young alabaster of poetry". He sinks down in despair before the gateways of annihilation, but in brief, divine moments he also feels a liberation in his faith that all recollection is "a seed of life, a tiny spark from the sun of truth, that nothing lived can die."

To continue our felicitous chronology: after only two years another author enters the stage, a man who was to become a storm-center in Norwegian culture for almost two generations, a healthy salt in our public debate, and a teacher of fearless sincerity, Arnulf Øverland (1889 — 1968). His poetry, almost ascetically free from cliches and empty phrases, extends from the period of his youthful nostalgia and lonesomeness, through his struggle for social justice at home and against tyranny and suppression of freedom in the world, to his shining verses of opposition to the German occupation and Nazism during World War II, during which he spent several years in German prison camps.

During World War I Olav Aukrust (1883 — 1929) appeared, perhaps the foremost artist using "nynorsk" (a form of country speech), an ecstatically visionary poet who continues the great European tradition and the impulses from Edda poetry and the folk ballads, Voluspa and the Draumkvæde. Aukrust himself said that he "sucked honey wherever he could find it.". One of the impulses behind his powerful poetry is that of Rudolf Steiner and anthroposophy.

This impulse is even stronger and more obvious in Alf Larsen (1885 — 1967), the poet of beach and coast, for many years publisher of "Janus", a magazine which played an important part in the Norwegian cultural debate. As a lyrical poet Alf Larsen is sometimes uneven, but at his best he is one of the peaks in our poetic landscape, immortal as long as the waves will thunder against the coast he loved and celebrated in his poetry.

Steiner and his spiritual and intellectual influence have also been at work in poets like the fine, deep writer Per Arneberg (1901 —), and in André Bjerke (1918 —), a master of form and the poetry that celebrates the joy of living with many undertones to his strings, as well as in Jens Bjørneboe (1920 — 1976). In the latter part of his life Bjørneboe steered the ship of his poetry by somewhat different lights — social indignation and a desperate desire to unmask the evil of man throughout history. But at every stage of his life he remained a good poet. The prominent and original essayist and philosopher Aasmund Brynildsen (1917 — 1974) also published poetry, and his background contained strong elements of anthroposophy.

But we should not forget other important currents in our poetry during the first decades of this century. One of those who were already well on their way at the turn of the century was Nils Collett Vogt (1864 — 1937). He is, among other things, an exponent of the strong national enthusiasm which culminated in the dissolution of the union with Sweden in 1905, and which left traces in all of our culture, science, and art during the following years. He also feels a strong social commitment, with poems proclaiming an uprising of the working classes. "It is ours, this earth, my comrades, ours unto its farthest bounds."

160

In the social struggle, partly with a revolutionary content, he is followed by i.a. *Kristoffer Uppdal* (1878 — 1961) and *Rudolf Nilsen* (1901 — 1929). Uppdal is the poet of the railroad and construction workers. But his great social epic also gives us intense descriptions of the leader, the pioneer. In the powerful poem "The iceberg", one of the greatest in our entire literature, we again meet the unifier, the genius, in a form which is both magnificent and frightening. Rudolf Nilsen, a city poet and poet of Oslo, was not yet thirty when death reached him. But his fine and well-planned snapshots of the city and its people, and his pure and courageous revolutionary poems assure him a place in Norwegian twentieth century lyrical poetry.

A number of original talents made the years before and after the middle of the century very thrilling. They are all essentially lyrical poets, often poets of protest, sometimes satirists and humanists. A vigorous, representative élite whose lives and work really merit a broad presentation which cannot be fitted into a short preface. But *Aslaug Vaa* (1889 — 1965), *Nordahl Grieg* (1902 — 1943), *Emil Boyson* (1897 — 1979), *Ernst Orvil* (1898 —), *Jacob Sande* (1906 — 1967), *Halldis Moren Vesaas* (1907 —), *Inger Hagerup* (1905 —), *Tor Jonsson* (1916 — 1951), *Gunvor Hofmo* (1921 —), *Paal Brekke* (1923 —), *Astrid Hjertenæs Andersen* (1915 —), and *Einar Skjæraasen* (1900 — 1966) must be mentioned.

Even so we have as yet failed to mention two of the most important: *Tore Ørjasœter* (1886 — 1968) and *Gunnar Reiss-Andersen* (1896 — 1964). Both had deep roots in a humanistic philosophy with Christian influences, and both achieved a poetic diction of their own, recognizable among all others. In other respects they are different. Ørjasæter — an inland farmer, a native of the Guḍbrand valley; Reiss-Andersen, a city boy from Vestfold, a beachcomber and cosmopolitan.

So far we have not said much about the form of the poets. By and large traditional verse constructions were used up to the Thirties. But already Wergeland had written "modernistic" verse, although here the term is somewhat misleading. Nevertheless it is possible to distinguish a fresh tone in the palette of poetry in the early Thirties. In 1933 *Rolf Jacobsen* (1907 —) makes his debut with the volume "Earth and iron". Here the subject matter is new, to begin with. The products of modern industry are brought into the magnetic field of poetry. Gradually Jacobsen develops his own special close-up technique for photographing the world and the many small details which give us an unexpected perspective. A small lamp post, a pavement stone in the street, or a snail on its way in the dew — everything becomes a fact that speaks of man and his destiny. In recent years Rolf Jacobsen has received European recognition, and is now represented in anthologies in many languages.

About 1940 *Claes Gill* (1910 — 1973) published his two small volumes of poetry "Fragment of a magic life" and "Words in iron". His poetic technique works with parenthetic statements and allusions; there are elements in his poetry that remind us of both Yeats and Eliot, and Gill united in a very personal way the European and the Norwegian background. Rolf Jacobsen and Claes Gill introduce new tones, tones that gradually come to be heard both among the poets we have mentioned and among others. A fine lyrical poet like *Peter R. Holm* (1931 —)

shows aspects that bring both to mind. *Erling Christie* (1928 —) is another important "modernistic" name.

At the same time new and valuable things are created in what, from a formal point of view, is a more traditional manner. *Hans Børli* (1918 —), *Olav H. Hauge* (1908 —), and *Alf Prøysen* all represent "rustic Norway", and give us, each in his own way, valuable contributions of intimate passion, humor, and identification with "the man in the street."

Around 1960 *Georg Johannesen* (1931 —) and *Stein Mehren* (1935 —) make their debut — two of the most interesting names in recent Norwegian poetry. The former, a political ultra-radical with a very fastidious poetical form, laconic, even mute, and at times full of Old Testament wrath. The other open, here and there perhaps somewhat indefinite, but with the passage of time appearing more and more as a poet in the Wergeland line, a cosmic poet of ever increasing stature.

About 1965 there occurs a certain change in poetry as well as in the other forms of literature and in the general cultural climate, in Norway just as in many other countries. The Vietnam war, political radicalism, student revolts, hippie culture, other sub-cultures and anti-cultures, are a few indications of this. De-mythification of the author's role is another indication of this change. We get a "neo-simplistic" poetry with such names as *Paal-Helge Haugen* (1945 —) and *Jan Erik Vold* (1939 —). Often the simple poetry turns into a loud and sometimes one-sided political message. We may mention such names as *Tor Obrestad* (1938 —), *Stig Holmås,* and, in part, *Einar Økland* (1940 —). But poetry is still being produced which cannot be classified and stowed away in any particular box — e.g. *Anbjørg Pauline Oldervik* (1918 —), *Kolbein Falkeid* (1933 —), *Arild Nyquist* (1937 —), *Jan Erik Rekdal* (1951 —), *Åse-Marie Nesse* (1934 —), and not least *Tove Lie* (1942 —). Opinions meet and struggle, goals are proclaimed and attitudes criticized, in poetry as in the rest of literature. Great, divinely inspired fighting poetry, such as Øverland gave us in his white-hot wartime verse — this we must do without for the time being. But we believe it correct to say that up to the last quarter of the 20th century poetry in Norway is both many-strung and many-colored. Much of today's verse is no doubt worthless scribbling, but much remains which can be enjoyed. A main tendency seems to be desire for contact with the reader. To quote Gunvor Hofmo, one of our most original and most sincere poetic voices: "I want to come home to human kind."

Eilif Straume
Oslo
Norway

162

KNUT HAMSUN (1859 — 1962)

Island off the coast

Now glides the boat to
the coastal island —
a blue sea island,
a verdant strand.

The flowers stand there
for no one's eyes,
they stand like strangers
and watch me land.

My heart becomes like
a magic garden,
with flowers just like
the island's now.

They speak together
and whisper strangely
like children meeting
who smile and bow.

Perhaps I was here
at the dawn of time,
a white Spiræa
that is no more.

I know the fragrance
from ancient times,
I tremble amid
these dreams of yore.

The night is thickening
over the island.
The sea is thundering
Nirvana thunder.

M.A.

NILS COLLETT VOGT (1864 — 1937)

Pan is dead

No longer are they fighting by our side,
the noble gods, who in man's morning rose
from his desire to live free, fair and wise.
They walk no more with us: long since they waned,
when sin's dark doctrine fell on weary men,
with coward thoughts of terror and remorse,
and Death first entered an enfeebled world.
Now every hour he lies in wait for us,
and mocks us, like the serpent's baleful eye
which watches scornful o'er its destined prey.
The whole creation travaileth in pain,
and through the woods at evening runs a sigh:
The mighty Pan is dead ...

But still He lingers here, that mystic, pale,
forlorn, deserted form from Galilee;
and where his hand is stretched, there fades away
the smile of confidence — resistance dies,
and man, abashed and fearful, slinks away
to clammy shadows, where no sun dares shine.

G.M.G.

SIGBJØRN OBSTFELDER (1866 — 1900)

The rose

The rose!
I love the rose!

All the world's young lips are
kissing roses, kissing roses.

The trembling dream in the maiden's heart
— none may ever know it,
none but one,
the rose.

164

Every woman on earth has blended her breath
with the rose's perfume, and whispered with trembling lips
the lovely words, the burning words that no one knows,
no one but the rose, itself the most burning tremor.

C.N. M.A.

Helga

Helga!
Oh look at her bright gay eyes!
Quite
black her gown today,
eyes that shine with a thousand lies ...
Light — so light ...
she waltzes away.

She has such jet-black eyes!
Black, intoxicating lies!
Will they catch her?

I think she is happy,
— not tired, not ill, —
I think she can twitter and sing
I think she is warm,
warm to the handsome,
I think her arm
is strong and still.

Now she is through,
— blushing, fair!
And now she brushes back her hair.
The dance was lovely?
Your heart was there?

She is still alone.
Ah, her dewey eyes!
Like a soul that knows
rainbows
between the words of men,
in the smile that glows.

M.A.

Can the mirror speak?

''Can the mirror speak?
The mirror can speak!
The mirror will look at you every morning, searchingly,
look at you with its deep, wise eye
            — your own!

165

Greet you with its warm, dark blue eye:
        Are you pure?
        Are you true?

M.A.

Hymn

When the first tear melts
then sorrow breaks.
O God, give me the first tear.

In me the tear is ice
and my sorrow the rose of the ice.
In me the tear is ice,
and my heart is cold.

M.A.

VILHELM KRAG (1871 — 1933)

The cry of a bird

The cry of a bird on the ocean waste
        far from land
crying so sorely the grey fall day,
failing wing-beats dying away,
        sailing on jet-black wings
far o'er the waste ...

C.N. M.A.

KRISTOFFER UPPDAL (1878 — 1961)

The starling

The starling he sits on the roof
a-playing his love-song there.
And she who will soon be his wife,
she thinks his song is most fair.

On silver shoes dance the notes
and sing of the warm nest in store.
But once he has captured his wife
he never will play any more.

M.A.

166

Working hard

Working hard they sweated both
day by day all through their life.
They sorrow knew and happiness.
He was man and she his wife.

                                    M.A.

The voice of the generations

Life has faded, life has budded,
life has lifted tide on tide.
Like the springs and falls it changed,
son was born and father died.

                                    M.A.

OLAV AUKRUST (1883 — 1929)

Bliss

When eyes plunge deep into fearful eyes
that never, never will reach the deep —
and see the light in eternal skies, —
when up and up all their love must ever
surge and sweep:
When joyful souls have each other found,
their minds so close to each other bound
in starry light that never can fade,
how blissful them to be man and maid.

                                    M.A.

A naked branch

A naked branch with berries red,
and one in leaf and flower,
may each, if love is judge, be said
to beautify their bower.

Her lovely scent she gives, the one,
and sweet her flowers fair.
Blood from the other's heart must run
in fall winds raging there.

She shines and glitters now, the one,
the other ripens, burning.

167

And finally her blood must run
where, pregnant she is turning.

I gave you one with flowers on.
I gave you one with berries.
It shall be known to you anon
which richer harvest carries.

                                        M.A. I.W.A.

OLAF BULL (1883 — 1933)

Powerful pain!

You powerful pain! The wild caress of death!
How burning hot he makes his love to *us*
in order that we soften in his arms,
that life's defiance may be crushed in us!

O man! His breath has fanned you to a flame,
his wild, enthusiastic breath upon your brow,
and in his arms you stammer in your shame
and giddy agony: "Yes! Take me now!"

I trust the hand that strokes my eager flesh,
I die when on my limbs I feel your breath!
But hold me not, my love, do not enmesh
my great and burning love, O royal death!

O man! When, all obedient and numb,
he left your body, and your word believed,
and waits with open arms for you to come —
was ever any lover so deceived?

                                        M.A.

To the brave

He who felt that no justice
          in life was planted —
He whose impotence weighed
          in every detail
his own against *others* — to him
          it was never granted
to force to his own advantage
          the hand of the scale — —

He who, shy and pale,
        astonished and cold,
wished that his flesh by
        animal blood were swayed —
Who never could grasp that
        his own presence told,
and heard that his name was
        called, but never obeyed — —

He whose deepest anguish
        was the word *chance,*
who only from sensitive
        chasteness would dismiss
approaching delights at
        twenty yards' distance,
and felt he was too exhausted
        to hold his bliss —

He has been struck by nature!
        He crumbles down
like a decaying wall in
        river slime!
Evil that man's renown, brave souls!
        Evil that man's renown!
He is food for the lowest
        algae of time!

                     M.A.

Tricks

How sweet she was with her lowered eyes!
But her words were like needle pricks
as I eagerly sought my prize:
"I think I know your tricks!"

I felt a chill in my burning blood.
She knew my tricks — I say! —
— And I understood what *she* understood
and wearily walked away.

                     M.A.

The ruin

There stood a temple once
in hundred-pillared grace,
and all around it teemed
the busy market-place.

But those who moved beneath it
in divers useful trades
had little joy or profit
from marble colonnades.

In days when trouble reigned
the ninety-nine fell down,
but one erect remained
at evening in the town.

How fine its leaves did seem,
how graciously upthrust!
The idea was supreme.
The rest lay in the dust.

                                        C.N.   M.A.

Chopin next door

That wretch is playing Chopin again,
and I must finish off this poem soon!
God damn it — now I found a fine refrain;
my feeble doubt is turned into a tune;
now music rapes this poor word, and you,
my desk, are trembling like an organ too!

My pen is beating time to music fine,
Chopin and I are brothers — and divine;
a strange and wondrous rosy bloom in bud
on stalks of music in my paper glade;
but if he stops one moment — O my God,
my great inscrutable mysterious God —
then over tombs of white they all must fade!

                                        M.A.   T.F.

Over a glass of wine

Soul, part those curtains of thine;
cold is the night and fine —
the moon is pouring out herself in your wine!

'Twixt your red wine and heaven's space
the world — a barren place;
this life's quintessence in nectar and sky I trace!

Like thousands of islands the stars now lie
in seas of ethereal sky —
O friends, upon this moment we should die!

                                        M.A.

OLAV NYGARD (1884 — 1924)

My only song

I cannot be glad
for one single day
as long as it's unborn,
my one, only lay.
It burns in my blood
and it weighs on my tongue,
it groans in my heart
and quakes in my lung.

It frolicks with joy,
it bends under strife,
it quivers with power,
it flashes with life.
It gushes like steam
from boiling hot pans,
like falls in the mountains
in gay, singing dance.

It's soft as a murmur
o'er a mountainous trail,
it's still as the earth-spring
deep in the vale.
It's free as the farewell song
souls are sending
to earth, when back to their
source they are wending.

It is still unsung,
it never found word,
it hovers in visions,
in earth it's interred.
And this is my fear,
that gone is the thirst,
the song never freed
when life's thread shall burst.

C.N. M.A.

ALF LARSEN (1885 — 1967)

The crows

Winter birds, birds of my winter!
How their black wings
master the solid air!
In the snow light, palely lying in state,
I see them like great flakes of soot drifting through the air;

the fire of life is still reeking!
The sky mixes the colors of death:
flesh blue, black, and cadaverous shades of violet.
And the earth conceals in white her lean shame.

This is the ultimate age,
the end of the soul's apprentice years,
and the birds of heaven shall be its last masters.
They sit there in mute flocks
on the stiff flax.

Their deep, black eyes:
O winter founts, alive and shimmering,
wellsprings of life!

But deepest down in the dark waters
I see

both fear and rapacious courage.
There is a sword's point at the centre of life's pupil.
That is how it should be!

Winter mornings with suns of ice
and white worlds. Time of crows.
They rule over the snowy fir forests
where no bird has a home any more,
and they lay hold on the birches of the landscape
with fantastic weights of snow falling
from their fine branches ...
Never did the slender birches
carry more beautiful burdens!

M.A.

Walking in the night

Beneath the mighty crown
with the stars scintillating through
the leafy roof above my head
my foot is arrested.
Here I stopped on the road
here in the quiet dark
as if confused
by the peace of a mystery.

What is your word to me, shadow
that lives by the starlight?
What is your message, spirit
that lives in this tree?
— Haunted wanderer, I am
the shimmer that awes your soul
under every tent where you rest.
Now go on toward the stars.

M.A.

172

HERMAN WILDENVEY (1886 — 1959)

Nature

I saw from a garden gate like snow
chrysanthemums billowing white.
I was not looking, as far as I know,
for poems to write.

But poets are poets and flowers flowers
in gardens that father the wish —
I dreamed a dream — something in those magic hours
chrysanthemumish.

There suddenly sprouted, or seemed to sprout,
a bark from the blossoms uncanny,
and lo, a little white poodle bloomed out,
one blossom of many.

A poodle in the chrysanthemum bed,
all white and woolly and curly!
Sure, a botanical quadruped —
it looked like that surely!

Or else the white botanical glitter
of blossoms, albeit not yelping,
seemed animal blooms, a whole damned litter,
a soft woolly whelping!

Woolgathering words you well may say —
heaven knows they will not bear shouting
like those of Goethe ... O Wildenvey!
A white poodle sprouting!

J.A.

February dialogue

They are two:
"What month is it, Mary?"
"Don't you know? You do!"
"February?"
"Queer. So short."
"Very."
"And bare."
"Yes. And rare —
No snow, no sport."

The Holmenkollen car
stops, and there they are.

She is young and fair and bright.
He's all right.

How lovely to walk
and not talk
while snowstars mild and meek
melt against mouth and cheek ...

"Look sharp now."
"Get going."
"Snow."
"It's snowing."
They smile ...
Silence for quite a while.

It is one of those nights
pastel blue:
the city in view,
the city lights,
the fjord,
hills and heights ...
A way
and they
and not a word.

Enchanted and hushed all;
over the path the snowstars fall:
looking back
he sees their track —
hers like a bird's
beside his ...
How thrilling it is! ...
And no words.

She stopped and said,
"Do you love me, Fred?"
"Yes."
"But do you love me?" he says.
"No."
"Oh."

After all how lovely to walk
and not talk
while snowstars, small and meek,
melt on the flaming cheek.
They walk, breathing deep:
"Is it leap year this year?"
"It's a cheap year, my dear."
"Sheep!"

That was a damned smart sentence.
But she'll be repaid:

she'll be brought to repentance
for what she just said.

He tried in vain to be clever —
no use whatever.

Then stopping, she said,
"Do you love me, Fred?"
"No."
"You said Yes a minute ago."
"But you said No."
"I meant Yes."
"So did I, I confess."

No doubt, so did Mary, so sweet and so cruel,
who made Fred an April fool
in February.

J.A.

ARNULF ØVERLAND (1889 — 1968)

Little Adam

Little Adam's largish head
perches on his neck's thin column.
Briskly and by no means badly
little Adam does a solemn
waltz, and then with heart of lead
makes his bow and sits down sadly.

"Girls take partners!" Not a chance
now has he to get a dance.
Sitting on his lonely chair
he may look at friends more lucky.
Skinny has been asked by Claire,
four girls make a rush for Ducky.

Home he turns him, sick and sore,
life's great lesson has begun,
One gets five, and one gets four,
one gets one, and one gets none;
that's the way the cards will run.

Fickle fate with laughter ribald
plays him false, it's clear to see;
and at home will soon be scribbled
his first lines of poetry.

C.W.S.

May 17, 1941

This day is freedom's feast no more;
against a plague we bar the door.

But still its poison entry finds,
and the long darkness slowly blinds.

Here books are on a bonfire hurled,
and lies are bawled across the world.

Free speech is stifled. All the press
extols a traitor's faithlessness.

We batten on ''defenders'' kind
eating the scraps they leave behind.

We move to factory or to shack
with bayonets against our back.

They lead us into slavery
proclaiming — Now we set you free!

Here Kark the thrall his triumph shows
by savage kicks and cudgel blows.

Cells of the Hird with shrieks resound,
but never any corpse is found!

Crepe soon will vanish from the land
for mourning signs are strictly banned!

This day is Freedom's feast no more;
against a plague we bar the door!

*

But though the last illusion fails
our fighting still prevails.

And we may starve or bleed, but still
the name of Norway nought shall kill!

Though all our towns in ruins lay
we'd build the houses, clear the way.

And though their mines our ships should sink
of giving in we'd never think.

Let thy right hand defenceless be
if still we keep fraternity!

What matter gyves or ankle-chains
while nerve to speak the truth remains?

So long as in ourselves we trust
we yet shall conquer, and we must.

Though some play false, though some may fall,
we still hold out, in spite of all!

While reason and respect for law
have still the strength their breath to draw

while there's a spark of common sense
to spread and share intelligence,

while still our hearts beat true and strong
and for the spring of Freedom long,

bomb us, imprison us, as you will,
we shall endure, unconquered still!

Till we ourselves our flag haul down
we never can be overthrown!

G.M.G.

The servant

My name was called in the night.
But when I whispered in my bed:
Father, I am here!
I did not call, he said.

Again a voice did call.
I answered, but it said:
I did not call you, my child.
You just go back to bed.

I was really made to taste
a powerless longing that burned.
Three times I was wakened,
and three times returned.

My god had not heard my voice,
my father did not call.
Nothing was asked of me
but I would have given all.

Now I am calling in the dark.
What will the answer be?
Will there be someone asking:
Were you calling me?

M.A. R.L.

GUNNAR REISS-ANDERSEN (1896 — 1964)

Annunciation

Wrapt in all the summer's sweetness,
words that I have whispered now
into flowing summer winds
in your sleep shall visit you.

And the summer wind that sways
apple boughs against your window
lays what I have whispered now
in the first white apple-blossom.

Hide your face in fragrant blossom.
When it brushes by your window
it is like a shining angel
sprinkled by the dew of morning.

At your heart it seeks to place
the sparkling message of its flowers.
It shall slumber by your heart
like a child, an unborn joy.

M.A.

To the hearts

Forget her never
who never met you —
perhaps she meets you
once after death.

Forget her never,
the one who maybe
waited to meet you
through all her life.

Forget her never
the one you long for.
Forget her never
for her you love.

Forget her never —
for she alone is
the one you love in
the one you love.

C.N. M.A.

A shooting star

A shooting star! A firestone fell
in midnight's huge and jet-black sea.
This streak of light — could this be all?
Could this perchance like dying be?

The star made ring upon black ring
of silence that was mirrored long
where nothing mirrors anything
and he who sees himself sees wrong.

O you who call the midnight *great*
and call this shooting star a *fall*,
and ask in awe — your words can wait.
Be quiet, quiet. All is all.

                                        M.A.

TARJEI VESAAS (1897 — 1970)

Snow and fir forests

Talk of home —
snow and fir forests
are home.

From the very first
they are ours.
Before anyone ever said it —
that it *is* snow and fir forests,
they are here within us,
and then they remain
always, always.

Yard-deep drifts
round the dark trees
— That is for us!
Mingled with our own spirit.
Always, always,
even if no one sees them
snow and fir forests are with us.

Yes, snow-clad mountain sides
and trees and trees
as far as we can see
— wherever we are
we turn to this

and have a promise within
to come home.

179

Come home,
go over there
—and feel with a shiver
what it is to be where you belong.

Always, always,
till the light is gone
in our inland hearts.

M.A. I.W.A. K.K.

Once upon a time

There was a little birch
was promised new leaves
when May came.
She was hardly here on earth
because of that
and because she was so slender.

And the promise came true
— a May wind
he made her quite giddy
and sweet of bark
and sore of all her buds.
A bird came too, and sat
on a naked twig,
said it was snow —

She knew nothing then,
on that day.
But when evening came
the thin green colors
were all over her naked slenderness,
strange and changed.

Dizzy, alive,
she freed herself gently.
Was quite free from her roots, she thought.
Sailed like a bright green veil
toward the hills.
Gone from here forever
— thought the birch.

I.W.A. M.A.

The glass wall

Between me and you
stands a soundless wind
as a glass wall.

180

This is the day of the glass wall.

Each time I look at you
you open your mouth
and call,
but not a word reaches through.

Your eyes widen
and read from my mouth
that I also
bitterly call.

Yes, in such moments you
press your face against the glass
like a wild child,
and become disfigured as a result.
Swollen and distorted by desire
you lean against the other side
and all is mute.

F.F.

EMIL BOYSON (1897 — 1979)

Army hospital death

A glimpse of the moon racing in terror between the clouds!
Then the night nurse, leaning over him, noticed he was cold.
Stretcher wheels echo in dull brains.
Pause. — Morning sun on the bare rectangle
of a bed removed.
On the floor a broken watch glass,
the latest movie magazine left behind without an owner,
and sleepily a mild morphine voice asking: "Who was that?" —
It was the soldier who died when all were asleep.

M.A.

Contact useless

In the Magnito-Gorsk of the Giant's Mill
I met (and this is one of the lesser dreams)
the beast we have reared, the machine-ape phantom,
the anthill king, killer of embryos,
the concentration camp experimenter,
God of the strongest battalions,
professor of Man-of-flesh-and-calculation.
"All that you know" — was my word to the beast — "I know too;
but you do not know the world I love."
The beast replied: "I will destroy the world you love."
I answered: "You will, but you cannot know it."
The conversation ended with no result.

M.A.

Norway 1941

My country, mutely guarded by the stars:
ere I resign myself to the mirage Sleep
slowly turning to thee I summon my soul,
scrutinizing myself before thy tranquil face.

The brotherly silence of spirits that Death made pure
looms in my mind, reminding me of thy fate;
those who died for thee did share death,
their loneliness with thee, therefore I am lonely.

Empty and weaponless is my hand:
but this I know, that fathered by thee my will,
mute and austere like the stars, desires
to serve thee, fighting in thy holy war.

Grief and patience are the portion of the living:
but though I be never elected, may at least
the icy clarity of these starry spaces
strain, like the steel of a sword, my soul!

Soon my will, still watching thee, shall drown
deedlessly in Sleep that wipes out all.
Fidelity be my last prayer! Soon only
thy honor immaculate mirrors the guardian stars.

                                                    E.B.

Before the ship sails

The signs of impending departure are many now;
you see them with a stranger's eye, even if your thought
had sometimes journeyed to those distant lands.
As if the port, the sailors, and the waiting ship
were your native soil and home for ever
your toil adds day to day in bland succession,
but your senses, wiser than you are,
realize that soon the ship must sail.
It will not be when you are done and ready;
more likely when your soul, one sunny morning
or starry night, in contemplation sweet
has wrapped itself around a moment's beauty —
    then, all at once, short words of command
and sudden haste will usher you aboard
without farewells; and before you fully understand
that the signs had told the truth, the ship puts out
and takes you away — to the lands beyond the sea.

                                                    M.A.

182

Old age

When we were young, we often sat like this
alone in the dark — which is still the same;
the house was quiet, and great and strange thoughts
visited our sadness, and our hesitant, groping words
(yours and mine; we wanted to share Everything)
tried to interpret our fate in shy wonder —
     love and death.

This evening, too, there are holy thoughts that come
to our quiet souls: that your flowers
have fresh buds, that our room is clean and tidy,
that the canary can shut its eyes in safety
behind the curtains where the moonlight dreams;
that we are close, and that your tired hand
     can find mine in the dark.

M.A.

ERNST ORVIL (1898 —)

A nuisance

A magpie in an ashtree top,
a black and white old nuisance.
It flutters up
and makes a flop.
And listen — scream and scream it must
of vice and fraud and hairy lust.
Then it flies back —
a white and black old nuisance.

M.A.

ASLAUG VAA (1899 — 1965)

Bat letter

I once imagined that you had left me,
that you and God had of all bereft me,
and made me least of the things created.
Within the house was a nameless dread;
out in the garden all was dead:
grass a-dozing in meadow patches,
water stagnant in marshy blotches.
Within the forest nothing rustled,
and through the moorlands nothing hustled;
it wasn't still, and it wasn't live;
to be alive was a very hell.

Then came the message that you were biding,
that you would meet me, that we'd go riding,
that you would talk with me, you would have me,
that you would walk with me, you would love me.
Then dawned a spring on the withered moorlands;
then roared a tempest through dying woodlands —
and I arose in a blazing song,
a sapling birch like, so sure and strong —
How warm and tender the springtime air!
How blest to wait for one so dear!
— So still it was and such throbbing life.
It was a heaven to be alive.

E.H.

EINAR SKJÆRAASEN (1900 — 1966)

The word of God

The word of God is she whom you love
she who met you with a smile
and body to body, soul to soul,
gave you to know
that the circuit of longing between man and woman was closed.

The word of God is the child you conceived with her
the son who clings to your legs
and calls you father,
and after you is the next step
on the way from age to age.

The word of God is the thought that breaks
away from your happy safety
to stretch its arms round the world
and live and suffer there
— Yes
to be with all
as if it were your own.

The wrought metals,
the wreaking, plowing, harrowing steel
you use
the grain that runs from your hands,
the field that rises in billows
of golden harvests under the sky
— these are the word of God.

Flowers and insects and stars
and all the things whose names you cannot tell,
whose laws you do not know,
and all that lives in you
so small that the heart can close round it,
so great that the seas and mountains are as nothing,
these are the word of God.

The word of God is the final white expanse
where the whirl within us shall fall
like snow in the snow,
where you yet once more, before the tracks are lost in the dark,
must turn about and *see*
— and render thanks for all that in your heart
was the word of God.

The word of God is the time after snow-time
when some shall be spellbound
by the twitter of migrant birds in the trees
and growing things in the sunny slopes
and think they remind us of you
— — — for you were a lover in the world.

I.W.A. M.A.

RUDOLF NILSEN (1901 — 1929)

The voice of the revolution

Give me the pure and the straight, the men who are steady and strong,
those who have patience, and will power never in life to go wrong,
and for my great thought will fight to the death and never sell out
        for a song.

Give me the clever, who know I am real, give me the cool, give me those;
more than for many who say they believe, my need is for someone
        who knows.
The promise of love is a message on sand, wiped out by the wind when
        it blows.

Give me the bitter, the brisk, whose face is not twisted by fears,
give me the godless, the proud, untroubled by mystics and seers,
who shall boldly build a heaven here after their own ideas.

Give me the burning hearts who never by doubt are oppressed,
who are never cowed by despondency and never anxious for rest,
but meet every victory and every defeat unwounded and unsuppressed.

Yes, give me the best from amongst you, and I shall give you all.
No one can know till victory is mine how much to us shall fall.
It may be it means we shall save our earth. To the best goes out my call.

A.T.

Christmas on the dole

We who're condemned to live
in grey and ravenous slums
celebrate now the sun feast
of him who from heaven comes.

They gave us twenty dollars
to celebrate Christ's return.
For that we have bought a Christmas tree
and some wood to burn.

For that we have bought some beer;
a pound of horse-flesh too.
The latter recalls the manger
where Jesus was born to you.

The master and lord of the poor!
To sorrow and grief he came.
They hanged him at last on the cross
right between sin and shame.

It's good that it's only a tale
that Christ has returned from the sky.
That's one of the poor people less
to torture and crucify.

We of the sombre alleys
feasting on Christmas pie —
at Christmas it's twenty dollars,
at Easter: Crucify!

M.A. I.W.A.

Confession

You feel there's no meaning in life?
We're born and we're buried too
but is there a goal in the world,
a meaning in all that we do?

I know of a meaning in life.
It is that you do your part,
your duty in all to your class —
in action, in thought, and in art.

It is that you never give in
contented with laurels won,
but fight with defiant hate
for justice and peace for your son.

186

For you can have nothing to hope for.
Happiness is not for you.
Your toil is for future ages,
and all that you plan and do.

I know of a meaning in life.
It is, in the nameless throngs
to fight for the working class
with rifles and thoughts and songs.

M.A.

The rival

The whistles were screaming at last
that now it was five again.
The workers poured out from the mill.
You ran out ahead of the men.

You happily gave me your hands
and smiled at me: What a surprise!
But under your smile was fatigue,
and shadows surrounded your eyes.

I picked up your hands in mine
and felt they were tired and sore.
You came from machines, whose marks
of brutal caresses you bore.

M.A.

PER ARNEBERG (1901 —)

Heart and hands

Here I walk, eternally man, my hands
bursting, ready to embrace
all that was touched by beauty,
life's eternal woman,
forests and blue violets.

But my hands are tamed and heavy,
there is no heaven in them,
no hell,
only my heart,
long lashed by god and devils
has a proud, unyielding defiance,
an unquenchable fire.

Alas, my heart,
alas, my hands,
what are forests and blue violets to a woman,
and the heart that is only burning, burning
— a heart without hands.

C.N. M.A.

Shield your eyes

Shield your eyes,
protect them from thoughts.
Thoughts come and say:
Do you see what others saw?

C.N.

NORDAL GRIEG (1902 — 1943)

May 17, 1940

Bare today is the flagstaff
where Eidsvoll's trees show green,
but never as now have we fathomed
what the blessings of freedom mean.
A song through the land is swelling,
of victory's hour it spoke,
though only by closed lips whispered
under the foreign yoke.

A faith has been born within us.
Freedom and life, we find,
are one, by a need as simple
as breathing to human kind.
We have felt the menace of bondage,
and gasped in a stifling throe
like men in a sunken U-boat —
and we will not perish so.

Worse than the flaming cities
is the war which no man sees,
which spreads as a slimy poison
on meadows and snow and trees.
By terror and base informing
a plague in our home is set;
but the dreams we have dreamed were other,
and these we cannot forget. — —

G.M.G.

Hope

Now is the time for the miracle on earth,
now hope conquers.

Yes, through all that lives hope streams:
the tender grass, the buds turning green,
the young girls with leaves in their arms,
and mothers smiling at the children's eyes,
all is hope!

But through the happiness rises a cry of anguish,
a groan of pain, a life that is doomed:
that all is hopeless.
A man who loved, dreamed, fought for his own,
but now only with an eternal echo —
that it is hopeless.

And she whose soul was hope, the young mother,
just now smiling at the life she bore,
she hopes no more; she carries within
another burden, growing and gruesome.

O life out there —
with leaves and bird-song and sun and laughter —
is not everything evil and meaningless
when people among us whom we love
let hope be murdered?

But we who walk in the rays of life
have the power to turn all the light against the darkness,
the power to turn the rays of the sun against death.

Now it is *we* who must speak the word of creation —
the loneliest, the weakest can speak it:
Let there be light and hope!

For each of us can give his gift to the light,
can become a part of spring's victory on earth,
a part of *hope*!

M.A.

The sprinters

Owens, the nigger, sprinting.
The Aryans fall in turn.
The fair-haired stadium wonders,
the Fuehrer's face grows stern.
But cheer up, thinking of many
Jewish women and men
who ran for their lives in the streets —
them you could catch again!

M.A. J.H.

189

SIGMUND SKARD (1903 —)

New York, N.Y.

Far out at sea
you met me again,
and I sniffed you in with open nostrils
and said: "Howdy" —
Breath of land after days at sea:
stench of cars and drifting flowers
asphalt and sweat
and a whiff of hot stone,
manifold and sensitive like the body scent
of one whom you love,
and I said: "Howdy — it's you, is it!
I guess we feel the way we used to
about each other."

You scared me the first time
you know
with your giant limbs
and your mixture of curses and breathless caresses,
but you got hold of me anyway
and never let me go,
for you are different.
You are different right through.
I remember you still,
that first skyscraper morning:
the rain drifted down between your icy summits,
and the fog hung black under your mountain sides.
Deep in the canyon purred the river of cars,
heavily, with a stony murmur underneath.

And I shuddered, and trembled violently,
and shivered: "By God you're ugly, my love,
but it's you."
Now I know you, and you don't scare me any more,
except once in a while.
Now I walk on your streets
as if I owned them,
and you grin at me as to other lovers,
harsh, but not unkind.

Your mornings are glorious,
with the sun rising over misty roofs
all the way to the horizon,
playing over raven-black gorges,
lighting the cairn on the Empire State,
moving its shadow down grey abysses,
painting a streak of light on bushes and mountain plants
in a crevice about the 60th floor —
victoriously down to the stone valleys
where it awakens life and the scavengers

and those who were sleeping on the fire escapes,
and sweeps over a lonely green tree
trembling with glittering light
under the slopes of Rockefeller Center.
Toiling and tearing — of course!
You hear seven million people
brushing their teeth and buttoning their pants
and painting their lips and going to work —
and I like the sound of it,
but sometimes it drives me deaf and crazy.
I like the thundering wheels,
the patter of gliding rubber,
the screeching din of the els and subways,
and the swish of countless pairs of feet
ebbing and flowing in Fifth Avenue:
girls rocking their breasts before them
in the morning sun,
perched on the curb like mountain swallows
two inches from death —
hurried striped trousers
with briefcase and diplomatic glance,
and men who long forgot
to care
I like the long dragon of cars
biting its own tail,
the trucks under smoking chimneys,
two-decker tourist buses
like one big skyrift on wheels,
and the gal in the '50 Packard
picking her way through the traffic
with a windblow and old eyes
steering with lazy hands
enamel, nickel and horse-power
and Nicaragua mines
with hosts of perspiring dagos.

I.W.A. M.A.

INGER HAGERUP (1905 —)

My love

My love came home last night, and there
were sparkling snowflakes in her hair.

My love is no longer my own.
Another has her heart alone.

My love herself has been beguiled.
She wept last night just like a child,

when in her sleep, close to my ear
she whispered: "Dear, I love you, dear!"

T.F.

Dies Irae

Mute is the final hour, and all that lives
drifts helplessly to its destruction then.
The earth itself kneels down, awaiting mute
the final portent and the final death,
while men with narrow, scrutinizing foreheads
and thin lips, work with test tubes and with plates.
They make their dreams of the catastrophe,
unbarring great apocalyptic gates.
Then breaks earth's brittle shell, and dire
combustion joins all elements in fire.

M.A.

Love itself must also die

Kill me, she said, for death must
master us anyhow.
Rather than living deserted by life
I will desert it now.

Love itself must also die
and never return again.
Love, let me lead our way,
let me be dead by then!

M.A.

I trust —

I trust in many things. In blood. In fire.
I trust in paths that drown us in the mire.
I trust in dreams that make us far aspire.

I blindly walk. Oh, do not lead me home.
Let darkness lead me on where'er I roam.
There is a door ajar in pitch-black gloam.

Some place where spirit and the body meet,
some place where time itself is at my feet
— surely there my heart the fire would greet? —

But heed me not. The words I speak today
are dangerous prophets who only lead you astray.
You must not think I am the one I say.

M.A.

We hold our life

We hold our life within a tight clenched hand.
Such is for ever our heart's demand.

It gladly suffers scorn, affliction deep,
if there is something it may always keep.

A man, a child, a dream must ours be,
and measured out in years, eternity.

For in our dread perplexity and blind
to conquest or to prey turns all we find.

By day and night eternally we meet
the pallid fear of our heart's defeat.

C.N. M.A.

The crazy boy

The crazy boy in the other house
was shackled fast. At night it was that we
would hear him howl. I whispered in my pillow:
Thanks, dear God! At least I'm free.

The crazy boy no longer shrieks,
but still on starless nights when I'm alone
I'm wakened in the blackness by a scream.
The scream is not the boy's. It's my own.

H.P.H.

I am the poem

I am the poem never born,
I am the letter someone's torn,

a path that no one walks along,
a melody without a song.

I am a prayer that's heard by none.
I am a childless woman's son,

193

a string no hand has drawn up tight,
a fire that will not ignite.

Leave me! Release me! Let me flee
from soul and body, rock and tree!

But nothing answers when I plead.
I am those things that don't succeed.

T.F.

Emily Dickinson

Very slender. Very small.
Always neatly dressed in white.
Through the house one heard her steps
always perfect, always right.

Dusting shelves and watering flowers
with her busy little hands,
baking bread and taking walks,
writing cards to distant lands.

Loving sister. Loyal daughter.
So the doll's house days went by.
But the hidden fire ravaged
and the muted heart must cry.

And behind the bolted door
of maiden room in childhood home
lay a stranger no one knew.
All too brave. Too much alone.

Lay a surgeon cool and listened
to the pain, the naked smart.
While the pillow mutes her cries
she dissects her dying heart.

M.A. R.L.

JACOB SANDE (1906 — 1967)

Mary-Ann

Mary-Ann is that pale little child,
      poorly dressed and plain.
Mary-Ann has heard them say so
      and stoops with the cruel pain.

She quietly leaves the others,
　　lonely, blushing and hurt
outside doors that are locked to her,
　　where words would be distant and curt.

She knows that her hands are red
　　from work in the freezing air,
and her skin very coarse and sallow
　　from neglect and poor man's fare.

Those eyes in their heavy sadness
　　her silent pain betray.
But longing and deep within her
　　the girl's soul is hidden away.

Sensitive, shy and humble,
　　a dreaming flower of night
that breathes in the air of dusk
　　and quivers in morning light.

M.A.

ROLF JACOBSEN (1907 —)

Pavement stones

Trample us under foot, jam us down and forget us,
but our muscles carry the whole world
and feel their strength growing under the pressure.

Paper, banana skins, black gutters,
and neon lights, dazzling department stores.
Lo! Our armies reach to the end of the world.

Silently we carry New York and London.
We keep quiet under the limousine
and stick together till our knuckles whiten.

Children of granite. Cast in volcanic forge.
Hewn from the bones of the earth to carry.
— You found us in Rome and in Niniveh too.

We were present in the blue Atlantis.
We saw the birth of new continents,
shaking off the waves, facing the light.

And if one day we hear the world booming
with heavy boots marching to the new age,
— O, grey brothers up there, let us follow.

M.A.

Landscape with excavators

They're eating my forests.
Six excavators came and ate of my forests.
Good God, what misshapen things! Heads
withour eyes, and their eyes behind.

They're swinging their jaws on long bars
with lion's teeth at the corners of their mouths.
They eat and spit out, spit out and eat,
because they don't have a throat, just a huge
mouth and a rumbling stomach.
Is this some kind of hell?

For wading birds? For the all too wise pelicans?
They have blinded eyes and chains round their feet.
They will work for centuries chewing the bluebells
to asphalt, covering them with clouds of greasy fumes
and the cold sun of their searchlights.
Without throats, without vocal cords — and without complaints.

M.A.

Blizzard

In the morning a blizzard fills the streets
like a mental disease in the light
— someone trying to play the flute with amputated hands,
trying to cover up the traffic lights with laced handkerchiefs

but like every attempt at changing our world
it fails and is itself
changed
into waste oil and urine seeping down into the sewers

Butterflies in chloroform are not sufficient,
or slowly moving a sponge over the foul picture,
when the hand hesitates, unsure of itself,
and the picture is of iron.

M.A.

But we are alive

— But we are alive
right through the supermarkets and the cheese racks, and we are alive
under the jet con-trails in the golden month of May

and in smog-enveloped cities,
we are alive with coughing carburetters and slamming car doors.

196

We are alive
through the TV evening of the golden century,
on the asphalt, behind the weeklies, and at the gas stations.

We are alive
in the statistics and social security numbers, in election years, we
     are alive
with a flower in the window,
in spite of everything we are alive under
the threat of nuclear annihilation
by the hydrogen bomb, in-
somnia, we are alive
side by side with the hungry who
are dying by the millions, alive
with a great fatigue in our thoughts, still
alive, alive
magically, inexplicably
alive
on a star.

M.A. R.L.

Sorrowful towers

The slaves had massive hands and built sorrowful towers.
They had hearts of lead and shoulders like mountain walls and built
     sorrowful towers.
They had hands like stone hammers and built mountains of silence.
They stand in Burgundy and Baalbek and Xeres de la Frontera,
ash-grey walls over the forests, foreheads of stone and melancholy eyes
in many places on the earth
where swallows form large arcs in the air
like soundless whiplashes.

J.S.

HALLDIS MOREN VESAAS (1907 —)

Happy hands

Happy hands!
From deed to deed, waiting there
only for them
they move all through the day.

It is given to them to serve at the source of life.
The hands make bread,
give out food at laden tables to hungry mouths.
Cloth glides through them, is turned into clothes,
clothes glide through them, become clean and smooth

fragrantly enfolding our bodies,
and lie shining white on bed and table.
Spots and dirt and dust disappear under the hands,
they want everything around them to shine.

Happy hands!
They live in water, and holding wood,
iron, and many kinds of metals
cold and hot,
lighting candles, making warmth.
Flowers they may touch, and all that will grow,
stroke the fur coat of an animal,
support a plant that was bending,
hold cautiously a costly book.
All day long the hands are full.

And evening brings them
new gifts:
clothes, water,
pillows to smoothe,
a child's fine skin and soft hair
to touch lightly,
a loved face
with weary features.
And when night comes
they sleep in the dark,
quiet and warm
in two other quiet, warm hands.

Happy hands!
What happiness one day
to rest forever.

I.W.A. M.A.

OLAV H. HAUGE (1908 —)

The schoolyard

When the bell rings
for the first class
the schoolyard is once more
like a concrete poem.

Close groups together
at the front door
coolly discussing
moon shots
and seconds in St. Moritz.

Half finished snow men
left behind
by the youngest kids.

Round the walls
footprints left by loners,
he and she were there.

On the outhouse wall
a mess of snowballs,
a broken window in the toilet,
over the headmaster's door
a contemptuous fling.

Letters in the snow:
Solveig + Knut,
Åse + , — he just managed
to erase it.

Out in the yard
marks of a fight,
drops of noseblood
and a green mitt.

                    M.A. R.L.

The weather-cock

The blacksmith wrought him
with tail and comb.
High up he went
the world was new
and many the winds.
He was a keen one,
strutting, crowing
and ruffling his feathers
to every gust of the wind.
In the storm he stretched out
his long neck.
Until one day he rusted
and got stuck
halfway north.
The wind was mostly
from that side.

                    M.A. R.L.

Today I saw

Today I saw
two moons,
one new
and one old.
I have great faith in the new moon.
But I suppose it's the old one.

                    M.A.

The scythe

I am old.
My scythe and I are one.
It sings quietly in the grass
and one's thoughts can run.
And it doesn't hurt
says the grass
to fall for the scythe.

M.A. R.L.

And I was sorrow

And I was sorrow and hid in a hole.
And I was pride and built beyond the stars.
Now I'm building in the nearest tree
and when I wake up in the morning
the fir-tree threads its needles with gold.

M.A.

ÅSMUND SVEEN (1910 — 1963)

Black wings

The god in me grows smaller and the tone
withers.
The vampire at my heart has sucked itself to power.
Now he overshadows me with his long wings
and a big friendly, evil smile.
His snout finds my solar plexus
gently as a kiss
and I give him my blood.
Each time the god grows smaller
and the tone more weary.
One yellow morning on a green day one red evening
in a blue night — farewell.
The vampire smiles:
break the flute of childhood.

M.A. R.L.

ASLAUG LYGRE (1910 —)

I'm going to the night

I'm going to the night
beyond all the borders.
She who is in black seas
and extinguished lights —

and I will glide blindly
into her embrace.

I will look for sleep,
a sleep without dreams,
and just as I put my clothes
on the sandy beach on a hot summer day
I will step over my body
and forget it.

I will sink into the night
and all that is in me and outside me
will whirl away
like a breath over the ocean.

I'm going to the night
beyond all the borders
and I will give her my burdens
and the flood will carry them away.

But as the light
loosens itself from the dark
and the land from the ocean,
so I will loosen myself from this ocean
which is night.

I will rise from the waves
and sleep will drip from me like foam
and I will walk toward the east
toward the first rays of the rising sun
and find myself again on the beach
when day ebbs.

M.A.

Hungry sea

The winds roar round the tower.
The beacon blinks in the night.
— Someone is waiting with anxious eyes.

The ocean snaps with its lipless
teeth — then sates its hunger
churning in satisfied peace.

Taciturn winter gulls
limn their cross against the dawn
— Day rises over vigil and waking sorrow.

The ocean has black waves,
the women black clothes.
The sky, with silent thoughts over the deep.

M.A.

CLAES GILL (1910 — 1973)

Morning by the sea

Coming in from the sea, with morning sun
    in your sail and blue mountains ahead —
a shining silver arc against the sky, did you see it?
    The sea-trout leaped!

So leaps your thought, buoyant and gracious,
    and knows no other limits
than the limits nature wisely made:
    a well-ordered world!

But net and bait? — Yes, how insignificant!
    A captured trout, have you seen it close
hard its jaws, bitterly, like one who has
    some secret knowledge:

One tears at the net, one at the bait — but thousands
    cleave the deep and the sounds
teem. Who stays the sun in its course?
    Who binds thought?

M.A.

Vanishing youth

Vanishing youth!
    A hind
hunted by a pack of
    howling hounds

The great hunter
    at his post
coolly musters
    his hands

M.A.

ASTRID HJERTENÆS ANDERSEN (1915 —)

The poet recites his own poetry

I.
The poet turns and twists on the straw mat
with eyes crossing.

He would most like to walk backwards into the ocean,
or be a rolling echo
from the rock breast of night.

He would most like to be quiet and mute
like the lime-white moon in the dark,

like one of the other petrified,
dancing, egg-white moons
out there in the night of the hall.

But the song of a bird
makes its way through his throat.

There is a bird on his heart's branch
doomed to survive.

II.
The poet swings to the left
as if toward an invisible wall.

The poet swings to the right
as if dancing with his own shadow.

Now he holds his breath.
Now he is drinking rain.
Sometimes he stands on tip-toe
with the morning breeze round his ankles.
Sometimes he grows like a tree
with a trunk and a rustling crown.

It works: he sees again the blood-rusty ground
and the brain's fossil on the barren beach.

He recognizes the strip of grass under his feet
and the cloud of night round a human embrace.

It works: there is a bird on his shoulder.
It took wing in a landscape of quiet and brightness.

M.A.

TOR JONSSON (1916 — 1951)

Unborn god

A seed lies in the heart.
The heart is cold as ice.
The seed — it is your hidden dream
of paradise.

But ice will melt in fire.
O fire, burn on then!
Life breathes joy and gladness into
all honest men.

Toward a Holy Place
in earthly garb we plod.
Life is ever yearning for
an unborn god.

M.A.   J.H.

The rapids

Death calls all.
The day is heavy with the struggle
against the powerful arms of the undertow —
heavy with time.
I row against the current,
my arms grow numb and the boat is drifting —
the rapids will stand as an exclamation point
after my life —

I turn my eyes to the rapids
and the rainbow above.
It is like a great church choir —
the vapors are rising — it is the priest blessing
the poor earth.

I struggle against the undertow and its hidden forces
but cannot turn round.
My consolation in death is the dream,
the dream of the day when man will remold
the rainbow into a bridge.

M.A.

AASMUND BRYNILDSEN (1917 — 1974)

You are in my blood

You are in my blood
you are in my lung
as it expands
to breathe.
You are the tear in my eye.
You are the hymn in my soul.

You are.

Only I am not.
I am nothing but blood
and a throbbing heart,
a sigh during the hymn, a breath.

M.A.

ANDRE BJERKE (1918 —)

Light thoughts on a soap bubble

A game of suds and soap: that's all. No more.
A glittering rainbow of bright color lies
in airy velvet bubbles — these replies
must make a decent barber good and sore!

And still: the bubble's movement has a score
of poems, visions; and its beauty dies
like happiness, to all but seeing eyes.
It's like the earth, with a transparent core.

It is like poetry itself, that springs
in form and color freely into space,
but bursts when it must touch the world of things.

May some find soap-suds useful for their lace —
forgive a poet who forgets his troubles,
forgets his reason too — just blowing bubbles!

                                          M.A.   J.H.

        To a determinist

We have abolished Free Will thoroughly.
Instead a happy message you have sent:
that our inheritance, environment
condition our least activity.

But if your brother sins — just wait and see!
You'll talk about his soul's Rearmament
and even cry aloud for punishment,
and force yourself to think his choice was free.

You judge him hard — for having so abused
a freedom which he never once possessed,
and which is nothing but a phantom sad.

I think you would be slightly less confused
if you would urge immediate arrest
because his parents' chromosomes were bad!
                                          M.A.

        The little man

My fear of offices — federal or state —
is fear of cold eyes that penetrate.

That X-ray glare from the bureaucrat's glasses
can frighten me more than a war of the classes.

And whether my business is short or long
I stand at the bar, and I feel I've done wrong.

It's like being caught by the headmaster's eye
which always detected the tiniest lie.

I feel that my mind must be falling apart.
Now all is exposed in my dirty old heart!

Full name and address? — Oh my God, this red tape!
You feel like man who is caught in a rape.

Your name? Occupation? And year of birth?
Have mercy! Take all that I have on this earth!

And where are you going? — Oh God! That to boot!
I'm sentenced to death. And they're going to shoot.

But then there are quite friendly goggles that say:
Call in for your passport on the fourteenth of May!

M.A.

The last joy

A man who didn't feel quite up to scratch
once had his doctor visit him. He said:
Say doc — I hope there isn't any catch …
The doctor said: You're practically dead.

But if you want to live you must not taste
a drop of alcohol of any kind,
no more your money on tobacco waste,
no more exert your body or your mind.

And as for women — do not even touch
them. Save your feelings. Yes, it's tough: all sorts
of little pleasures that we value much
are banned to you: no pictures, books, or sports!

This rule is most important of them all:
if any food tastes good — then let it be!
Your diet will be this: just one fish ball,
one glass of water every day. You see?

Yes, thank you, said our plucky man and bowed.
But tell me, honest — is there any reason,
my dear sir, why I should be allowed
to have a Christmas tree this coming season?

M.A.

Hurry!

Your homework, kids! Competition is hard in
the world today. You must study like crazy!
If we're to better the balance of trade
you boys must improve every single grade.
Society needs you! Your childhood is not
productive of anything much. So hurry!
Yes, try to get childhood over with —
                    fast, fast!

And then you grew up? But you're still too poor.
Your standard of living had better improve —
for what is your moped to Meyer's Bugatti,
and your wife's fox to Mrs. Steen's chinchilla?
They made you a manager? But no peace in your soul
till Hansen retires, and you may stick
the DIRECTOR'S silver plate on your door —
                    quick, quick!

Make haste! Make haste! Reassuring sound
the wheels of the train: your speed is good.
You must get to the terminal on time if you can
with a granite block over six feet of dirt.
And what did you see? This country out there,
your life. Was this all? A few looks through the glass —
like poles on the line your days disappeared —
                    fast, fast!

Now hurry — and drive off the road in the curve
and end in the ditch. You will miss your plane,
but instead you will see the butterfly's wing,
the grasshopper's leg, and a cloud in the sky.
It's drifting so slowly. Why don't you relax in
the grass — it's quite sufficient to know:
you *are* alive, and your life is now.
                    Here. Now.

                                   M.A. R.L.

        Bill of Rights

    You have been given the birthright to be
    dead or alive, or imprisoned or free.

    Choose to be wise man or fool, if preferred,
    fire or water or viper or bird.

    Choose to be something that others can buy!
    Yours is a privilege none can deny.

    If you prefer what is shameful or trite
    that is your holiest personal right.

Yours is the choice if you dig your own grave.
Choose your destruction! Decide to be slave!

Feather or sword? Which of these is your soul?
Which of your choices shows you as a whole?

You bear the guilt for what you've come to be.
You were the chooser. The choosing was free!

T.F.

ANBJØRG OLDERVIK (1918 —)

Oh, my beloved

Oh, my beloved —
do not come when I call you
you were never more marvelous
than in my longing

never richer
than as the one I miss

never more beautiful
than being invisible

Do not come when I call you
because you can be closer to me
than in your body

do not come
— this is your existence

this is *my* existence
— as a dream of you

M.A.

HANS BØRLI (1918 —)

Makeba sings

Your smile runs
like a gazelle in the rushes
round the long
corners of your mouth, Makeba.

And your voice:
the quivering fear of the antelope
at the water holes
when the scent of a leopard
darkens the wind.

Beauty
which like the stars
needs the darkness
to shine.

Makeba singing — —

Put down your coffee cup.
Put your teaspoon
by the pastry on your plate.
Miriam Makeba is singing on TV —
and we are educated people,
we have a *soul* — sure,
a first-class durable
European soul,
not black, not white,
but old and yellow
like rancid fat.

Listen! Her voice rises
in anger. It's as if
it could see us sitting here,
dead with welfare. A panther's claw
glimpsed
in a soft paw, a piece of chalk
in the dust on our hearts:
''all the dark people,
one big team ...''

                                        M.A.

TORMOD SKAGESTAD (1920 —)

                The year after

Boys were playing at marbles
in the spring mud behind a cart.
Girls skipping rope in sunshine.
Kari did not take part.

Why don't you join us, Kari?
And then the girl quickly said:
— I don't want to play with you any more.
She quietly turned her head.

A German came down the road.
Children's faces set.
Kari defiant, straight as a rod!
Her eyes shone clear and wet.

The German on the road
softly stroked her blonde hair.

The soldier's steel helmet glittered.
Guttural, strange his words were:

— Ach Himmel, solch ein Mädchen
hatt' ich im deutschen Land. —
Quietly turning away from her
his eye to the roadside went.

He straightened up, weary and cold.
No smile. No answer. He knew.
Judged by two clear bright eyes:
— I once had a father too.

M.A.

JENS BJØRNEBOE (1920 — 1976)

The song of Hiroshima town

It was a lovely morning
in Hiroshima town,
a summer morning nineteen forty-five.
The sun was shining
from a blue and cloudless sky —
a summer morning nineteen forty-five.

The little girls were playing
among the trees and gardens green
and doing everything like grown-ups do.
They dressed their tiny dolls
and washed them very clean.
The women sliced their bread on kitchen tables.

And many little children
were still asleep in bed
for this was very early in the morning.
The sun was nice and warm,
the dew was on the meadow,
and little flowers were opening their crowns.

It was a lovely morning
in Hiroshima town,
a summer morning nineteen forty-five.
And the sun was shining
from a blue and cloudless sky —
a summer morning nineteen forty-five.

M.A.

We

We of the suburbs, the new suburbs
where everybody hears each other's radio

in the same apartments, with the same words,
with the same lives, with the same
streetcar in the morning. Where we
smell each other's dinner,
where we smell each other's lives:
movies, radio, cancer.

There are no temples to Apollo here.
No Saint John lives in this desert.
No vines grow round the hearts.
No fisherman by Lake Gennesareth.
Not a chip, not a splinter
of a classical pillar.
No emperor here.
But we do have cancer, radio, movies.

Strangely enough we got cancer —
in return for almost everything else.

The aqueduct, broken, alive in the landscape.
The overturned pillar of white marble,
smothered by efeu and wild vines.
Golden sails against the dark, dark sea.
And the Sun.
We have cancer, radio, movies.
We of the suburbs, we are what we are.
And you won't overturn us
with a hymn to Apollo.
There are no accidents in the suburbs.

M.A.

GUNVOR HOFMO (1921 —)

The night

In the empty streets there wanders
a child, and it is blind.
It brushes by your window —
it is sweet and kind.

It creeps into the room —
close by your cheek its breath.
In cool and fragrant wind
sleep pain and fear of death.
Its cold and slender hands
are softly giving you
a gift that is forgotten
when light of day breaks through:

depth behind the image,
unbounded tenderness.

Deep, unutterable
flaming loneliness.

The empty streets are whistling
a brittle tune and shy.
And what you think is darkness
is children walking by.

I.W.A. M.A.

CARL FREDERIK PRYTZ (1922 —)

The wind-bent

who feel a little helpless in the morning
or in the evening and dutifully get up early
and stand in line for the feeder bus and sit
with a worried look on their faces in the subway
full of responsibility for their job and their spouse
or the kids or their old aunt
or mother and father and God and someplace
far into you or far out it dawns on you
that you should probably have taken responsibility for something
within yourself too but it's too much
as it is and now there's this report
which the boss wants today and actually
you should have taken a call for someone
who asked you to remember something and the errand
wasn't there an errand you were supposed to do today to
buy something for one of the kids because the kids
must have what they need and the rent
and the boss suddenly standing there and what's this
you forgot or took down wrong and what
will happen if you can't manage any more
because you're so tired and the papers are full
of all the waste which is piling up and where
does one put it and all the things
that have to be dusted and washed and
moved and all the paper and all the wrappings
and the weeklies if you can't cope with it
another week or two it'll soon fill up
every corner and where does one put it all ...

... and all the others in this ward
are so good at talking about
all their problems and I don't get to
say anything because it's all just a big knot and
I have all the symptoms I recognize them
every time the others mention them and everywhere
is fear and worry about all the things I haven't managed to do
and hopeless and inefficient and I

212

have always been like that and dear God
where are you now because you knew
that I was always trying to do
my best but it was never
good enough for the boss and the spouse
and the kids and my parents and God
you've simply disappeared from me altogether
and I'm all alone always
all alone ...

M.A.

HARALD SVERDRUP (1923 —)

Kimono

I open your kimono
      within
your nakedness shines

I open your body
      within
the streams branch, the sea spreads

     beyond
awaits a pattern of lime-white bones
a timeless immeasurable darkness

I close your kimono
      outside
it burns red-green-orange, blue-violet-yellow

We close our love
      within
a sun-god dreams forth a rainbow

L.A.M. H.S.

Flying fish

A flying fish in flight!
A paltry second of sunshine
a wingéd dance of light
before the ocean will teach you its dark law
against the moon mouth of the shark.

M.A. R.L.

Spitzbergen

Here on the barren beaches of Spitzbergen
there are larch trees from the Lena-Jenisei-Ob

trees flayed by the Siberian floods
bared of the crown's song and merry cones
cleaned of root insects and dark dreams
gnawed and chewed at by stone jaws
with the bark's living hieroglyphs
peeled off
trees enclosed in miles of ice
and slow years across the polar ocean until they finally appear
here in the sun and the storm,
huge organ pipes
of knuckle-white heartwood,
death-organ
and God's instrument in the sand
I hear anthems to the sun
ice hymns, star hymns.

But among these organ pipes I found
a child's ball with remains of bright paint
maybe lost on a village bridge
on the Lena-Jenisei-Ob.

M.A.

PAAL BREKKE (1923 —)

Where all paths are lost

The man who killed on Tuesday
was he a murderer on Monday?
And waking on Wednesday at a grey window
with the shots forlornly driving through him
who is he now

the man from yesterday?
when the stone raised his hand to the blow
or the man he was the day before yesterday who

when was the day before yesterday
He remembers the light from the piano lamp
and hands on the keys
yes Handel
And a heavy grey stone, crushing
He stares inward
where old eyesights are dissolved in the shots
changing their form and place
And looks at these hands
whose are they!
a stone which they threw away into a ditch
or Handel, Handel

who rose from the piano
without looking at him
and lets the door close

And only the hands remained
                    borrowed used

They're like stray dogs
wailing on a barren moor
toward Thursday Friday

                              M.A.

            Ecce Homo

    Ecce homo, said the poet
    decoratively posed against the grand piano.
    I saw my face
    mirrored in a soup spoon
    Ugh!
    Take this cup away from me

                         M.A. R.L.

        ARNLJOT EGGEN (1923 –)

    Village in an underdeveloped country

    There was tuberculosis
    in my village in Norway too
    Young girls cried out in fever
    that they didn't want to die
    Most of us lost our teeth
    before we were twenty
    The draughty old houses there
    were picturesque
    to the tourists
    We played poker for a fag
    sat on a step and spat
    to while away the day
    No prospect of further schooling and out of work
    There was "such peace everywhere"
    like in this village here

    Here is like coming home for a visit
    in strange clothes
    I have been away about twenty-five years
    living in a land that was never ours
    Do you still know me, brothers

                              C.J.

FINN BJØRNSETH (1924 — 1973)

We were the young shock troops

We were the young shock troops who lifted the earth
and put it on our index finger to spin around,
what a gorgeous red and yellow balloon to delight
the children in the front row round the arena.
We were the lament of the west wind at the branches that split
our song into vain, powerless tears —
it should have carried us round the earth and all the way here
where need and want are crowned in beautiful steel and plastic flowers,
we were those who didn't take the homeward road
to the fleshpots, we chose the oblivion of a desert death without a fait
not for the sake of the land we would find
but because we could no longer stand the voices
monotonously preaching the blessings of progress.

                                                            M.A.

FINN STRØMSTED (1925 —)

The stern hour

It is a night with brass in the moon,
it is a night with scattered stars
like dust on the gown of a judge.

The dead hour
when horses heavily change their resting position.

The cold hour
before the fish bite,
before the lights on the coast are extinguished.
The stern hour before the hunt ends.

An early hour without a shadow
before death comes to fetch you.
The barren hour
before the attack.

The stern, biting
hour of judgment
before the cock crows.

                                                            M.A.

Sun bridge

A cloud is raining itself bright
as milk,
and the sun-cat is spinning on a half-wet rock.

216

That's all. All.
Enough for today. Let nothing else come
between the unattained yesterday
and the vague round
taste of salt water and oranges
you suddenly placed on my closed mouth.

M.A.

ARNOLD EIDSLOTT (1926 —)

Three sermons
Second Kings, 19:3

The child has reached the womb's mouth
but she has no strength to bring forth
Is there no one in heaven or earth
who will give her the strength to bring forth
The need of the foetus is known from the fibres
and the veins and the swelling breast
Is there no one in heaven or earth
who will give her the strength to give birth

M.A.   Gab.B.

Portrait of a girl

She worships Chopin
slowly stirring
the waters of sleep.
She is alone
with the mustard seed
in her breast.

M.A.

Sabbath

God stopped the world with a kiss
cycles and blind acids
rested in their own beings
Motionless
the arc of the swallow
The ocean's mill
was locked under the coasts
and the falling fruit
did not reach the ground.

M.A.   G.S.

217

ERLING CHRISTIE (1928 —)

Lone wolf

Roger, the lonely wolf
is hunting under the neon lights —
feared from the square to the Grand Hotel.

Chewing his cold contempt
he snarls at all the smiling couples
angrily invoking a curse on the world.
While he is coldly murdering
those molluscs with his eyes

he expertly boards No. 5
and rushes home quite beside himself
to his couch at Sinsen
where Marilyn has long been waiting
with hungry lips and demanding breasts.

M.A. R.L.

GEORG JOHANNESEN (1931 —)

First lesson

I teach the ant to think
that there is no spruce
just brown needles and too many ants

I fly after the fly
I ape the ape
I cut off my hand and give it to the dog

I teach the wolf to howl quietly
I teach the sparrow to find the hawk
thinking that a bird is a bird

M.A.

The full moon

Fifteen earth diameters away
the moon with its ruined face
sucks the ocean a yard toward her

The leper king out there
is treated with sunshine
in the vacuum night

while a full-size globe
is rotating slowly
in a cover of wind

M.A.

218

PETER R. HOLM (1931 —)

Granite

Like walking about on a
stage: the rocks in the port, the lamps
which extend from them
on ugly steel tubes which give off
a zinc-white reflection, We can
put the palms of our hands on granite
and wonder which performance
this is, Suddenly
the rocks are tuned to the factual
vagaries of imagination, and
in the dark turn into backdrops
for our life. They remain there
after us when the lines
have been spoken and our moments
are gone, just resting there
enduring for ever, granite.

M.A.

KOLBEIN FALKEID (1933 —)

The horizons

The horizons hold out their hands to us
in all things.
Now come on, they say, come on.

Like little tots who let go of the table leg for the first time
to wobble out across the endless floor
we put out toward the ever receding edge of the horizon
where Berenice's hair
falls like silver rivers in the clear, frosty new-moon nights
and the mysteries beckon like a sailor's ocean mirage.
Come on, they say. Everything says, Come on.
And lo, we are always on our way,
life's eternal travelers
with no other baggage than thirst, hunger, and longing.
Plato's cave-dwellers
with memory like a never extinguished fire in us.

No, I'm not talking of conquests
but of the journey, the duty to travel
into all that exists.
For all things have horizons.
Man, love, his working days.
But also the tiniest things.
The distance between the atoms in a drop of water is greater
than between the stars in the universe.

219

And the horizons call us all.
Come on, they say, come on.

Come on, say the horizons of a righteous world.
Come on, say the horizons in the people around you.
Come on, say the horizons in the seconds.

The unattainable horizons.
The world would die without them.

M.A.

ÅSE-MARIE NESSE (1934 —)

Marc Chagall

Garlands of lovers
spun round the earth
celestial rhythms
gently rocking them
to sleep on a star
where time has stopped:
the heart's second
is Eden and eternity —
hear the violin
from the roof of time
the rabbi is dancing
with wings of laughter
Solomon's temple
floats in the sky
with golden gateways
god in the green
the blue mixed
of dust and longing
fables and fruits
the reddest shade
jubilation. Sela

M.A.

STEIN MEHREN (1935 —)

Where the path ends

Where the path ends
Only there will the hidden
be revealed
A rock — the memory of a face
or the petrified
final beats of a heart
Roots — veins in a bony hand

220

secretly carrying the forest
Masks — faces resembling expressions
deep in you yourself

Where the path ends
you can find: log piles
still glowing like burnt-out fires
Stumps where the resin is still flaming
like a light from the earth's interior
Lumber, wells, far into the forests
like a fever, the wounds of incurable
beauty in death and lava
from life slowly dying
Life starting afresh!

Where the path ends
you must really move on. Push
the branches aside and walk
out into the world
Isn't it like conquering yourself,
going deeper into yourself?
And recognizing there
all that surrounds you: the moment
when you can put your mouth to this well
and be the well yourself ...

                                        M.A. R.L.

Gobelin-Europe

There's a Europe gathering moonlight, a Europe
of monuments ruins crumbling columns arches
— entire landscapes gathering moonlight, nights when
seeping light in dust and web of starlight
around the themes, weave gleaming lands of the past
into pale gobelins. But then the threads begin to glow
— one night when the moon rises from the sea like a red boil
suddenly pierced. And the sea fills with blood

a sudden earth-colored living battlefield, a wild
and heathen landscape under the veneer of classicism, a
primaeval tapestry where glowing fir-cones open their petals'
darkness, where haw-drops trickle around night's thorns and
shadows of pine-wood writhe like tentacles, as I walk
by the pool's slimy green: a gurgling mirror
where plague bubbles, a witches' brew where water-lilies suck
a childhood's feeble light from black and poisonous sludge

Gobelin: I live your lightening darkness your dark light
your black sun in your dazzling night, your past is
more than legend, is bread and wine, my wings with their
roots in you, your black faith, your shining doubt

the more I accuse you the more I am guilty of you
In your colours are my poems; like wars massacres
revolutions crusades and saints, witches and graves and
violence, inquisitions and plagues, science superstititon belief

— I drink your black pagan water, I cry
dripping candles, your longings, the humble faith of your
moderation, beauty of your violence, your past which congeals
and suddenly glows in me, in thoughts and buildings words
cathedrals and bourses, in all I see, it's as if death
is looking at itself, as if life's bursting forth towards new
ideas discoveries words, new frontiers of the times; Gobelin-Europe
woven afresh tonight in colours glowing with past!

P.F.

Casa Nova
(The white castle at the horizon)

He was to her
the King of Hearts who rides by
blue lagoons out toward the white
castle between the mountains, he
was a name that foretold storms
in the weekly horoscope, and who came
to kill the dead men, her
childhood heroes, committing murder
every night in Casa Nova

She was to him
an ever faithful refugee
and his Yes to bliss, in all
the lagoons the sun was in her
image with a heart of gold, she was
the writing that betrayed him, the girl
with blonde hair and the Queen of Spades hidden deep
in mazes of mirrors, if he rode
toward her she would just recede farther and farther back,
and finally became his search for happiness: the horizon.

Maybe he was a stiff consonant
on a skinny nag of a table
of the contents of the weekly true stories
He had ridden through all the possible words
of the possible sentences, language after language,
and seen them decay into ruins of
stereotypes facts and dead games, theories,
cryptograms, secret signs, Now
he was wandering restlessly
between computer programmers and readers of the weeklies
and maybe he had a vision of the language turned to face
the language: the white castle at the horizon

222

She — maybe a homebody vowel
a song from the innermost room in the dark
she was the colors of the wind, and the wind from
the changing light, she had walked in and out
between the consonants, driven from sound
to sound,
but always with open hands
and unruly hair, waiting for the rhythms
that would dance her through herself
rhythms that would dance together with the computer programmers
and the readers of the weeklies, dance
when language turns language
against itself, in the tower of Babel ...

                                        M.A.

ARILD NYQUIST (1937 —)

Oh, Santa Claus!

Oh, Santa Claus — send
me a raincoat
without holes! Send me
a 25 cent ball point pen
full of ink
and a monkey wrench
so I can repair the world
a little!

                                        M.A.

Four birds

Four birds landing
in a tree.
On the ground below
thaws the spring snow.
Then one of them
flies off, and there are
only two because my uncle
plays the harmonica
and me, I don't.

                                        M.A.

Under the sun

The sun
opens
its eye
and says:

I
see
you
Arild!

M.A.

Bumble-bee in bed

In the middle of the clover meadow
sleeps the bee in his bumble-bee bed
dreaming of fleas
and beetles and lice
dreaming of cookies and figs
and snuff.
Then he wakes up in the clover meadow
and climbs out of his clover bed.

M.A.

Apple stealing

This is a poem.
It came to me last night.
It came on a billow
and walked slowly across the paper
with small, delicious steps.
Must I walk straight? said the poem.
No.
Is it very far to Africa? said the poem.
Well, rather.
What time is it? said the poem.
Five minutes after four.
Are you all right, Arild?
No, said I.
I will give the last word to apple stealing, said the poem
happily.

M.A.

TOR OBRESTAD (1938 —)

Song to art
Extract from a poem
written for the 1970 Harstad festival.

Serve the people! But what people?

For whom these pollen seeds
that drift on the afternoon breeze
and lie yellow on the window sill, for whom
is the sky full of whirling flower seeds?

224

Is it the flowers on Consul Holmboe's brocade
and is it the cultural emblem of Mr. Fangel, the Manager?
Or is it fuel in a blizzard
on the Bidjovagge waste: the Lapps drive their herds
against the weather. The workers work the profits
in the copper mines. Whom shall we talk about?

Shall we sing about the metropolis
and the profit rates on investments in the periphery?
Shall we talk about the reindeer hearts at six crowns a kilo
at Johnsen's at Grorud? People in Svolvær
never heard of deepfreeze reindeer hearts
from Finnmark? On the express train a picture of a ram goat
looks at us from the wall

M.A.

JAN ERIK VOLD (1939 —)

Oh, well

Today the paper says
there were 24,975 spectators
at the Norway—Bulgaria game
at Ullevål stadium yesterday.

If I hadn't been there
there would have been 24,974
spectators. Oh, well.

And the game ended 0 — 0.

M.A. R.L.

It means

I'm sitting in the sand, drawing
a circle round me.

This means that I am caught.
Then I get up and walk

out of the circle, just like that
— like crossing the equator. Cheers!

M.A.

The day collapsed

the day collapsed like a house of cards
I woke up at the bottom of the ocean

stuck like seaweed
swaying in the distant swell of the foghorn

until I slowly lost my hold and rose
like a lazy fish

sniffing the rock wall
up and up

as if I were drawn by the sun
out of the ocean into daylight

where all was light without a sound
and I twitching on the hook

free

M.A.

EINAR ØKLAND (1940 —)

I was there

Rocks with salt on them.
A blue beach
and sheep in the woods.
A little boy takes this just as it is.

He came from his home
alone. Does he want to look at the sea,
do you think? Or play?

Another rock, fresh sun.
Dangerous depths
below the cliff.
Breeze and dazzling light,
warm wood with sheep.
A little boy with a serious body.

M.A.

TOVE LIE (1942 —)

Afternoon verse

When I had a glass of red wine
on the porch this afternoon
all the deep meaning disappeared
from my life

226

Peace be with it

What do I care about deep meanings?
The sun shines crimson in the glass
and the birdsong is meaningless
the grass and the trees
shine meaninglessly — O, life
so this is joy

— that nothing really
has a deep meaning —
what a relief!

M.A.

HELGE RYKKJA (1943 —)

Sweden

Sweden, such a beautiful country, I dream of you.
Bjørnson was in Sweden and others too. It is the
deep Gulf of Bothnia that's fine, the sea of flames
at Kiruna, the sister city of Gjøvik. High mountains,
not as high as Galdhøpiggen, but high enough.
An infinity of highways.
The national anthem is very old.
Why do we love Sweden now?
Because it has such pliable children.
The Swedes can't take much, can they? They
really get beaten up. We like patience.
I think we love them because they get beaten.
Haparanda.
There's something wrong with Sweden.

M.A.

PAAL-HELGE HAUGEN (1945 —)

Didactic poem on dust

All this fine, drifting dust.
It's ours because we were born down into it.
Our feet walk in it, we draw it down into our lungs
with every breath.
All that rises from living and dead things
and all that creeps and is slowly sucked
off, a grey stream of dust.

We know the coarse dust, the rock splinters,
the sand, the clay, the coal particles from the great furnaces,
the dirty rust from the storage yards and garbage piles.

227

We love it and hate it, dig it with our hands,
let it fill the pores of our skin.

But the invisible dust is different and unknown,
full of strange life, microscopic animals and plants.
Alien, close life.
We see it live in the sun's rays in dark rooms
but we don't know it.
It wells up incessantly from the ground,
from our clothes, rises in a mist from our skin and mucous membrane.

Around us and inside us.
You can depend on it. You know that much.

M.A.

JAN-ERIK REKDAL (1951 —)

Dublin — the city with the green mailboxes

Dubh linn — dark spring
Baile Athe Cliath — the town by the willow hurdle ford
in your dark eyes
run threads of blood
a westward longing in stained letters
expressed in funny little turns of phrase
far from the glib-tongued English of the telephone operators
letters with green bank notes
for the ones that were left behind out there —
filling your mailboxes
flying west like pigeons
black shawls waiting by stone fences
the grey knock-kneed homespun pants
waiting also, but half hidden in the doorway
when the pigeons arrive as buses
and the drivers coo like pigeons:
"Dia's Muire dhuit, a Cháit, seo litir agat, a stóir"
far-off Ireland where Irish is still spoken

Dublin you smother your child
there's stagnant water in your springs
you're feeding your child English dish-water
but the child needs goat's milk, cow's milk, buttermilk
hold your child to your breast
and learn from it your morning song
sing no lullaby
but a morning song, a lark's song,
the wind organ of the stone fence will accompany it
and the donkeys will bray
in spite of the hawking of the English
and the loud market noises of Europe

228

You, city under a Celtic name
your speech is that of a foreigner
but your laughter is fresh and your own
your smiles, your worries and your tears

Do not cling to the frozen image of your lost self
for the grass is the wave
that carries
the ocean is the spring
and the dream is life

                                        M.A. R.L.

SWEDEN

SWEDEN

The modern breakthrough in Swedish prose — including the drama — occurred in the 1880s, but the beginnings of modernism in poetry were to come one decade later, in the 1890s.

The three first Swedish Nobel Prize winners in literature all belonged to the period usually referred to as the Nineties. Selma Lagerlöf was a prose writer, but *Verner von Heidenstam* (1859 — 1940) and *Erik Axel Karlfeldt* (1864 — 1931) were both genuine lyrical poets. All these authors felt strong roots in their home provinces in Sweden, and each of these writers claims his own "province" in the literature of the country. From Värmland, Selma Lagerlöf's home, came *Gustaf Fröding* (1860 — 1911), together with Carl Michael Bellman the country's most popular poet through the ages. Fröding gained his great popularity not least by his incredible virtuosity in rhyming, and by his melodious rhythms. The Swedes are a singing people, particularly fond of lyrical poetry set to good music. The popularity of Bellman's successors among the troubadours, *Birger Sjöberg* (1885 — 1929) and *Evert Taube* (1890 — 1976), bears witness to this. Medieval ballads, incorrectly called "folk songs", have maintained themselves in the oral tradition until our own day. They are still being recorded, e.g. by the troubadour Gunnar Turesson (b. 1906), whose music for Gabriel Jönsson's literary text "Backafall Lassie" is so well loved that it has become a kind of folk song.

The most popular Swedish lyrical poets — Fröding, Taube, Ferlin, Gullberg, Martinson — usually sold more than 50,000 copies of each of their volumes of poetry, which is remarkable for a nation of only eight million. Naturally, this would not be true of the more "difficult" poets. At the beginning of the century the first Swedish "modernist", *Vilhelm Ekelund* (1880 — 1949), wrote free verse which seems rather easily accessible to the present generation, and yet each of his books sold only very few copies. Angered by the public's lack of understanding of his poetical work, he turned away from the "ding-dong" tomfoolery of poetry to devote himself to more manly forms of literature, such as essays and aphorisms.

The key word of the Swedish Nineties was "beauty". In one of his "Thoughts in loneliness" Heidenstam wrote (1888):

> Round half the earth I have searched for
> a place I most beautiful could call.
> So beautiful were they all
> that none of beauty had more.

— and to Fröding the whole of life was so beautiful that you could find beauty even in the smallest and lowliest things:

> even in a louse,
> and in a green leaf behind the secret house.*
>
> *(Drops of the Grail, 1898)*

The generation which succeeded the Nineties lacked the enthusiasm, *joie de vivre,* and faith in the creative power of the imagination of the previous decade. The turn of the century in Sweden, as in the whole of North Europe, was a period of melancholy, fatigue, pessimism, and paralysis of the will. ''I believe in the lust of the flesh and the incurable loneliness of the soul,'' Hjalmar Söderberg, one of the most typical authors of the period, confessed in his play ''Gertrud.'' *Bo Bergman* (1869 — 1967) found the true symbol of man's lack of freedom in ''The puppets'', the title poem of his first volume of poetry (1903). Vilhelm Ekelund expresses a similar pessimism in his image of the ''tired trees.''

But only a few years later the atmosphere of Swedish poetry is again very different. Now there is a new faith in the individual's ability to shape his own destiny, joy at the good things of life, and an almost humorous view of evil. There is a cosy realism about the picture of their homeland which several of the poets draw. *Anders Österling* (b. 1884), for many years Secretary to the Swedish Academy of Letters, and an annual orator at the Nobel Prize ceremony, was the Nestor among these writers. In an early poem he speaks of ''the brave beam of good will'' which is victorious when dreams die, and which accepts reality as it is.

World War I could have meant an end to all optimism, and it did bring a change of climate even to neutral Sweden. But this change of climate was temporary and individual. During the war *Pär Lagerkvist* (1891 — 1976) published his poetic volume ''Anguish'' (1916), which expresses the contemporary feeling, and where his style, a moderate expressionism, broke with Swedish tradition. But after the anguish of his expressionistic period, Lagerkvist came to adopt a renewed ''faith in life''.

In the midst of a world destroying itself in hatred, annihilation, and denial of life, Österling wrote his volume ''The book of idylls'' (1917) in which he turned his eyes to the ''small world'', the idyll, the quiet moments, the sleeping villages. This new provincialism is often reminiscent of the ''home town'' poetry of the Nineties. Indeed, Österling has been called the Karlfeldt of the wealthy southern province of Skåne, until 1658 a part of the Kingdom of Denmark.

During the Twenties a whole movement in Swedish poetry followed in the wake of Österling. To this poetry of the idyll, this ''intimism'' — which had many counterparts in other forms of contemporary Swedish art — belong Birger Sjöberg's Frida poems, and Gabriel Jönsson's ''Backafall lassie''. Some older, politically radical poets like *Erik Blomberg* (1894 — 1965), and *Ragnar Jändel* (1895 — 1939) were also briefly attracted by idyllic motifs. More importantly, these autodidact authors belong to the first generation of ''proletarian'' poets, like the pioneer
* Swedish outdoor toilet.

Dan Andersson (1888 — 1920). The latter, who rose from the depths of the people to the Swedish Parnassus, expressed himself mainly in verse; the next generation of proletarian authors (Vilhelm Moberg, Ivar Lo-Johansson, Eyvind Johnson, etc.) wrote almost only prose.

Gabriel Jönsson (b. 1892) came from a small idyllic fishing village on the Öresund coast opposite Denmark, and is very typical of the trends mentioned above. But *Birger Sjöberg* (1885 — 1929) had many other strings to his lyre than the purely lyrical ones. In his book "Crises and wreaths" (1926) Sjöberg introduced a powerful Swedish modernism which discusses questions of Weltanschauung and political philosophy in an ambiguous and fragmentary, but at the same time expressive and concrete form. "Crises and wreaths" did not provoke much interest — the reading public only wanted to see Birger Sjöberg as the poet of lovely "Frida" — but its importance became very clear during World War II, when the anguished visions of the poet became a deadly reality. The so-called "Poetry of the Forties" harks back to T.S. Eliot as one of its chief sources of inspiration, but also has roots in this earlier Swedish expressionism.

In historical perspective, the Swedish Twenties appear as a period of experimentation. On the other side of the Gulf of Bothnia, in Finland, one sought models and inspiration in such writers and originators of new forms as Södergran, Diktonius, and Björling. American Modernism — Diktonius had opened the door in his volume of translations "Young ocean" (1926) — became very important especially to a group of Swedish poets who in 1929 appeared in a joint manifestation ("The Five Young Ones"). Foremost among these were *Harry Martinson* (1904 —1978), and *Artur Lundkvist* (b. 1906), who both made signal contributions to the renascence of Swedish poetry. While Lundkvist in his symphonic verse, and in his omnivorous appetite — he represented, among other things, the modern cult of the machine which found a number of devotees in the poetry of the early Thirties — Martinson is an explorer of a much more personal kind. He first champions a new internationalism under the aegis of the "World Nomad", and then issues many warnings against the coming rule of the technocrats. "Aniara" (1956), which was turned into an opera by the composer Karl -Birger Blomdahl with a libretto by Erik Lindegren, is a lyrical piece of science fiction, a space epic, which may be seen as the negative counterpart of the atomic age to Dante's Divine Comedy.

Both Lundkvist and Martinson were for a time influenced by the sexual romanticism which produced enthusiastic protagonists both in Swedish prose and Swedish poetry ever since the end of the Twenties. Although D.H. Lawrence was the admired model, many poets went directly to the source, to Sigmund Freud, and bored down into the abysmal vegetation of the subconscious. *Karin Boye* (1900 — 1941) early had herself psychoanalyzed, and her poetry shows a sampling of half understood dreams and complexes. She was never able to cope with her personal and sexual problems, and finally chose voluntary death. This happened during the early part of World War II, when she also saw all humanistic values threatened by totalitarian movements such as Nazism and Bolshevism. In her last big volume of poetry "For the tree's sake" (1935) Boye employs the conceptual framework of depth psychology and achieves a concentration of language which she had announced theoretically in "Language beyond logic".

There is a strong religious tendency in Karin Boye, just as in the playful capriciousness of *Harriet Löwenhjelm* (1887 — 1918). A basic religious experience is also the starting-point for *Johannes Edfelt* (b. 1904) and *Hjalmar Gullberg* (1898 — 1961). The religious commitment, which often finds expression in direct references or allusions to the Bible or to the great spiritual leaders of Christianity, is, however, in these two poets often spiced with irony, everyday slang, and anachronisms. Gullberg is a modern mystic with all the mental reservations of the academically schooled sceptic. "Spiritual exercises" and "Conquer the world" are typical titles of Gullberg's works. As regards his form, Gullberg is the most virtuose of Swedish poets after Fröding, not least in his techniques of rhyming, which makes him very hard to translate.

The religious and mystical tradition in which Gullberg worked is continued in more everyday language and in simpler rhythms by *Nils Ferlin* (1898 — 1961) In some poems with a mordant satire of the modern welfare society of Sweden he approaches the vaudeville hit. The satirical song hit, whether aiming directly at a theatre public (Hasse Alfredsson, Tage Danielsson, Povel Ramel), or with literary ambitions as with *Lars Forssell* (b. 1928), has learned much from Nils Ferlin.

Religious poetry has always had a great and grateful public in Sweden. Even proletarian authors like Bengt Jändel wrote religious lyrics. *Anders Frostenson* (b. 1906) has become internationally known as a Christian poet and hymn writer. This tradition is equally strong in our own time with poets like *Ebba Lindqvist* (b. 1908), *Helmer V. Nyberg* (1907 — 1980), *Helge Jedenberg* (b. 1908), *Östen Sjöstrand* (b.1905), *Maiken Johansson* (b. 1930), *Bo Setterlind* (b. 1923), and *Ylva Eggehorn* (.1950), who each have their own very personal profile.

Gunnar Ekelöf (1907 —1968) is also a mystic. He is Sweden's most personal and "different" poet in the 20th century, and cannot be classified in any school. His debut "Late on earth" (1932) is marked by surrealism and the doctrines of André Breton; Rimbaud, whom he translated into Swedish, is the most important inspiration of his early poetry. Later Ekelöf became more and more influenced by Oriental modes of thought and poetry whilst, at the same time, he was always looking for "something else". Ekelöf was a poet who loved to destroy everything traditional ("Smash the letters!" he exclaims in his first book), but who also possessed a deep cultural consciousness, and made allusions to older poetry with the same obvious ease as Mr. T.S. Eliot. His poetry is a cave of echoes with sounds and reminiscences from Oriental and classical poetry, as well as from such Swedish poets as Bellman, Almqvist, Stagnelius, Fröding, and Ekelund. He also worked with simple, and even "folksy" poetical forms. The "many egos", the thousand slumbering possibilities of the subconscious, have indeed been realized to an amazing degree by this many-facetted poet.

In the shadow of World War II Sweden developed a "poetry of anguish" which became more intensive, more ambiguous, and more experimental than that of Lagerkvist twenty-five years earlier. Its foremost representatives were *Erik Lindegren* (1910 — 1968), and *Karl Vennberg* (b. 1910). These two were soon followed by several younger poets, *Werner Aspenström* (b. 1918), *Stig Sjödin* (b. 1917), *Elsa Grave* (b. 1918), *Gösta Oswald* (1926 — 1950), and *Staffan Larsson* (b. 1927). Most of these poets soon left the style of the Forties behind: one may perhaps best call Aspenström a late-born symbolist who likes to create personal myths out of simple, earthy things like Boy Granite Rock, as contrasted with heaven-aspiring Icarus, who was a symbol of the surrealism of Lindegren attempting to remake reality. Sjödin's finest poems are portraits of workmen from Swedish industry, often created in strong indignation at the capitalist destruction of human beings.

But the most typical expression of the mood of the Forties came with Lindegren's "the man without a road", which at first met with no understanding and had to be published privately by the author, but was later seen as the introduction to the "fashionable anguish" Even older poets, and particularly *Bertil Malmberg* (1889 — 1958) were drawn into this form of modernism. Malmberg had made his debut in 1908 in the decadent manner of the turn of the century, and had written much poetry where the superiority of beauty and the world of ideas is contrasted with the illusions of the world of reality. Now he is ready for a fresh demolition of the world of values, this time directed against his own earlier beautiful forms, as well as against their all too cliché content.

Martin Allwood (b. 1916) also made his debut in the spirit of the Forties with "The cemetery of the cathedrals". It appeared in 1945, at the end of World War II, and while it is marked by the anguished Forties, it also denotes the first departure from the poetic fashions of the contemporary generation. Allwood speaks for a new internationalism; he hopes that "the international of human beings" is on its way. He pours out his irony over careerism, social climbing, and strivings to achieve a false "standard of living".

Different poets sought different ways out of the Forties. As we have seen, some found a religious road. Others chose romanticism, although in a modern form (*harald forss*, b. 1911). Some tempered their anxiety with irony (compare the reactions of Birger Sjöberg and Hjalmar Gullberg after World War I). Lars Forssell followed this road; his mouthpiece becomes the unhappy, but cleverly loquacious fool (the title of one of his volumes of poetry, 1952). Some found anchorage in a new worship of form, which also implied a new feeling for classical motifs and verse forms. This "metapoetic" line attracted Majken Johansson and *Göran Printz-Påhlsson* (b. 1931). These poets freely admit their dependence on tradition, and not least on Anglo-Saxon tradition (Dylan Thomas, William Empson, and others).

Surrealism too, with its provocative dream worlds and the receding horizons of its hidden egos, attracted some poets, e.g. *Ingemar Leckius* (b. 1928) and *Lennart Dahl* (b. 1922). Nature, the classical theme of Swedish poetry, offered an escape to others, such as *Staffan Larsson* and *Björn Julén* (both b. 1927). The latter is a fighting humanist with classical connections.

But the poets could also be released from their problems by penetrating to the eternal wellsprings of poetry. Already in the Forties *Sten Hagliden* (1905 — 1979) — a poet with a most personal profile — began to look for a form of his own, perhaps partly inspired by Birger Sjöberg. He excels in energetic concentration and surprising new creations, whilst at the same time imparting to the most commonplace elements of reality a fresh lyrical significance.

During the Fifties several poets appear who attempt to conquer the language of "pure poetry". French poetry again becomes more important than Anglo-Saxon as a model (Eluard, Célan). The most prominent representative of this "pure poetry" is undoubtedly *Tomas Tranströmer*

(b. 1931). The poetic production of *Lars Gustafson* (b. 1936) also belongs to this ascetic school.

The poetry of the Forties had been powerfully moved by the anguish and problems of the age. Politically and socially committed poetry, in a more direct and less poetic form, dominated the Sixties and maintained its hold on a fairly large group of radicals into the Seventies. *Göran Sonnevi* (b. 1939) assumed the role of a moral conscience for Sweden in his poem "On the war in Vietnam", which expressed the anguish of many Swedes at oppression, war crimes, and torture all over the world. He has continued this versified political message (e.g. in "The impossible", 1975), and has also shown an interest in language as a semantically alluring phenomenon. *Göran Palm* (b. 1931) too, has written energetic poems of contemporary commitment in terse, simple form. In Sweden this type of poetry is often referred to as "neo-simplistic".

The women's liberation movement has had a number of eloquent representatives, e.g. *Siv Widerberg* (b. 1931), and *Sonja Åkesson* (1926 — 1977), both very critical of the deficiencies of the Swedish "People's Home" welfare state. Another ironic spectator of the "People's Home" is *Björn Håkansson* (b. 1937), who wants to call his own poetry a "critique of values", a questioning of all conventions.

Perhaps these versified debates find their most original form in the work of *Sandro Key-Åberg* (b. 1922). His first stylistic models were Birger Sjöberg and Elmer Diktonius, in particularly graphic descriptions of children and forgotten people in a naivistic, but not sentimental manner. In his later work Key-Åberg has developed an unusual style which uses everyday language but at the same time constantly exposes the hidden depths both in our language cliches and in our value judgments.

During the Sixties "concrete poetry" for a while found a number of verbose representatives. The notions of these poets were transferred to the written page with apparent automatism. Among the best known concretists are *Jarl Hammarberg-Åkesson* (b. 1940), *Carl-Fredrik Reuterswärd* (b. 1934), and *Bengt-Emil Johnson* (b. 1936). With a certain justification this catalogue poetry has been ironically referred to by *Karl Bolay* (b. 1914) as "pop poetry".

Life in "welfare Sweden" has been so thoroughly documented in Swedish poetry, that poetry can well compare with prose in this respect. The life of a fisherman in a small Swedish west coast town (Lysekil) has been well described by *Sebastian Lybeck* (b. 1929). *Jan Mårtensson* (b. 1944) has given us ironically lyrical reportages from another small town (Tidaholm). The Swedish landscape has always had a strong fascination for the country's poets, and this fascination has by no means become less potent in the so-called "Green Wave" of the Sixties and Seventies, which actually made some poets leave the big cities in protest in order to start a new life in the country, e.g. *Jacques Werup* (1945 —).

But "typically Swedish" elements are perhaps less typical than ever in the history of Swedish poetry. The Swedes have always been open to impulses from abroad (their originality is often far less than the country's inhabitants have supposed), and with the onset of large-scale immigration after World War II the image of Swedish society and Swedish culture has changed considerably. Sweden now has a rich immigrant literature, richest perhaps from the contribution of the Baltic refugees who fled from Russian annihilation, and who have published much both in their own languages and in Swedish. But there are also authors from many other countries. Some have come from Nordic neighbors — *Ulla Olin* (b. 1920) and *Sebastian Lybeck* (b. 1929) from Finland; *Maria Wine (b. 1912)* and *Jørgen Nash* (see Denmark) from Denmark. Some have come from more distant countries — the many-sided lyrical poet Karl Bolay from Saarbrücken; *Nicos Kokkalis* (b. 1918) from Greece; *Lütfi Özkök* (b. 1923) from Turkey; *Nenad Andrejević* (b. 1931) from Yugoslavia; anbd *Ilse Edström* (b. 1941) from Germany, to mention but a few.

The provincialism which has so often characterized Swedish literature is doomed to disappear. Swedish poetry has received an international vitamin injection: it will certainly look quite different already in the next decade.

Helmer Lång
Helsingborg
Sweden

VERNER von HEIDENSTAM (1859 — 1940)

After a thousand years

A quiver in distant space, a memory
of the farm that glimmered among the huge trees.
What was my name? Who was I? Why did I cry?
Forgotten all, and like a mighty storm
disappears among the spinning worlds.

M.A.

From the Forest of Tiveden

From the fir-trees a doleful music comes,
with horns in the minor and muffled drums;
the words only trolls of the wild could devise
and witches sing with shrieks and sighs.

The dancing midges here astir
seem ghosts of the time before men were.
Ancestral forests of fern grow tall
and massive moss-grown boulders grim
pile up in cyclopean wall.
A rotten tree-stump at the marsh's brim
like a sea-monster sticks out,
lifting aloft its dripping snout.
Scaled reptile-like, the pine-tree's root
is set in the mud like a saurian's foot;
or is wrenched from the soil, like spider, to cling
to an edge which the giddy to death would bring.
But quiet now. For a hairy head
breaks the network of branches spread,
and dry twigs crack on the heathery earth.
It is the elk: ponderous, of giant girth,
a mastodon. His thirst in the marsh he slakes,

then contemplates a wall of crag upreared
wild-eyed, as water drips in silver flakes
from panting muzzle and ragged beard.
The haughty pine, as if in fear
of heaven's light creeps on gravel here.
No mountains are there white with eternal snow,
no pinnacles, just ridges grey and low
that squat like bondmen in cloaks close-wrapped,
soiled and colourless and lapped.
The farm-hand shares his dark rye-bread,
his plough rattles over a field stone-spread.
All words for dark and heavy you could take
would be of insufficient worth
to paint in truth this parent earth
which preaches its eternal creed: forsake.
How low, how grey, how empty of all joy
this clime where I was born, and lived a boy.
Greeting you give me.
In your rags and poverty.

K.L.

GUSTAF FRÖDING (1860 — 1911)

Three lasses were strolling

Three lasses were strolling in sunshine
the highway at Lindane Lea.
A-swinging their skirts, they were so fine,
and singing were all of the three:
  Tra-la-la, la-la-la-la-la, tra-la-la-la-la, etc.

Like soldiers they marched there in strict time,
and then they would waltz down the lea,
and ''Johnny is not worth a half dime''
a-singing were all of the three.

But when on their stroll they had come to
the bend down at Lindane Lea
they all of them cried ''That's the cuckoo!''
and then they were silent all three.

They shut up as hard as the dead men
and blushed crimson red all the three.
But why were they all of them red then,
and why were they silent all three?

Three students stood there in the bend too,
a-grinning like mad all the three,
and aping their song: ''That's the cuckoo!''
a-singing were all of the three.

M.A.

242

Grey rock song

Stay
grey,
stay
grey,
stay
grey,
stay
grey,
stay
gre-e-e-y.
That's the grey rock song
very l-o-o-o-o-o-ng.

                                                    M.A.

ERIK AXEL KARLFELDT (1864 — 1931)

The sea voyage of Jonah

See the ship at anchor riding
under verdant headlands hiding,
and the skipper shouting on the deck: "Blow, west wind, blow away!"

Hey, ye bos'ns and ye yeomen,
it is time to quit your roamin'
and exchange your turtle doves for seagulls o'er the salty spray.
Here we see the noble vessel plowing through the brine
with the native Dalecarlians in charge of block and line,
while behind a sail on deck
with a backward tilted neck
lo! the captain has a few for luck and feels uncommon fine.

But the beasts of all creation
spew and howl their indignation,
so the rattled skipper drops his bottle in the roaring sea.
And he cries: "The ship will founder!
We must jettison some bounder!
Let's toss overboard our fattest man, whoever he may be."
Over there stands Jonah, most respectable of men,
although somewhat chubby, as behoves a solid citizen.
Oh, his face is very white —
how he holds his belly tight!
He is doubtless sick and wishes he were back ashore again.

And they grab him without heeding
his insistent, frantic pleading:

243

"Can't you see I am a prophet and a holy man at that!"
But they answer: "Where you're heading
you can practise water treading
though undoubtedly you'll float, O prophet, on your priestly fat!"
Upside down is Jonah in the midst of his descent
with his frock coat round about his head and flapping like a tent.

In the horrid depths below
we behold a double row
of the gaping monster's gleaming teeth on bloody murder bent.

As to farmers, I might mention
that they have no comprehension
of the evil creatures lurching in the ocean's slimy dark.
And they would do well to ponder
on the fate of seamen yonder
who are often swallowed by some predatory whale or shark.
Here we see poor Jonah in the belly of the whale;
he is sicker now than ever, and his face is deathly pale.
We can understand his feeling,
it is cramped and low of ceiling,
he can't even straighten up, our prophet, in this smelly jail.

But we know the good book's story:
how he fled his purgatory
after days of drifting far and wide upon the churning brine.
And the monster's jaws in shutting
did a proper job of cutting,
making of his frock a jacket ripped into unique design.
Here we see our Jonah strolling on the verdant shore.
He is smiling sweetly at a sign above a swinging door.
Jonah climaxes the tale
toasting heartily the whale,
and I wish the same for everyone and many, many more.

T.F.

BO BERGMAN (1869 — 1967)

At a milestone

Not happiness, but yearning,
desire for it makes us sing.
But he who suffers exile's sting
will sing in deserts burning
of Eden's glorious spring.

Condemned men's curses ever
the brand of death reveal.
If your desire for life is real,
leave hidden things and never
disturb their kindly seal.

244

A man should say in parting
farewell to bygone things, and make
a clearcut, a decisive break,
and bravely face the smarting
sharp blows he still must take.

                                        T.F.

VILHELM EKELUND (1880 — 1949)

For no one my verse

For no one my verse —
for the wind that wanders,
for the rain that weeps.
My song is like the gale
mumbling and moving
in the dark autumn nights,
speaking to the earth
and the night and the rain.

                                   L.E. M.A.

ANDERS ÖSTERLING (1884 —)

Psalmodicon*

A crofter plays the psalmodicon
in his cabin by firelight,
and tunes about Salem and Lebanon
enliven the barren night.

In the friendly light from window and fire
he fumbles with clumsy fists
and the psalm is blended from forest and mire
with autumn's rustles and mists.

And who would hear what the crofter plays
if God didn't lend an ear?
In its humble garb it's a hymn of praise
and naught for the world to hear.

Just an ageing, forgotten man who plays.
But maybe the Lord above
feels lonely, too, in these evil days
and welcomes this gift of love.

* An ancient stringed instrument.

Infinity magnifies little things —
as long as his music sounds
the world is more than a ball that swings
through space on desolate rounds.

T.F.

Starry landscape

Late summer night, where glittering jewels freeze —
the earth becomes a magic, secret place.
Now fell in dizzy blue Atlantic seas
a silent star. Into what time and space?
But underneath the stars in twilight sleeps
a little roof that o'er the song-birds' nests
and o'er my children's beds its nightwatch keeps.
In there my weary thought from roving rests.

This gable I can proudly call my own.
Infinity ends here, this point is sure.
To those who dwell within my steps are known,
the handle of the door meets me secure.
And e'en the stranger among midnight suns
has found an earthly refuge 'neath their dome,
where Öresund its childhood ditty hums
to budding trees and willows round my home.

M.A.

BIRGER SJÖBERG (1885 — 1929)

The time when first I saw you

The time when first I saw you, it was a summer day,
the morning sun was high in heaven's blue,
and all the meadow flowers in colors fresh and gay
stood round and bowed politely two by two.
So soft the wind was whispering, and down upon the strand, dear,
the rippling wave crept fondly toward the shells along the sand, dear.
The time when first I saw you, it was a summer day,
the first time that I took you by the hand, dear.

The time when first I saw you, bright shone the summer sky
as dazzling as the swan in white array.
There came from out the woodland a sudden joyful cry
where forest fringe was green against the day.
'Twas like a song from Paradise, and there above us winging
far, far away and hard to see, the little lark was singing.
The time when first I saw you, bright shone the summer sky,
its gentle warmth and light about us flinging.

And now whene'er I see you, though winter wind be chill,
when snow lies deep, all glitt'ring white and cold,
I hear the summer breezes, the lark above the hill,
while plashing wavelets murmur as of old.
I think I see the grasses green and smell the fragrant flowers,
the clover, too, that charmed us, and the summer-scented bowers.
The summer sun is beaming in your bright features still
and glows for me through winter's longest hours.

H.A. M.A.

The green-eyed monster

"What makes you mutter so madly
and sigh all the while so sadly?"

Oh, nothing for a *lady* to bother her head about!
She'll find some jollier *gentleman* to wait on her, no doubt.
More elegant companions, hereafter!
Haha!
My scorn I show to Frida in laughter.
Haha!

If this would make her happy, quite willingly I'd try it — —
I'd muddy up the water in our little crystal bay.
'Twill bubble for a moment, then at last be calm and quiet,
while rustling reeds the funeral music whisper as they sway.
No billows mark this lonely grave.
A straw hat floats upon the wave.
When time has passed
beneath a stone is found at last
a note with message fateful:
"For what has been, I'm grateful!"

"You jest so gloomily, mister!
I'm going to fetch my sister ..."

Oh no, I am not jesting, I only would tell you this:
a *lady* finds consolation in the pressure of a kiss.
A *gentleman* will offer it gladly.
Haha!
My scornful laughter rings rather sadly.
Haha!

And while the crowd is searching and shouting on the morrow
and frantic boats are churning up the water's surface gray,
a *lady* — I shall name no names! — may feel the weight of sorrow.
But not for long — a *gentleman* soon comes along the way.
And while my hand, so white, is caught
in rushes' roots — his hand has brought
a bright bouquet.
She holds it, rosy red and gay.

Round me, so slowly sinking,
the little fish are blinking.

"I'll stop my ears with my fingers
as long as your voice still lingers!"

By all means do, but leave just the tiniest space between
so she may hear the willows sigh as o'er the grave they lean.
No "sweetheart" the engraving is naming:
Haha!
"The Glee Club raised this stone", it's proclaiming!
Haha!

And now the grave is quiet, where foliage is gleaming
and rustling in the autumn wind, when leaves are gold and sere.
The little bird that lingers on has long been fondly dreaming
of flying to a southern land where waits a sweetheart dear;
but chirps to me, "I'll stay with thee
a little while. So bitterly
you turn to dust! ....
To dust, to dust, for love's lost trust ...
Let earth's sweet sleep relieve thee.
No more may sorow grieve thee!"

"All this because he sweetly
helped fasten my cloak more neatly!"

What he has done or may do is not a concern of mine.
Congratulations I offer for her "Musketeer" so fine!
I see the bridal veil float about her.
Haha!
With scornful laughter loud, hear me flout her!
Haha!
— — —

Don't cry! ... If to my Frida 'twould give any pleasure
I'd gladly reach my hand to her to make our peace anew ...
Her vase of blue with mignonette I'd fill in heaping measure,
and list to "Hearts and Flowers" while we walk in evening dew.
Forget the scenes of dismal death
I painted in my jealous wrath!
Those small pearls hide!
From coffers blue so fast they glide ...
And oh, they taste so salt, dear ...
'Twas all my foolish fault, dear!

                                                        H.A.

From Convention man

Then came a time that stamped so heavily the earth
that all traditions cracked and were exploded.
And violence slaughtered hopes of peace like chickens,

killed off their frightened cackle and fluffy down.
Up sprang humanity — a beast in terror
with wounds that flowed from breast and sides.
Earth, hot with cannons, drank ...

— — —

My strength gave out. I could not any more
sum up the letters of our life anew:
"Black letters mostly — red ones not a few ..."
But no — the black ones got the upper hand
and threw the red ones out.

I had to make a choice: strong civil servant
heroically calm in crises — or
a fiery apostle rushing out
into the market-place to tear to pieces
starched rags, ecclesiastic symbols stiff,
with flashing cry:
"O, let me be the spirit's torch!
Attack, my mind!
May dust be flame and prayer 'mid yells and pain!
Wake up, and kneel for the Avenger's pardon!"

— — —

I too became a member of conventions.
We moved in a procession fine
from church into convention hall,
and from the hall back to the church.

Thus here on earth the question is of order
constructed all of steel, but spirit yearning
is woven of transcendent purity
baptized from a hopeless combination,
for hard and fast words cannot show our dreams.
And so they mingled iron girders strong
of years of service and bank accounts and tenure
with silver beams of stars and airy music.
And all their proud and lucid stellar discourse
and sky-high controversy, they did spice with
pedantic dots and rounded paragraphs
and passed them then with gavel carved of ebony.
And zealots here play zealous patty cake,
and highness punched his highness on the nose.
But I, who felt the spirit burn within me
in agony beheld my white wings nailed
to the convention's solid oaken table.
At times it seemed as if the Great Avenger
'mid this calm honesty of the convention
and in these very regular proceedings
was a deputy whom they had missed,
on paper crowned, but never called to serve.

— — —

And yet!
No better kind of meeting has been found,
for dust and stars were given each a round.

I wanted to cry out: "I wish to raise
right now point zero one thousand nothing!
It runs as follows: "What's the Lord's opinion?"
For in the head I carry on this journey
I've packed down every horror of the age.
Now bray the cities like wild beasts
and states are swooning.
Now the Manger burns at Bethlehem.
The royal star is fouled with greasy smoke,
the earth aflame,
the homes aflame where soldiers do not bother
to count how many were in a day impaled
on worn-out bayonets ...
I thought that I would roar: "I wish to raise
my urgent question now!"

The secretary then with little ado:
"A simple luncheon will be served at two."

A nice and simple meal with Peter's fish
that had been fried and turned on crackling fire
and done a waltz in fat.
A sober little glass of decent stuff
where nothing hissed or rippled of the devil ...
Now came with Bacchic cheek
and imitating with his outstretched hand
enjoining words: A blessing upon thee,
a swift-eyed ganymede surrounded by
little black servants carrying the dishes.

I saw the apostolic table — and
my eye across the table-cloth did move
to where I thought to find a Highness
in reveries, encircled by a halo —
and found instead a fat and prosperous colleague.
He seized a dish, and dropped an awful brick
when, smugly innocent, he spoke to me:

"I tell you, colleague,
the lamb is really better plain
than stewed with vegetables ..."
And full, but not of food, I trembling learned
the curse of our flesh's vexation.
And agonized in burning hopelessness
I went to drink the bitter cup of passion,
to lift in stark anxiety my hands
in loneliness of heart on darkening strands.
Then suddenly the gates were opened wide
that hold the chaos of our hidden impressions:

Crazy seven-colored streams of
dreams that rumbled their tornado

now gushed forth and mingled
with real life and things.
Reason's rule and golden mean
feverishly were evicted,
teaching schedule, expedient rates,
engineers' rings.

Dredgers with their dripping buckets
cast up visions from the mud.
Look there, raw flesh crudeness!
Look, a white and mangled hand!
There on murky swell are lifted
broken limbs of fallen gods,
tattered proclamation posters.
Naked rose the hidden news
of terror in our age again,
threatening with whitened hands,
staring out with bursting eyes.
Gone was all — and yet not gone.
And then a futuristic school
in the midnight gallery of
hearts exhibits fearful things:
lips, too cowardly to speak,
hands that killed for filthy gain,
eyes that sting with cruelty ...

M.A. B.S.

TURE NERMAN (1886 — 1969)

The finest of all of the love songs

The finest of all of the love songs
no eyes ever read.
It was left in a dream at Montmartre
by a poor young student's bed.

That song would have shone o'er the nations,
forced spring to her knees to pray;
and a world to its heart would have taken
a new, a new Musset.

Along the old quays he'd have wandered there
with a pale little blue-eyed Lucile —
and whispering of violets and kisses sweet
through the April night still.

The finest of all of the love songs
no eyes ever read.
It lies in a graveyard in Flanders
with a student from Paris dead.

M.A. J.H.

251

HARRIET LÖWENHJELM (1887 — 1918)

Beatrice-Aurore

In Stockholm town at Kornhamnstorg
in Hallbeck's second hand book store
I bought an ancient dream-book once
composed in days of yore.

Then I lay dreaming all last night
of Beatrice-Aurore.
She was a one time love of mine
whom I lost long before.

She stood so close, she took my hand,
she whispered: "Come to me."
At once I understood and knew —
my only love was she.

We wandered down a linden walk,
I wept and I was sad.
The autumn leaves were wet and sere
and yet my heart was glad.

We walked and held each other's hand.
Like children's were our words.
And then we reached a quaint old mill
with many singing birds.

I said: "Will you be mine alone,
say, Beatrice-Aurore?"
"Then catch me if you can, " she cried
and left me at the door.

And I ran in and searched and searched
in every nook around,
and cried — but Beatrice-Aurore
was nowhere to be found.

I woke up crying bitterly
and in my heart a sting.
And in my dream-book then I searched
but there was not a thing.

M.A.

DAN ANDERSSON (1888 — 1920)

Sailor Jansson

Hey, yeo-ho, sailor Jansson,
now the morning wind is blowing,
now last night is past forever

and the Constancy must go.
If you've kissed your mother's cheek
and mingled tears with Stina's, flowing —
If you've had your swig of brandy,
then sing hey, yeo-ho!

Hey, yeo-ho, sailor Jansson,
do you fear your little lady
will betray you, yes, betray you
for another sailor beau?
Though your heart is beating fast
as twinkle stars in dawnlight shady —
turn your nose out to the tempest
and sing hey, yeo-ho!

Hey, yeo-ho, sailor Jansson
maybe Fate will have you falling
not among the lovely ladies
but where sharks swim to and fro;
and among the ragged coral
maybe death awaits your calling —
he is hard, but he is honest,
so sing hey, yeo-ho.

Maybe some day you will have
a little farm in Alabama
while your hair is growing greyer
and the years are sifting slow.
Maybe you'll forget your Stina
for a girl in Yokohama —
that is careless, but it's human,
so sing hey, yeo-ho!

H.A.

Saturday night in the log cabin

Hence, yearning and weakness from soot-blackened breasts,
no more cares in our snow-covered home.
We have fire, we have meat, we have liquor for guests,
there is peace in the deep forest gloam.
Sing, Björnbergs-Jon, with your full-throated calls
of love and of roses and springs!
String your fiddle, Brogren, and play us a waltz
to eery blue moon-lighted things.

It is miles upon miles to the houses in snow,
the frost lingers sullenly there.
Here is fun in the log fire's yellow glow
that trembles in midnight air.
As you play on your black violin
for food and for liquor, forgotten the shame,
and your forehead is free from its sin.

When the stars of the morning grow feeble and die
and the vapors are turning to freeze,
and the dawn is on moor and water and sky
we'll slumber in freedom and ease.
We are sleeping on branches of soft fir and pine
and dreaming of pale maidens' eyes.
Then we turn, and our snoring is manly and fine
while the log fire is crumbling and dies.

M.A.

Epilogue

Good night — good rest I wish you,
O all you wandering men!
We sing no more, we say farewell — why care
if never we meet again!

I have sung a little something and poorly of all
that soon burns low, yet burned with me,
but the love found there no destruction knows —
Good night — good rest to you!

C.S.

Now darkens my way

Now darkens my way and my day's work is done,
weary my heart, my seed I have sown.
I stand — a beggar, O God, at your gate,
and blood roses grow in the path I have gone.

C.S.

BERTIL MALMBERG (1889 — 1958)

My room is no longer in its house

My room is no longer
in its house,
surging
with a rocking floor
it sails alone in the cloudy sky.
Borne by what?
Drifting on towards what?
No fettering cord,
no anchor's weight
held it down to its place.

The room reels. The door opens
on failing hinges.

254

O, mildest mirage,
Sister Asteria,
white as snow on the threshold.
Behind the white shape:
abyss and flying night ...

L.F. M.A.

EVERT TAUBE (1890 — 1976)

Calle Schewen's waltz

On Roslagen's isle, in a flowery bay
where ripples wash in from the sea,
the reeds slowly rock, and the sweet new-mown hay
is wafting its fragrance to me.
There I sit alone 'mid the trees by the way
and gaze at the sea-birds on high.
They dive to the water in glittering spray
and feed, while I watch them and sigh.

I'm lacing my coffee quite freely with rum
till the strength and the flavor are right!
The accordion's measures alluringly come
from my cabin so gaily alight.
I feel like a boy, though a granddad am I —
my spirit my grey hair belies.
I only get worse as the years pass me by
with waltzes and maidens' bright eyes.

Look — there is a gull with a fish he has caught —
but I'm caught by arms soft and white!
My heart is so happy, my years are as naught:
then play, for I'm dancing tonight!
The sea sends a song, and its fragrance the glade.
Tonight you must stay as my guest.
Here dances Calle Schewen with Roslagen's maid,
the sunset is in the northwest!

My flowery isle on your bosom you hold,
you tranquil and darkling blue seas,
while June twilight shadows so tender enfold
all the slumbering bushes and trees.
You're dancing so silently, sweet little miss —
we men are all ogres, you say.
It trembles, the small childish hand that I kiss,
while in minor the waltz dies away.

But hey, all you fellows who visit my bay,
I'm really a sober old man.
When morning has come I must stack up my hay

and catch all the fish that I can!
The deuce take you, twilight; the morn you disclose
in firtops agleam one by one.
Here dances Calle Schewen with Roslagen's rose,
he dances while up comes the sun!

H.A.

Bride waltz

Sound accordion, clarinet, fiddles and flute —
come and waltz with me, sweet, because you are so cute!
Only rarely one dances
at weddings and balls
with such sweet ladies as here in these halls.

But you are one of the few
who are sweetest, it's true,
in this business of choosing I'm older than you.
For the sweetest brunette in the Nice carnival
did a waltz once with Rönnerdahl!

Hush, the players have changed to a low, minor tune
that makes goblins and pixies dance under the moon.
And in meadows and fields round our house gay with light
fairies dance in the dawning spring night.
Flowers cover the earth for our bride
who expectantly blushing would hide.
Let us play, let us dream then where happiness dwells —
how our next meeting falls no one tells.

L.F. M.A.

Fritjof and Carmencita

Samborombon, where dwells my sweet inamorata
lies not so far from busy Rio de la Plata
on the romantic beaches of the Atlantic
with the Pampas behind it for a hundred verdant miles.
There I came riding while the April moonlight smiles
for I wished to dance the tango.

Fiddle, accordion and mandolin
sound from the tavern and I eagerly step in.
On a bench, in a mantilla, with a rose on her breast,
is that adorable little Carmencita!
Mamma is sitting there on guard —
gladly my cloak and whip and pistol I discard.
Then I bow, and Carmencita says:
"Si gracias, Senor! Vamos a bailar este tango!"

"Carmencita, little girl,
you have got me in a whirl!
I should like to tell your papa and your mamma
that I want to marry you, Carmencita."
"No, Don Fritjof Andersson,
just forget Samborombon,
if you fancy, Fritjof, any other plan for me
than to dance the tango!"

"Ah, Carmencita, do not say that you refuse me,
I'll get a job here in the shop if they can use me.
Plodding and slaving, only working and saving,
never gambling and drinking — just loving all the while!
Oh Carmencita, how i love you when you smile,
oh, and how you dance the tango!"

"No, Fritjof, music you may know,
but I'm afraid you'd find a job too slow,
and besides I think I heard my papa say, just today,
that he knew someone who soon might wed his daughter!
One who has twenty thousand cows,
and an enormous hacienda, he avows,
he has bulls that win first prizes, he has oxen and fine pigs,
oh, and how he dances the tango!"

"Carmencita, little friend,
you beware of wealthy men!
Happiness is not in cows or pigs or oxen —
it is something you can't but with his money!
I can make you rich with love —
I shall get the job I told you of!
Then when we are married you'll have small ones of your own
who can dance the tango!"

H.A.

The ox-driver's song

With oxen ten I parted
from city joys and blues.
At nine o'clock we started,
our goal was Santa Cruz.
With four tons fully laden
and guitar in my hand
the Lord I'm serenadin'
and Pampas lovely land.

Refrain:
Pull, pull, my good old oxen!
Now, do your very best!
That's fine, my good old oxen.

257

At home there's feed and rest
and moan and groan and quiver.
Old wagon, we'll go far!
And shiver, quiver, shiver
each string on my guitar!

Rich ladies may be resting
in fancy castles, but
me and my Lila nesting
in our old bamboo hut.
Have poverty to share with,
but she is young and hot.
No pillows can compare with
the bosom that she's got.

T.F.

The ocean never shimmered so bright

The ocean never shimmered so bright
the beach was never so glorious and free,
the fields, the meadows and the trees were never so fair
and the flowers never so sweetly scented
as when you walked by my side
toward the sunset
that evening
the wonderful one,
when your tresses shielded me from the world
and you drowned all my sorrows
beloved
in your first kiss.

M.A.

PÄR LAGERKVIST (1891 — 1974)

Anguish

Anguish, anguish is my heritage
my throat's wound
my heart's cry in the world.
Now congeals the lathered sky
in the rough hand of night.
Now rise the forests
and stiffened heights
barrenly against the sky's
contracted vault.
How harsh is all,
how stiffened, black, and still!

258

I grope about this darkened room
I feel the sharp stone's edge against my fingers,
I tear my blood-stained upstretched hands
against the clouds' frozen rags.

Oh, I tear my nails from the finger-tips,
my two hands are mangled, sore
'gainst hill and darkened forest,
'gainst the sky's black iron
and against the cold earth!

Anguish, anguish is my heritage
my throat's wound
my heart's cry in the world.

                              M.A. E.W.

A letter came

A letter came. It spoke to me
of spring wheat, currants, cherry-tree,
a letter from old mother dear
in sprawling script and queer.

Word after word stood flowering field
and rye and clover, the summer's yield,
and He who guides all far and near
from year to year.

Sun-bathed, secure, farm close to farm,
lay 'neath the Lord's protecting arm,
and peeling bells sang full of mirth:
Peace be on earth!

There was a breath of garden air,
of evensong and lavender
and Sunday quiet as she wrote
to me her note.

It had been speeding day and night,
never resting, so that I might
know from afar — O mystery! —
that which is of eternity.

                              M.A. C.A.

The sun is loosening her light blond hair

The sun is loosening her light blond hair
in the early dawn's first hours.
She spreads it out on the ground in the springtime air
where gleam a thousand flowers.

Thoughtful she walks and poses
her hair where brightly the dew drops gleam,
she loosens it from the thorn of roses,
but absent-mindedly, as in a dream.

She lets it caress the forest, and sad
with the wind she lets it go.
It's caressing the children in their beds
and the wrinkled cheek of the old bent low.

But her thoughts are far away from all.
What does all this merriness entail?
She is dreaming among the stars that fall
and enlarge life's mysterious tale.

She loosens her hair, and spreads it out still more
in dawn's sacred hour in a dream.
She walks among the worlds that have gone before
and where new ones with longing gleam.

B.Sw.

The people in the churchyard

They sit by the family graveyards
awaiting the service hour.
Their hands in their laps are folded,
the hymnbook their only power.

The flower-vase, upset in the tempest,
stands upright now with a host
of hollyhock and bleeding heart from
the island, their home on the coast.

Toward heaven the windows are opened
up high, and resounding bells
ring out to the grey, cold rocks and
the ocean that no one compels.

The hymnbook pressed hard in their hand
they slowly ascend to the height,
and faith with its dazzling white sail
sets out across seas of light.

M.A.

NILS HASSELSKOG (1892 — 1936)

Fall — a humoresque (To Miss X)

Now fell the year's last and final plum,
fell heavy with the dew that now has come.

Yes, summer gave us now her final kiss.
It's fall, as it has been for centuries.

I walk in garden gravel wet and thin
around your home, the comfortable inn.

Approach, beloved, to the window-pane
where tenderly I hold the plum in rain.

A token of my gratitude I bring
for what you gave of warmth, for everything.

Your love, since you were blinded by its heat,
is like a plum deliciously complete.

And in your being — may't remembered be —
at bottom dwells a core of poetry.

Yet — sighs the fall within your father's garden,
and it is time for us our hearts to harden.

But give me, ere the last plum I dismember,
your word of honor that you will remember.

                                        M.A.

GABRIEL JÖNSSON (1892 —)

Backafall lassie

Backafall lassie, the schooner Three Brothers
is cruising tonight the Caribbean Sea,
and there's a land wind that blows from the southern
coast up the island, past home in the lea.
Fragrance of sweet scents the evening air hallows,
but I'd give all the sweet scents back again
if I could stroll through the Backafall mallows
with the old moon keeping guard over Hven.

Ellen, I cannot come home in the May night,
then I shall still have the Line in the north.
But as you stand by the church in the twilight
fancy I come like a cockchafer forth,
who without leave touches lightly your shining
hair — while your sweet little hands it pursue,
and finds its way down below your blouse lining
while the old moon in the sky watches you.

For the intruder would only be feeling
if your round breasts are like mallows in bloor.
each time you know that my thoughts have been stealing
home from their guard in the hurricane's boom.
Feel that it's only your boy who is sending

greetings tht once as a captain again
back to the Backafall shores he'll be wending
— with the old moon keeping quard over Hven.

M.A.

FRANS G. BENGTSSON (1894 — 1954)

A ballad of the French king's bandsmen

From Burgundy we come and from Guienne,
from Brabant, and the green realm of Normandy.
We have never seen those pleasant lands again
since we drumméd for King Charles's Company.
        When the snowy Alps defied us
        sounded ''Come!
        With our Oriflamme to guide us
        on to Rome!''
In the blue Italian air
waved our standards everywhere —
Lo, their Tuscany a lily-field in bloom!

We have music for the march and for the ball,
droning litanies and lays of Charlemagne;
we can sound the clavicord and virginal,
hymns to dawn, and old romances of Bretagne.
        We have rhymes of Blanchefleur
        and Herr Floris,
        and refrains about the Sieur
        de la Palice;
and the Pope his blessing gave
on the Courtesans' Conclave
to the tune of our ''Les dames du temps jadis.''

We blow, and keep in time, and thump the drums,
spite of swelléd cheek and fast-increasing girth:
still from us the call to boot and saddle comes
though the Maréchals we followed rest in earth.
        Beneath vic'try-waving lances
        we appear,
        or at festive torchlight dances
        here and there;
and we still go marching by
with our bonnets cocked awry,
and our burial-equipment in the rear.

Is a woman left that minds us in Guienne?
Blows the spring still green in ancient Normandy?
We have never seen those pleasant lands again.
To Rome we go with Frundsberg's Company.

'Twixt Oriflamme and sabre
march we on!
For d'Orange we strike the tabor,
and Bourbon;
and whate'er in our advance
we thought worthy of our glance
we have transsubstantiated to a song.

C.D.L.

UNO ENG (1896 — 1972)

Still life

A glass with dirty flowers sinks in the sand,
the withered stalks in thick and rusty water.
Faint furrows from a rake are to be seen.
Scared — scared and helpless must have been the hand.

A withered wreath. The ribbons stiffened, and
a broad Farewell in faded, gilded letters.
Bewildered ants are running on the name.
A host of ants are plodding in the sand.

M.A.

EBBE LINDE (1897 —)

In time with the rain

No girl in the green park
and it just rains, rains.
A leaf falls over the yellow dragon's mouth.
Fall, fall, fall, rain! cobblestone grey.
The soul walks alone, sits and shivers
sick for duplicity and intimacy.
All over. Alles aus. Already closed for the season.
And nowhere the warm corner of childhood
where you sat and painted with water colors.

R.B.V.

HJALMAR GULLBERG (1898 — 1961)

I'm planning to set out on a long journey

I'm planning to set out on a long journey,
it will probably be some time before we meet.
It's by no means a sudden decision, I have thought about this for quite a
    while
though I couldn't say it openly to you until now.

263

I've arranged about lots of details,
I have seen to 'most all but the route itself:
where it finally will end I shall have to find out by and by.
I'm leaving to look for something in myself that I never could capture
    here.

I think they are calling for me far away, I must go.
I feel that I'm able to face quite some inconvenience in order to get there.
I'm feeling so free today, a weight is lifted from my chest.
It is as if a great joy were waiting for me somewhere.

M.A.   R.L.

The reflective country postman

A simple country postman I,
tramping ice and snow;
and just this daily wayfaring
is the best life I know.

The world may go from bad to worse,
my job is free from shame:
among my predecessors
Mercury I could claim.

Yet mine's a humble calling;
upon these feet no wings,
though messages from soul to soul
my mediation brings.

Of happiness each one should have fair share.
Last week it cut me to the marrow keen
when I took cash to one already rolling,
demand-notes to a chap without a bean.

I saw myself as love's postilion go
to a village maiden fair across the heather,
yet to his girl maybe the lad had sent
a heartless note that ended things for ever.

Gold and diamonds I longed to give
to him who after ploughing, stones had reaped.
But often black-edged letters I have carried
to one with griefs already overheaped.

To feed the hungry, give the thirsty drink
— with some such task was I not meant to cope?
I make my rounds with fate inside my bag,
but there's a seal set on each envelope.

Master, whose errands here perchance I go,
why are some lives so cheerless, so distressed?
For once just give me leave to intervene,
just once, so I can fix things for the best.

                                        K.L.

The lake

That holy man, Sire Bernard of Clairvaux
bade me, his squire, to the stable go.

His gift for silence is a wondrous thing;
he spoke not of our journey's purposing.

He rode beside the crystal lake's bright brim
— he bowed and grey, I youthful and more slim.

I thought when we had rid the whole way round:
my master cannot be on business bound.

I thought, as thrice in circuit we did fare:
my master knows the value of fresh air.

The seventh time we reached the cloister pale:
Ah well! God's brave world doth his soul regale.

A lark o'erhead in laud of spring sang gay
the twelfth time that we rid the selfsame way.

Our long-kept silence then my voice broke through:
"Indeed, I think the lake is marvellous too!"

A sudden whip-lash powerless had been to make
me more amazed than his next words: "What lake?"

Outside my master's ken had been that day,
the glassy lake, the lark's sweet roundelay.

The selfsame route we took; but in what wise
he rode upon that day was past surmise.

A squire should well enough his master know,
but who can fathom Bernard of Clairvaux?

                                        K.L.

At Cape Sunium

This is the sea, youth's very spring,
Venus' cradle, Sappho's grave,
the Mediterranean, sea of seas,
glossed to a mirror without a wave.

Raised like a lyre toward the isles
Poseidon's temple ruins gleam.
The row of pillars, drenched in sunlight,
melodise the sea's eternal theme.

O hear the music of the marble lyre,
water-borne guest as you waywards fare!
Full of ruins the world you'll find,
none with the beauty of this to compare.

At the altar no longer the sounds of joy
or of grief the sea-god's temple fill.
Nine pillars only stand there
speaking the memory of his saga still.

May the thing you shape, with the jostle of men
around you, from dawn to evening red,
stand like a lyre against time's sky
when you yourself and your god are dead.

K.L.

Wanted

Childhood faith of the undersigned,
vanished from home, for all to find:
hatless, coatless, shoeless, blind.

Here, in hope to make it known
where in the world it may have gone,
is its description shown:

Voice like a bird's, two eyes of blue,
their glance so mild, but empty too,
that never earthly passion knew.

Who, before the owner dies,
returns the same, to him applies,
receives reward of ample size.

P.B.A.

Dreadful accident

Bird-song, evening in July
by a railway crossing (I
have taken from the daily press
scenery and time and place).
On the bank the cornflowers blow.
Suddenly a cry: "Lie low!"

Fling yourself upon the ground,
else your brittle bones are found
snapped off like a cabbage stalk
by this thing of fire and smoke.
Over you goes dancing on
a screaming steel-black skeleton.
If you stir a finger's end
the raging beast your heart will rend.

Over your shivering shoulders
fly the laughing ticket-holders.
What does their cheerful chatter know
of your terror here below?
This is your hour of trial;
press yourself a little while
to the ground, and soon you'll see
heaven shining splendidly. —
Time's express has passed you by.

                                        P.B.A.

NILS FERLIN (1898 — 1961)

In Arendorff's time

In Arendorff's time,
that's when life was sublime,
and the stars weren't so hard to get at.
There was joy and delight.
Were you locked up one night?
There was nothing peculiar in that.
It was class — though at times one's apparel
was rags, and one dwelt in a barrel.
And though famished and cold
one did not lose one's hold.
There was nothing peculiar in that.

Now existence is hard
in the street and the yard,
and saloons, where one formerly sat.
One sits silently, just
like a log or a bust.
Well then, what's so peculiar in that?
But in Arendorff's time one had entry
and mingled with barons and gentry.
Were you sassy, you lout,
you were soon booted out.
There was nothing peculiar in that.

They were good years, for fair,
but with plastered down hair
standardizing has altered all that,

and the new rules are these:
You're as like as two peas.
Well then, what's so peculiar in that?
One is docile with taxes and handouts,
though one never is classed with the stand-outs.
Now existence is flat
like a sat-upon hat.
I see nothing peculiar in that.

Yes, one lives and one tears
at the body one wears,
and one day one lies prone on the mat.
One is moved on one's back
in a broken-down hack —
there is nothing peculiar in that.
And some birdsong would sure be a blessing,
for the trip wouldn't seem so depressing
though the words of the priest
are the poorest and least.
There is nothing peculiar in that.

                                        T.F.

Through a wall

Count to a thousand — a thousand and one,
or a thousand and two, Mr. Anderson!
Take a sleeping-powder before you're done,
that would work better yet, Mr. Anderson!

What sort of life is yours — just a farce?
Is it drama — or farce, Mr. Anderson?
A complex perhaps, or your hair getting sparse,
—or is it your soul, Mr. Anderson?

It's your soul? Why that's swell! — Now we know all is well:
a mere appendix, Mr. Anderson!
Remove it tomorrow — and then sleep well,
we'll sleep soundly and well, Mr. Anderson.

                                K.H. G.K. M.A.

Gethsemane

He was such a feeble, confused artiste
that he felt quite hopelessly sad and triste.

He took up his No. 2 Faber and wrote
on one fine evening the following, quote:

In God's photographic salon there will be
a dark-room that's called Gethsemane

and there clear pictures will soon appear
to him who is quiet and sincere.

But he who is frightened of rod and ice
shall never have flowers in paradise.

His life shall be like a barren hell
where never a silvern tear fell.

Maybe the purple path he took,
but his look was always a beggar's look.

He ashes became, but could never burn.
The smiling moon from his hand will turn.

For he who's afraid of Gethsemane
shall never nor giving nor getting see.

M.A. T.F.

May I offer you some flowers

May I offer you some flowers,
a few roses in your care?
And you must not be so downcast, my dear,
for these roses I have brought from a royal garden fair.
It takes a sword to approach them there so near.

And one of them is white, and the other one is red,
but the third one is my best gift, my dear.
It cannot blossom now, for the giver must be dead.
That rose is strange and wondrous, my dear.

It cannot blossom now, for the giver must be dead.
It shall blossom very long then, my dear.

K.H. M.A.

Astray

The sun is setting, the moon appears.
Dreams have led you astray,
dreams from lily of the valley years
led you so far astray.

Paths on moors where the thistles bruise
now you must tread with tattered shoes.
Dreams from lily of the valley years
led you so far astray.

T.F. M.A.

269

And not even —

And not even grey little birds
all singing in green, green trees
there'll be on the other side —
it's a thought that can hardly please.

And not even grey little birds
and never a birch that is white —
but it happened on summer's most beautiful day
that I longed there with all my might.

                                        M.A.

Neutral

Mostly I remark: That so?
Chiefly because I feel as though
I'm not committed either way,
when that is all I say.
I go on digging in the soil
and keep my mouth shut while I toil.
My bible on the table lies
where it's visible to all eyes.
God protect both priest and state
and thanks for the dinner I just ate!

                                        T.F.

A waltz-melody

Day is asleep, through the night creep
street-girls, and cats and the stars.
Copshop and jail fill, without fail,
scum of the gutters and bars.
"See", dreams the child in the dead of the night,
"See an angel goes round our house with a light".
— And I fight in the night's lonely minutes,
a langorous waltz, note for note.
And my legs have become somewhat skinny,
and likewise my arms and my throat —
I have tailored my verse to the vogue of the times
and God may forgive me for some of my lines —
for my legs have become somewhat skinny,
and likewise my arms and my throat.

Old father Groan
via gramophone
churns out his marionette show.
Judas of old

played the same role —
just watch his bank balance grow!
All that I ask is a rhyme-word for moon
when I've already June, croon, spoon, soon and tune.
— And I fight in the night's lonely minutes
a langorous waltz, note for note,
and my legs have become somewhat skinny
and likewise my arms and my throat.
There is nothing to win in this world here for me
and soon in my grave are the earthworms to see
that my legs have become somewhat skinny,
and likewise my arms and my throat.

F.L.

An animal

The seven thousand flies we fail
to reach with our poor, tired tail
harass us through the days and nights.
Their never-ending buzz and bites
drive us from peace and grass, — and now
they've made of us a feeble cow
— the seven thousand flies we fail
to reach with our poor, tired tail.

T.F.

I could be ...

I am a hobo — what more,
I could just as well be a priest,
I could be a proprietor,
a farmer, a horse at least ...

I could be a swallow also,
a crow or a snook,
a snook — or maybe a flower,
a gleam of summer in a book ...

Yes — east begins in west
and south ends in north as well,
confused am I by all the questions
and my throat is dry as hell ...

... A hobo I am who is stumbling
on the highway gravel alone.
My heart is hot as an oven
and cold as an old people's home.

B.Sw.

With plenty of colored lanterns
I set out in the world one day.
They fizzled — unnoticed and soundlessly
and their beauty faded away.

I stopped, surprised and bewildered.
The radiance was no more!
But now, on this road from Nowhere
I've trudged, as I did before

far into the land of Noplace
in darkness and midday sun
without any colored lanterns.
It's hard — but it can be done!

T.F.

KARIN BOYE (1900 — 1941)

Prayer to the sun

Merciless one with eyes that have never seen darkness!
Liberator who breaks the ice with golden hammers!
Save me.

Straight as thin lines the stalks of the flowers are sucked aloft:
closer to thee the trellises must tremble.
The trees hurl their strength like pillars toward your glory:
only up there
do they spread their light-thirsty leafy embrace, devoted.
You drew mankind
from an earthbound stone, blindly gazing,
to a wandering, swaying plant with heavenly winds about its brow:
yours the stem and the stalk. Yours is my spine.

Save it.
Not my life. Not my skin.
Outward things obey no gods.
With put-out eyes and broken limbs
it is yours, who lived erect,
and with him who dies erect
are you, when darkness swallows darkness.
The rumbling rises. The night swells.
Life shimmers deep and precious.
Save, save, seeing god,
what you granted.

E.W. M.A.

Night's deep violoncello

Night's deep violoncello
hurls its dark rejoicing over the expanses.
The misty images of things lose their shape in floods of cosmic light.
Swells, glimmering, long,
surge in wave after wave through night-blue eternity.
You! You! You!

Light transfigured matter, rhythm's flowering foam,
soaring, whirling dream of dreams,
          dazzling white!
I am a gull, and on resting, outstretched wings
I drink the sea-salt bliss
          far east of all I know,
          far west of all I want,
and touch the heart of the world —
dazzling white!

                                        C.A. L.F.

INGEBORG LAGERBLAD (1902 — 1979)

Cast away I saw them

          Cast away I saw them,
          shunned and loathed
          like lepers,
          listless shapes
          prowling across the city tundra
          like silent cries.
          The eyes of the passers-by,
          cold as window panes,
          mirrored only
          the icy indifference of the tundra.
          Barricaded
          behind seven seals,
          sharing their loneliness
          with their companions
          they are drawn farther and farther
          into the spider's web,
          paralyzed by his coolly calculated,
          slowly killing poison.
          Out of the depths they implore us —
                              M.A. G.D.

JOHANNES EDFELT (1904 —)

Spring sacrifice

Spring, you closely knit death and resurrection —
grass you awaken from narcosis winter-dire;

green shoots have staged their insurrection,
and you have warmed the herb's root in voluptuous fire.

Crassly you join decay and transformation —
grey thoughts of yesteryear, the new glands' lay;
zenithward points the spring's oblation,
but moves toward nadir on its fated way.

In enigmatic travail, spring, you intertwined
the sap's exulting and its diminution;
all things which fumble now with fingers blind
toward life, are groping also toward their dissolution.

                                        K.O.

Pain is the greatest sculptor

Pain is the grestest sculptor,
            greater than Phidias:
shaping from shadow and blood
            monuments of regret.

Darkness that fills our breast
            is its living clay.
Skilled and sensitive hands
            shape the relief and the statue.

Inwardly grows its art,
            strange its material.
All that was wholly destroyed
            makes it a lasting image.

                                        M.A.

Life of life

Close to the breast of night
            wrapt in its tender breath —
arch of mildness its gaze,
            waves of peace its pulse!

Never could light of day
            give me a mother's arms:
now be your flowing hair
            flowery scent on my cheek!

Misery's daily law
            offered us stones for bread.
— Gateway of affirmation!
            Satisfy, Nyx, the returned.

Nameless and mute at your breast
    I am at one with your blood
like a salamander in fire,
    like the algae in its sea —

M.A.   C.A.

Archaic image

For whom that smile? O, was it the light of myths
that brought the smile upon those lips?
From silent centuries she smiles — did she
once know a splendor brighter than the sun's?
Did she have days of dew and diamond?
Her evenings, surely, must have been amber.
— A feat of saving light in seas of shade:
such is the common day. O, my companion,
might we be dazzled in the frosty night
by a message from your lips in mystic fire signs:
there is a fountain, and its murmur peace,
there is a smile, undying in the night.

M.A.   C.A.

The world is a dream of peace

The world is a dream of peace.
And you will soon be there.
The starlight makes your pillow
shine with silver rare.
— Plows, the swords
which faced you bare!

Bathed in moonlight, dreaming
stands the forest thorn
as if it held no ambush,
no treason and no scorn.
— Grant oblivion
to all that mourn!

Charybdis or Scylla —
in vain you raise your knife!
Blue space will fill our chest,
cool earth will heal our strife.
— How deep the soil
at the root of life!

M.A.

Places of rest

This long disease, my life ... basically true, perhaps.
Yet, at intervals, there are places of rest
where the pores of the soul drink the freshness of the light
when, like a cataract, it plunges over the oak-leaves,
while the garden warbler sings his blue ecstasy.
There is a precious vein of joy.

W.H.A. L.S.

Summer organ

Far beyond the scentless years
        the sacred aroma of summer:
cradling, intoxicating, gentle,
            it rose among the cherry-trees.

Far beyond soundless years,
        the apple-tree's music:
the leafy tree-tops, swarming with bees
            were turned into organs then.

W.H.A. L.S.

HARRY MARTINSON (1904 — 1978)

Farm maids

Remember the maids of my childhood
some of them souls
with desolate, sensuous eyes,
some of them high-bosomed mighty-loined warm testimonies
to their descent from corduroy countries of yore.
The shout of quick-tongued mouths at harvest-time;
maid-hymns sung together in the barn;
kneeling dreams among turnips;
sour milk in stone jugs at the field's edge.
The sullen muttering about Olga
gone off to Idaho.

Many vacuous maids were sitting
with drooping souls,
but many sat there proudly, wondrously childloving women
        with sullenly melodious voices
        muttering as if out of myths.

There were maids with virgin vagueness
        with legends in their shawls
        and weighty questions in fawn-clear eyes.

Many walked
with white breath
over the autumn-cold stage of the world.

There was the lamenting heaven-maid of the guitar.
The slovenly wench hankering after the dance
and the persistent sailor gal
— fetish worshipper of navy uniforms.

But strangest of all the enchanting nostalgic maid
of the autumn twilights,
the sad and heavy priestess of the separator
who bent down and pulled, and bent down and pulled
the milk-roaring Alfa-Laval
          with the stove fire mirrored
          in wondering eyes.

Then the arch-enchanting peasant in her sang
          like a heavy ore.
          Sullen spoke the voices.

The child lay wondering in the cradle,
the hound looked up from his basket.
Was it not like the song of eternal peasanthood?
Like the ore of the yielding earth?

                              M.A. E.W.

The cable ship

On latitude l5 degrees North, longitude 61 degrees West,
between Barbados and Tortuga, we fished up the Atlantic cable,
held up our lanterns
and pasted fresh rubber over the wound in its back.
When we put our ears to the injured spot
we heard how it hummed inside.

One of us said:
"It is the millionaires in Montreal and Saint John who are speaking
about the price of sugar from Cuba and the lowering of our wages."

In a circle of lanterns we stood there long and thought,
we patient cable fishermen,
then we lowered the mended cable
down to its home in the sea.

                              W.H.A. L.S.

Visual memory

Thin birches stood on Stockholm's nesses
I saw them nod one spring —
with brittle lines swaying in the water

277

broken, rocking zig-zag — white, white
like optic water-lilies.
And white gulls in keeping with it all,
and white terns —
when — plop — our black barge came in
so useful
with chug-chug and belly-cough and sixteen barrels of oil.

And the rainbow shimmer of the oozing oil
— a spectrum saga —
began to fight with the swaying white rods of the optic lilies.
They fought, they fought like China's exotic dragons!
They fought and they wearied the eye
till evening came with wind and billows —
but the woman of love tarried forever.

_M.A._

The goddess of complexion

What should she be called, the woman on the beach?
She is a victim of her own beauty
and the golden spider web of flattery
Perhaps the goddess of complexion.

When she has displayed herself to her admirers
she goes home to her altar mirror
to worship herself in the temple of complexion care.

She takes the short cut through the churchyard,
where she can mirror her whole body when passing
the bright monuments.

_F.F._

After

After the battle of Heligoland
and after the battle of Utshima
the sea dissolved the driftwood of men's bodies
treated them with its secret acids,
let the albatrosses eat out their eyes
and transformed them with diluent salts
slowly back to the sea — —
to a creating primordial water,
to a new attempt.

_R.B.V._

From Aniara

But all too late. I hadn't a chance to restrain
the people who pushed on toward Mima hall.
I screamed, I called to them to turn back.
But no one listened to me, for although everyone
wished really to flee in fright from Mima hall,
everyone was drawn, eager to see it happen.

A lightning-blue beam struck out of Mima's viewers,
a rumble rolled in Mima's halls
like thunder had roared in the valleys of Doris.
A stroke of terror ran through our group
and many emigrants were trampled to pieces
when Mima died in Aniara in space.

The last words she sent were a greeting
from someone calling himself The Bursted.
She let The Bursted witness on his own,
and stammering and bursted relate
how difficult it always is to burst,
how time rushes forth to prolong.

To life's challenge time rushes forth,
prolonging the second when one bursts.
How terror blows in,
how fright blows out.
How difficult it always is to burst.

F.F.

The dream city

The dream city looks quite different from what its blueprints indicate.
This bridge, for instance, so light and so cheap,
made of morning and evening mists painted with sunlight.
The houses are built out of dream material, beams of sunlight.
In their dream-kitchens you need only dream.
The traffic is controlled by huge soap-bubbles which burst on arrival
with no harm done:
there will always be fresh ones.
The streets are of water, crystal-clear,
and men know the art of walking on the water:
furthermore, their movements are more beautiful on the water,
and the movements of all the women are delightful,
the sure floating gait of a day-dreamer.
In the dream-kitchen a dream-clock ticks.
The city has no solid constructions, no troublesome pipes,
no wires, no dishes.
You can just sit there and let the city manage itself.

W.H.A. L.S.

The earthworm

Who respects the earthworm,
the tiller deep under the grass in the earth's soil.
He keeps the earth in transformation.
He works completely filled with soil,
mute from soil and blind.

He is below, the farmer downstairs,
where the fields are dressed for harvest.
Who respects him,
the deep, calm tiller,
the eternal little grey farmer in the earth's sod.

F.F.

We sat on the shore

We sat on the shore of forgotten words
and tired hands
where only the wind-blown sands are eternal
to those who build on sand.

In the dusk we saw from the beach
a boat fly out to sea;
a boat of burden
fled to be sea-borne.

And still men believe
the sea will bear them; the hope
of a new-built ship
rocked by necessity's law
borne by the bearing sea
toward day.

P.B.A.

ALF HENRIKSON (1905 —)

The limits of fame

When the famous Swede pays a visit to London town
he'll find that no one has ever heard of his fame and renown,
which mightily ought to purge and improve his soul
and broaden his view of the whole.

M.A.

Plastic flowers

Plastic flowers never wither, that's what's wrong.
Only mortal things are worthy of love and hate.

Spring won't be cast in a mold; it's gone — and returns with a song!
This is what plastic flowers don't do; they're deadly dull and sedate.

M.A.

Ancient China

"How many springs have you blossomed?" said Wu to Ping.
"Nineteen useless years I was a bore."
The conversation didn't produce a thing.
The strange thing is that anyone cares any more.

M.A.

Efficiency experts

Come on, let's now have an end to this mad economics —
in the long run it certainly cannot pay!
The business schools annually turn out their students,
their diagram wizards, their excellent Assistant Directors,
talented, rational-minded, who, using arithmetic,
production curves and beautiful tables, can show
that giant business is better than small, and mastodon hospitals
better than human-size plants, barracks than homes,
that outlying land should lie waste, the people of the North
should live in the South, and that Sweden's National Bank
should discontinue their service in X., and that the railroad
— unlike the highways — ought ot be run at a profit.
They talk so fast, and they count so well that they really believe it,
converting not only business and absentee-managed coops,
but Members of Parliament and union chiefs to believe in Mammon
and the short-lived latter-day paradise offered to city-dwellers
— to be paid for by coming generations — what a deal!
And the tax-payers sit there in little provincial places
with factories empty, no kids in the schools, and know
with utter conviction that rational calculation
is short-sighted — yet strangely profitable to certain parties.

M.A.

STEN HAGLIDEN (1905 — 1979)

Delta

Diffidently my furrow finds
various paths
across this sodden country.
I'm bogging down disgracefully
in marsh and mud.

Way back there: the downward dash,
the defiant challenge of the cascade
to the rough rock underneath!

281

Now I can only flow on flatly,
my hydra arms reaching out
toward you whom I would meet
'n high fresh falls
and silver streak.

> *M.A.*

From Cumulus County

For these cloudy peaks
of mist and bright glimmer
all eyes
all hearts have yearned

Here you shall all have dwellings
here in the boundless regions
whe e the wind demolishes all the cairns

> Escape, O escape here, earth's
> heavy-hearted little serfs!

> Believe us in Blueland:
there is an Above,
there is a Space County,
there is noble Peak freedom!

> *M.A.*

ANDERS FROSTENSON (1906 —)

Our faith in things eternal

Our faith in things eternal
went wayward and amiss,
God's peace forgot, we made for
the land of restlessness.

Forgot, too, God's great working;
to dust our deeds each day,
life slipping through our fingers
uneasily away.

Thy calling voice be heard through
our stress, anxiety;
O make us strong in stillness,
found only, Lord, in Thee.

> *K.L.*

GUNNAR EKELÖF (1907 — 1968)

Absentia animi

In autumn
In autumn when you bid farewell
In autumn when all gates stand open
      to meaningless pastures
where unreal mushrooms are rotting
and water-filled wheel-tracks lead
to nothing and a snail is on its way
and a tattered butterfly is on its way
to nothing, which is a wilting rose,
the tiniest and the ugliest. And the daddy-longlegs,
      the stupid fools
brittle-legged, intoxicated by the lamp light in the evening
and the lamp itself sighs fadingly
about light's sea of nothingness, the arctic sea of thought
in rolling swells
silently sizzling foam
of series divided by series
from nothing through nothing to nothing
thesis antithesis synthesis abrasax abraxas Thesis
(like the sound of a sewing machine)
and in the quiet night the spiders spin their webs
and the crickets fiddle
      Meaningless.
Unreal. Meaningless.

     In autumn
My poem rustles
Words do their job and lie there
Dust falls on them, dust or dew
until the wind whirls up and lays (them) down
     (and) elsewhere
he who everywhere seeks the true significance of things
     has long since realized
that the purpose of rustling is rustling
which in itself is something quite unlike
wet rubber boots through leaves
absent-minded footsteps through the park carpeting
of leaves, affectionately sticking
to wet rubber boots, absent-minded steps
You stray, go astray
Do not be in such a hurry
Wait a moment
Wait
In autumn when
In autumn when all gates
then in the last slanting ray
      after a day of rain
    with long intervals hesitating
      as if caught
a black bird left behind may sing in a tree top
for no reason, for his throat only. You see

his tree top against the pale background of the sky
next to a lonely cloud. And the cloud swims
like other clouds but also somehow left behind,
                    hors saison
            and by its nature long since somewhere else
and in itself (like the song) already something
                    other than
Eternal peace

Meaningless. Unreal.
        Meaningless. I
sing sit here
about the sky about a cloud
I long for nothing more
I long to be far away
I am far away (among evening echoes)
I am here
Thesis antithesis abrasax
You also I

Oh far far away
over a tree top in light skies
a cloud is swimming
in joyful unconsciousness!
Oh deep within me
an image of a cloud
is mirrored by the surface of the black pearl-eye
in joyful semi-consciousness!
This is not the existing
It is something else
It is in the existing
but is not the existing
It is something else

Oh far far away
in the far remote
there is something nearby!
Oh deep within me
in the nearby
there is something far remote
something beyond-nearby
on this side of the distant
something neither nor
in what is either or:
neither cloud nor image
neither image nor image
neither cloud nor cloud
neither neither nor nor
but something else!
The only existing
in the existing
is something else3
The only existing
in the existing
is what in this

284

is something else!
(Oh lullaby of the soul
song about something else!)

O
non sens
non sentiens non
dissentiens
indesinenter
terque quaterque
pluries
vox
vel abracadabra

Abraxas abrasax
Thesis antithesis synthesis that becomes thesis again
        Meaningless.
Unreal. Meaningless.

And in the quiet night the spiders spin their webs
and the crickets fiddle

        In autumn   *F.F.*

                    One after one

            One after one
            I see them expire, the lights.

            O Lights, hope of my life!
            O lights, memories of lights!
            No wonder I linger behind
            or grasp for a hold.

            Maybe my universe is darker
            or my dread of the darkness greater
            than that which others have known.
            It is always so far to the next light
            — they flicker in the sky far away:
            I hardly see them.
            Perhaps they will expire before I get there ..
            No wonder then I linger behind
            and grasp for a hold.

            O lights, memories of lights!
            Memories of those I have loved,
            memories of eyes, a short time faithful,
            memories of homes I thought I owned
            or homes of my hope!
            Yes, I long for home,
            homeless I long for home.
            Home to where love is, the one, the good,
            home to my real home!
            That home is bright.

In my mind I open the door,
see everything awaiting me there.

One after one
I see them expire, the lights,
one after one, through life
toward death, the last.

And yet it is here that I would live
here I wanted to settle,
here on earth, with men.
No wonder if I linger behind
and grasp for a hold.

L.F. C.A.

Five times I saw the star

Five times I saw the star
but on the sixth the moon stepped from the clouds
I stood my ground
he hacked at me
but I parried
            twisting my torso
That's why you can read this.

M.R. L.S.

Among the dead lives a notion of beauty

Among the dead lives a notion of beauty
Yes in their dead lives, a dream of beauty
He who has not seen, or felt the terror of
this evil life we have been born to —
has no dream of beauty
he has not seen the moonlight on the river
like a vision, like a dream of beauty
He has not longed to dive down for the moon
to dreams of death, in the dream behold sights of beauty
freshness happiness life falling in love, and a love
that is beauty
In this cruel life of ours
love is the dream of beauty.

Ri. L.

To Posthumus

Posthumus, you who in your electronic chair
can hear the murmur of the human past
as we on an old 78 record hear
songs of our youth, the top ten, forever receding
under the needle's tone a scratching in the worn
cracklings and clicks over notches and cracks,
or as we in the radio's program about space can hear

the rush of the Milky Way ... Hui Hui — Come! Posthumus!
Do you hear me as a click?
                                In the classical sea-rush
where the chains of ten thousand slaves jade to an itch
and the moans of ten thousand crucified along the roads to a scratch
and pleasure's moans, too, and sighings in a click-series:
Noete, lumen, va, va, usque va, Noete my light
come, come, you too! Hávete transistores
válete transistores! Posthumus! *Do you hear me?*
The classical record spins, we must help it over
the circular grooves where it sticks and spins for itself
The human hit parade breaks through. Yes *Posthumus*
I am signing off now.

M.R.

To see yourself in others

To see yourself in others
your condition
your need
your weakness
your humanity:
To be social in your heart
you others, all social in the head!
— And the heart is not an impulse of the moment
but lasting
The heart is not a business cycle.

M.R.

Heard in a dream

Heard in a dream in the year 63, on the 15th of the harvest month at
        night:
"You lie asleep in a sarcophagus with no bottom" —
Half-wakened by these words, neither asleep nor wholly awake
the marble coffin comes to my mind more distinctly
its shadows, its shimmering whiteness, a few clear details
first the rough-hewn inner sides, two long, two short:
The stone-cutter has not gone to much trouble here
everywhere chisel-marks show, the corners are round
He seems to have bestowed all his skill on the outside
with its fruits flowers birds dolphins bucrania
its fragments of myths: two figures sailing in scallops,
holding veils filled with wind over their heads
I am searching for my name — then with the clear logic
of the dream it strikes me: since the coffin has no bottom
it must also lack a lid. And he who rests there
lies with his back against Nothing and his face toward Nothing.
Only the force field of the four walls holds the sleeper
floating between the bare interior's demand to forego
and the power of the exterior, ornate with myths, to desire —
Virgin, O Atokos, when this force field will be broken

287

let me, in the dream, be neither reborn nor begotten
What came before this has no scars from chisels.
What is to come has no fruits and flowers.

Ri.L.

Have you seen the desert bloom?

Have you seen the desert bloom?
Tell me: Have you seen the desert bloom?
Tell me so I will know
how a blossoming desert looks
— I have seen the desert bloom
It was the face of the blind man
when, with his hand he felt
something his hand recalled.

Ri. L.

HELMER V. NYBERG (1907 — 1980)

You are Columbus

You are Columbus
— seek new continents!
Continents where no one will be baptized
by the sword
— where the color of the skin is invisible
— where gold is not taken in exchange
for lives
— where no one wants slaves
— but reconciliation!
O continent of continents
— we are all grand admirals
proceeding across immeasurable oceans
— do not bring me back
fettered in irons!

M.A. K.L.

He who loves is a sleep-walker

He who loves is a sleep-walker
ambulating safely on the tip of the tower.
He is the fakir by the Ganges
buried alive without dying
— the Shah of Agra building his Taj Mahal
under the starry sky of loss and longing.
He is the disciple speaking to the dead man
on the road to Emmaus,
and the grain of mustard lifting the mountain
He can carry a nightingale
through walls of concrete,

and when the fiery tongue
is over his head
he communicates in all languages
and every stranger
recognizes his own forgotten speech ...

M.A. K.L.

HELGE JEDENBERG (1908 —)

The precious poverty

That evening, the one I am talking about,
thousands of stars came out
beautifying like flowers the heavenly meadow.
Saint Francis had sat down to rest
under the trees of the blessed with their glittering crowns
by the side of the wintry road
and his birds were there too
resting in the branches of the trees.
Their song was muted. His breath
froze to clear crystal flowers.
Poverty never seemed so rich
never so precious as that evening.

M.A.

The poems of the cherry-tree

The cherry-tree scatters its petals to the wind.
Filled with barely discernible signs
the leaves heap in my cupped hands.
I do not understand the signs, and I don't want to,
overwhelmed by so much beauty.
But the wind tells me that now is the time
when cherry trees publish their poems.

M.A.

ASTRID PETTERSSON (1909 —)

You can't just ignore it

I know no short cuts, no retreats.
That would have been too easy.
You can't pretend it isn't there. The abortive foetus
lies dead in the mother's blood.
Prestige-hungry men do not understand.
They starved away their love
in some strange way
while they were climbing.
They got callouses on their elbows.
The next generation just means competition.
When no mother bears a fully developed foetus

the big climbers will be at their retiring age.
They lack a chromosome of imagination in their heredity.
In the farming community one never noticed it
because sowing and reaping took place in the same year.
Now the climbers can sell themselves to nuclear reactor construction
and poison the oceans and the wells
and have themselves buried under fine monuments.
The next generation will be stillborn.
Millions of incubators cannot save it.
Centralized birth clinics filled beyond capacity
but no flags flying at the home.
This is what the future holds in store
if we don't scrap the unimaginative plans of the men.
Retraining won't help the big shots.
Early retirement might be the right thing now.
If we stop the nuclear reactors now
perhaps we will survive.

M.A. N.O.

KARL VENNBERG (1910 —)

Timely answer

Those who still have the strength to believe
may try to pierce the torpor of the world
How ready we are to applaud
conviction's
heavily rolling tanks
with what shining eyes we will behold
the clever subversive activities of idealism

Let no one be deceived
by the fact that we ourselves prefer
to ride on the ridges of the roofs
let it not weaken the enthusiasm of any crusader
Why should not the beautifully
ornamented verse of the age
continue
to the jubilant refrain

Heroic courage os magnificent
let's just make sure
that no one chokes with it
when it flows too fast
let's make sure the vision is not impaired
in those who sat too long
with their heads down between their shoulders

Indeed
we must make sure
as truth and untruth
exchange their prisoners
that there is no mix-up

and that only those who have had their right ear branded
are turned over
to the guillotine's happy activities

M.A.

You must avoid

You must avoid
the farthest promontory
only there can you see
that the ocean
drowns in the horizon
and that all sails become uncertain

M.A. G.D.

We have all

We have all
done our best
and no one can blame us for anything
We sat patiently
in the easy chair or on the coach-driver's seat
went to bed with our women
and stumbled over our thresholds
Some cured themselves with hip-baths
and some even took part in church conventions

Our whole life
became a simple practical joke
a whistle through the emptiness
now all that remains is to be pensioned off
by a miserably poor
silent eternity

M.A.

ERIK LINDEGREN (1910 — 1968)

XXI (From The man without a road)

but when the morning dawns the city becomes quite different
the saboteurs' endless cheers ring in the ears of the celebration

parks and streets and houses drunkenly stray by
mumbling of merry memories from the time of the plague

scenes and landscapes and man shout trumpets
and crown everything dead into the charlatan themselves:

my eye deceived us it sought only the bottom
the wall to be able to stalk forth as conqueror

291

the offering lives my solitary life in a gravel pit
and the blood and the meaning trickle down into the earth

I compared me with us and nothing tallied
I killed you and me in order that we should live

with human lips heavy with death we were forced
to this smile of self-esteeming idiocy

L.S. R.B.

XXXII

o spasm of desire with jazz and plundering hands
and love breast to breast and the ether mask murmur

you the invalids' rival dance of death's small revelry
with terrors in advance and the bandage of simplification

you trampler of webs with hymn of high heels
and nothing which is able to reach meaning or end

your surprise gives us only the same well-known thing
the spirit of homelessness which visits our magnet

and seduction gives death and the space a moonshine solo
blue mantles of crystals which perhaps give coolness

to the green mesh of leaves where the caught eyes stares
at the fall of flesh-flakes from the clay of empty hands

when naked up to the waist we trespass in the house
in death's river and the overcrowded wards of pain

L.S.   R.B.

Cosmic mother

be in me the breathing of your galaxies
be in me what you already are and always have been
a dream beyond the mountain of dreams and beyond the
secret
something more real than reality
something I can neither forget nor remember
something like dark ships that wander up to the
lighthouse
something like clouds like bright rocks and rocks like
dark clouds
something that changes inconceivable cold to
inconceivable warmth
something that was in me and changed me
o change me

292

make me a harbor for the ship of my anguish
wait for me under the earth
find me in my urn
o change me and be in me
as I unnoticed rest in you
in unconscious dreams in the stars of your eyes

M.A.

HARALD FORSS (1911 —)

shy are your thoughts

shy are your thoughts
— for they brush by things that are desolate
and a wish rises in these that are shy —
to be desolate things
to be the rock that extends where the white lily is dreaming
— o that the rock were your heart and your eyes closed
then you could be the desolate, lonely things
that your thoughts brush by —
but in the waste land there is something that keeps you away
the immutable, that which you love, frightens you

M.A.

inalienable the right to silence

inalienable the right to silence
brooding closeness filled with enigmas and wonders
the voice speaking no threat now —
uninvited, I have stopped at the tower of questions
and, unrecognizable, I disarmed its dark skull-cap

M.A.

BERTIL GEDDA (1912 —)

The only strength

We may not judge whatever died,
whatever is weak and falls,
for life will always be outside
our strong palisades and walls.

We need to have great faith and care
to break the narrow ring.
Look, how the yielding bridge of air
bears the sparrow's wing!

Dying power shall more and more
make secret victory ours.
As the water supports the oar
so our weakness gives us new powers.

My strength must be your fragile home,
and my hunger your appetite feeds
as toward a distant harbor we roam
still borne by that which recedes.

M.A.

KARL BOLAY (1914 —)

Swedish reality

Saturday, August 9, 1969

Two youths got drunk
on fifteen cans of beer
and then went into a youth club and said:
''Come on if you wanna see how we knock down an oldster!''

The victim was 63-year old crane operator
TORSTEN ALGOT HÖGBERG

It was around nine o'clock last night
that Torsten Högberg took the short cut
from the last streetcar stop
at North Guldheden
to his residence

In his home his wife
was waiting for him.
She knew almost to the minute
when her husband would be back
he was usually punctual

But when Högberg came by the youth club
the drunk boys came out
and blocked his way
They knocked Högberg down
and when he tried to get up
they hit him hard over the head
with a bottle

In spite of the vicious assault
the 63-year old man got up
and tried to escape running
from his tormentors

Torsten Högberg fled for his life
with kicks and blows raining over him.
After thirty yards he could no more.
He fell on his back.

By then he was already dead.

M.A. R.L.

294

to create a poem

to create a poem
    is to compress
        the primary rock
            into the weight of a feather

to create a poem
    is to pour into the fleeting now
        the concentric heat of the sun
            through the cool of the burning glass

to create a poem
    is to explode space
        and build the dwelling of love
            in the luminous expanses of the void

                          M.A.

MARTIN ALLWOOD (1916 —)

I love America

I love America!
I can see all the things that are wrong with her;
can you see all the things that are right?
Are you strong enough to see the good in America
while not forgetting the bad?
I have spoken with anger and bitterness about this great country;
because my hopes were so high, my disappointment was so keen.
But let no one doubt where I stand.

America, only America, gave me freedom to speak and be heard.
America, only America, gave me freedom to work where I wanted to
    work,
and paid me well for my toil.
America never told me what to do; she trusted me to do my best.
America, only America, gave me a warm smile of recognition
and made me feel I was a man.
America accepted me as I am and wanted me to stay that way.
America, the hot and passionate, gave me the love that fears no ghosts
and doubts no dreams.

America gave me the larger view.
If I did not have America in my heart
I would never believe in the greater future of man.

If I did not have America in my dreams
the sky would never be so blue above my head,
my song would never rise so high!

                          M.A.

Not the same person

John Calvin and Jesus Christ were not the same person.
He was clever, O how clever ...
His thoughts were his undoing.
Jesus was not clever at all.
He never thought too much.

Martin Luther and Jesus Christ were not the same person.
He was angry and brave,
a thunderbolt in the night.
Jesus was not angry.
He struck no one with fright.

Vladimir Lenin and Jesus Christ were not the same person.
He was strong. He burned
for the downtrodden masses.
Jesus did not burn.
He was cool and mild.
He loved men of all classes.

The Pope and Jesus Christ are not the same person.
He sits on top
with the keys in his hand
Jesus was at the bottom.
The lilies of the field were his land.

I and Jesus Christ are not the same person.
I stumble and am nobody
in the larger scheme of things.
He walked straight.
He was somebody
in the larger scheme of things.

                                        M.A.

STIG SJÖDIN (1917 —)

Judgment day

O what a wonderful judgment day,
what final trumpets,
what whirls of liberated dust!

Lo, the prophets fool the god!
Lo, fire conquering water!
Lo, the lamb riding the lion!
Lo, the crutch supported by the cripple!
Lo, nobody is anybody else!
Behold them, behold them, behold them!

O what a wonderful judgment day,
what prophets of doom have
deceived us of this feast?

Lo, the seers in the corner!
Lo, the oracle tormented!
Lo, the depths rise up;
lo, the flight of black frocks!
Lo, the wreath lies withered!
Behold them, behold them, behold then!

O what a wonderful judgment day,
what fathomless seas
is the ship of morning now to behold?

Lo, the light is slain!
Lo, dalliance consumed by loathing!
Lo, the wine vomited from the glass!
Lo, the blessing strayed from its path!
Lo, the key locked by the gate!
Behold them, behold them, behold them!

O what a wonderful judgment day,
what revenges are here convened
to change all into contraries?

Lo, the virgin polluting virtue!
Lo, charity whetting the scythe!
Lo, honor in a begger's hat!
Lo, the palm shooting arrows!
Lo, the well become a desert!
Behold them, behold them, behold them!

O what a wonderful judgment day,
what final trumpets,
what winds of liberated dust!

M.A.

WERNER ASPENSTRÖM (1918 —)

Something's travelling past

It isn't you travelling forward
It's darkness travelling towards you
and past you.
It's those you meet who're travelling
not you, not here.
It isn't your boat moving forward.
It's the waves coming toward you
and past you.
Notice the shores, the too well-known.
Notice the drooping willows.
The water trickles from the oarblades.
Pitiful crying,
why should it move the heart of the sea?
Old women look at the sky and say
that someone's dead;

The carriage rolls softly across the edge of the forest
drawn by six black horses.
This happens every day.
How lightly death travels,
how heavily life!
Life rows its boat desperately,
with childish oars.
Life sets its sail
and the sail cries to the wind,
but the wind's tired right then.
Are there no waiting shores?
Are there no legends or monuments,
no rumors of forgotten cities?

Don't you have urns and fans in your room
and coins of foreign mintage?
Aren't these signs valid?
You don't know for sure.
You only know that a wheel turns slowly,
you know that something's travelling past, a darkness
or maybe a light that you don't understand.
From where and to nowhere.
From where and to nowhere.

Y.S.

ELSA GRAVE (1918 —)

Afterthought

And again they turn
their dark grey sails back
from air mass
after air mass
sailing counter-sunwise like silver vultures
spying over the icy wastes
and their hunger too
a slow swell

They have flown far
between winters and cardinal points
they have consumed streets
and solitude
and their cries of hunger
are long airy perspectives
behind the silence

M.A.

NICOS KOKKALIS (1918 —)

The tourist

A hotel in a foreign country
which is not yours.

Soft, fine sand on a beach
whose soul is alien to you.
A sea which you do not approach with awe,
trees whose names you have never heard.
Games you never played,
houses which do not speak to you,
scents of food which provokes no memories.
Words you do not understand.
Thoughts you might not even comprehend,
poverty which you merely pass by.
Two weeks as a tourist.
Swimming, sunshine and empty laughter
echoing in the dark.

M.A.

ULF PEDER OLROG (1919 — 1972)

The stork named Ibrahim

There was a stork named Ibrahim from Egypt's ancient land
whose district now included all of Mjösa's rock and sand.
He placed the wee ones tenderly with Peter and with Paul
and got so many orders he could hardly fill them all.

But Ibrahim the stork arrived in Hamar town one day
with shooting galleries, lively shows and games of chance to play.
He hesitated, thought a while — but then he said: Oh hell!
A little Löjten's aquavit would really ring a bell!

A snifter here, a snifter there, and when the count reached nine
our stork's respectability went into steep decline.
He ran the gamut — flying darts to random rifle shots ...
By five o'clock at poker he was raking in the pots.

Next morning, back at the hotel, this droopy, tired bird
reacted dutifully to the baby cries he heard.
He left his order pad behind and hastened on his way,
bearing his precious load aloft high over Mjösa bay.

From Minnesund to Toten and from Brumendal to Kapp
his blundering created havoc all over the map
He dropped one here, he dropped one there, — and sometimes three or
     four,
and almost gave old spinster Mo a heart-attack once more.

So Ibrahim flew back to his retreats along the Nile
pursued by gentle Mjösa's tears and curses all the while,
and now he stands on one red leg deep in the river's slime
composing this last verse as a confession set to rhyme:

"Oh, little maids with eyes of blue along the paths of spring,
we all can make mistakes — so just blame me for everything!
If ever you're in doubt regarding Jens and Joakim
repeat this simple song about the stork named Ibrahim!   *T.F.*

299

RAGNAR THOURSIE (1919 —)

Commencement

On the first day of summer, when the dust rises,
on the first day of summer,
the pastor, like a great black woodpecker, mounts
the prow of the sermon;
holds on to the banister with white admonitions,
black wings folded on his back,
lifts his beard and gapes red;
Oh, the first day of summer!
And through the dusty aisle of the church, in God's chest,
we all marched, the carpenter's sons,
three hundred singing
          without a voice
on the first day of summer.

Our eyes' consolation
twelve men of wood, with beards, staffs, crosses, keys, swords,
      and books,
while the water of the organ flooded
the summer season waiting at the entrance
in great joy and beauty.
The little lady in her bell skirt and cowslip hair
gnaws upon her lip.

This was the first day of summer. Then followed
the second, third and fourth and the dust
rose even higher.
We grew into men of wood, with staffs, keys, crosses and swords,
and eyes, watery blue and blind
blinking at the last commencement.

                                        M.A.

ANNA GRETA WIDE (1920 — 1965)

The star

On my toes I've tried to stand
and reach the dipper with my hand.
I had yearned so much
for a star to touch

I finally got hold of one.
Then I regretted what I'd done —
the radiance I admired
very soon expired.

So many things which in the sky
are bright and wondrous to the eye
in people's hands would just
be ashes, slag and dust.

                                        T.F.

300

STIG CARLSON (1920 — 1971)

To learn again

You are still fondling the worn-out
icon of your faith
and draw a warmth from it
which you have long lost
hoping to find in the petrified folds of the robe
a motivation
for your tottering uncertainty

shut out these thundering choirs of negation
catch in the black-out dive of the swallow's wing
the depth of freedom:
bleed and bleed to death in the hour of birth
in the throes of delivering the truth
from the withered death-womb of lies

fondle yourself far into
the face of new realities
where the eye of the sun, red with crying,
gives you desperate closeness
and cracked distance

o to proclaim
to be able to proclaim
finally the strayed
meaninglessness of the icon
o to learn again
to learn again with the burning zeal of discovery
to discover

o my life

M.A.

Enforced concrete thoughts

Man stands there alone, shivering, shut out,
viewing his work with dry eyes,
looking into the house of steel and concrete
which he built as a defense against nature
now turned into an implacable enemy
when the last remains of self-healing
were wrapped in hard, whitish lozenges marked "Secret"
The home turned into a bunker against all living things.

And the heavy, sealed houses wait like tombstones
for the moment when life will no longer demand its right
and enter into a fateful alliance with the concrete
which is mute to every lament
and will never dissolve to the salts of tears.
Already the eyes are burning dry in their stone setting.

M.A.

The short wrath and the long wrath

The short wrath
and the long wrath.

The short wrath is not a very solid foundation,
it passes like a slight giddiness
when its cause is fulfilled.

The long wrath, of which the revolutions speak,
has no beginning and can therefore have no end.
The long wrath is not satisfied with half-measures,
it must run its course to the end.
The long wrath demands a high tribute
but the short one may end in a laugh —
was it so simple!

The long wrath is the history of nations,
the short wrath is the history of its kings and courts.

You belong in the long wrath.
Never betray it —
it could betray you!

(Freely from Mao Tze-tung)   M.A.

ULLA OLIN (1920 —)

The child's gift

The child's gift to the mother is a home.
When it cries for help the child attaches
to itself the defenseless one as its protector.
And the night is no less night,
but around the child gone back to sleep
there is a peace that passes understanding.
                                        M.A. K.L.

The Italian

What could he do? It was not his country —
with thawing, wet roads and pale bushes
against the low row of houses. He stood his hurdy-gurdy
in a grey yard, setting astir
his melodies.

O heavenly sun, O sole mio!
A few silent children listening on the step.
Homeless strains snatched by the wind.

                                        M.A. K.L.

SANDRO KEY-ÅBERG (1922 —)

Life, man

Life, man, that's the fast buck!
Check the situation —
and pron o! Let's have the dough.
It's now when every hing
looks real good
that you want to blow it.
What the hell do I care about yesterday
any more than the Renaissance?
My old lady keeps chewing
her chi'dhood memories.
What the hell do I care
about the little shit who ran
around Stora Tuna and had
the same name as I?
It takes seven years to renew the human body.
I refuse to live as an heir
to the past.
Man, the thril of speed,
that's a lasting value,
it's great to feel time
like a wind on your face.
Life — it's real simple
if you stick to things
that you can tou h.
Don't give a dam
about al the cant about
alienated souls that thirst
for the meaning of life!
A shot down the hull
and a screw when the body needs it,
and that's all the tim —
that's the meaning of life!
Man, when your stick
is squirting into flesh
that rocks with pleasure
you're not lying there with questions
about what li e might
mean with this.
Take what you can take
from all the branches
wi hin your reach!
Get out as fast as hell
when the conscience dopesters
with their pious looks,
a social halo round their brow,
ngel incense round their mouth
and with dentures
dripping with democracy,
arrive to squeeze themselves
into your little heart

and infuse their shity
noble sense of brotherhood!
That kind of shot won't
make you high, take it from me!
Keep the fires burning
and to hell with death, man,
the parlor game of all the squares.
If all your cylinders are firing
it makes no bloody difference
if you are fifty years
or two hours
from your heart attack!

M.A.

LENNART DAHL (1922 —)

A culture salesman

A culture salesman
chased onto a rostrum —
so the poet appears.
Chanting his inaugural chant
here in the library
among the usual
attempts to rescue literature.
His distinguished poetic words
strut onto the stage
between rows of pale faces.
Relatives blow their noses
at heart-pinching
twilight words.
Plainville inauguration,
a city championship
in cultural surprises.
The poet, a nervous picker
among brittle words
a king
a shadow
walks home through a coughing November.

M.A. R.L. G.B.

Lily of the valley sadness

Lily of the valley sadness
rioting hooligans
intoxicating smell of mosquito oil
on Midsummer Eve
in the welfare state
holiday Sweden
a country with blessings
continually appointing committees to study its impotence
'Ere we go
round a juniper bush

M.A. R.L. G.B.

304

BO SETTERLIND (1923 —)

A song of freedom

There is an ocean no man sees,
there is a grave where no one dies,
there is a sun, which never sets,
there is a shore in every soul.

And if you wish to know your weal
and be as free as every cloud,
then build a world for living in;
this life's your own, your very own.

There is a world, which never ends,
there is a letter none has read,
there is a wind which comprehends,
there is a freedom unblemishéd.

P.B.A.

Love

Love
is a child.
If you can play
you'll have friends,
but if you hit them
you'll be alone.

M.A.

Death I fancied so

An agéd peasant went and sowed
and sung among the fields.
He held a basket in his hand
and sowed the word which tells
of life's beginning and its end
among the seed he sowed.
He went from dawn till dawn
of this our earth's last day.
And I, affrighted like the young
hare, trembled at his song.
He took me then and plucked me in
among the seed he sowed
and when I slept he walked again.
'Twas Death who sowed.

P.B.A.

LÜTFI ÖZKÖK (1923 —)

A cloud of dust

A cloud of dust gathered on my brow
The moss grew black on the rock of the days

305

My dreams melted in the dream
In this northern city my youth was erased

What happened to happiness? Now it is snowing
in the shade of my old poems
Days saturated with salt and a pale sky
are steaming over the streets of exile

Erased in this northern city
Answer me ye gods, sleepless with rain,
Why does he wind never catch fire
in this breast where homelessness pitched its camp

M.A.

HELMER LÅNG (1924 —)

To Arrabal

And if they handcuffed all the flowers
and if they put boots on all the blades of grass
and if they made machine-guns blacken all the walls
and if they put a knife into the eye of the only spy-hole
and if they forced a gag down his throat all the way down to the navel
and if they cut the tongue from the throat of the victim
and if they hung liberty with its head down
and kicked the stones out of its scrotum
and made the screw slowly slowly penetrate the soul's throat
to strangle the Word and tear out its breath

the flowers would shower their scent in desperate defiance
and the grass would grow through their boots like cross-bows
and the walls would flutter white with birds's wings
and the wounded eye shine inwards
and the mouth would spout the truth of the vision
and thousands of eyes bore new spy-holes through the walls
and the hanged men would deny the law of the body
and walk with their feet in the ceiling like flies
and the bloody bars would become a retina for new visions
and the hanging would be the execution of the hangman
liberty cries out if it cannot speak
the spirit of liberty wears no clothes
but it is like the breath
inseparable from the living man

the mushrooms of the nightmare grow in the prison's darkness
shiny like bulls' pricks (but edible)
the foolish virgins are constantly being violated
and still laugh at eternal innocence
the seven deadly sins parade like priests in ceremonial robes
handing out cowdung as consecration wafers
nettles sprout on the murderers' faces
and worms eat their way out through the asphalt of the eyes

306

but the dream of liberty grows like a water lily
a red water lily from the black mud
the man who was paralyzed by blows can again use his legs and rises up
the hanged man gets a new trial and rises
the prickless man gets an erection and rises
urine is pressed to wine
and the anthem of victory rings from the lacerated throat

M.A.

I am the fresh-fallen snow

I am the fresh-fallen snow.
Tramp your feet down deeper
the weight gets lighter and lighter
you will sing in me
I am no longer me
You are no longer you
we are both one
in a blazing grotto of snow

To fall softly
and become snow for you
to be totally consumed
and become fire for you
   heavy like fire
   hot like fire
   burning snow
   melting fire
for you!

R.L.

IVAR GRÜNTHAL (1924 –)

Epitaph

All that made music in the trees is silenced to bare
birches in a black and white truce,
even the longest detour failed us,
there was nowhere a golden life.

Falling leaves are a last decline,
divine grace is always too late,
let me reach out where the stars and the moon
and nature's wonders can never reach.

You were silent when I knew not how to act
but in the autumn night, almost black with darkness,
your gaze, my nightingale, is still a summer hue
although the southern rose has long since closed its eye.

M.A.

KERSTIN THORVALL (1925 —)

The dining-room of the Grand Hotel

The dining-room of the Grand Hotel is an ocean
dotted with white islands.
Shipwrecked grey-haired men
with their little shot of whiskey
and the latest sex murder in the evening rag.
Lonely men.
But tonight there's a dance
and the not so young girls
turn up with fresh hairsets and low cuts
and very modest demands
on the greyhaired gentlemen
at the white tables
at the Grand Hotel evening dance.

                                                        M.A. R.L.

ARNE LUNDGREN (1925 —)

After the collision

She was watching night after night
fighting the shadow by his side.
And then, suddenly, a bunch of carnations,
flowers of blood, a bundle of tampons,
the donor pale in his bed after the gift.

The head — a snowball; how innocently
hurled into unconsciousness!
The curtain no longer billowing.
Death is ready behind the rigid drapes.

                                                        M.A.

Eyes in the alley

The whites of the eyes roll over to
hunger, the stench and the putrefaction,
to the candle bits of the street vendors
and a smell of roasting meat —
O traveler through thought and space
cast your eye into the alley,
behold the image of the Lord:
yes, it is a human being, a child,
feet and skull of natural size,
the rest mummified (but not in a prison camp),
deformed by the diseases of malnutrition,
the skin taut over the chest of ribs,
knee-joints like those of a horse.
It's hardly worth while for death
to take over this body —
no, my child, stay in the alley where you are.

There is no food, no celebration,
it's not the Maharaja's birthday today.
The harsh smell of meat emanates
from a funeral pyre near by.
All is transfigured, your skin translucent,
there is no God but Allah
and hunger is his prophet.

M.A.

ÖSTEN SJÖSTRAND (1925 —)

This all too exposed heart

This all too exposed heart —
These eyes that have already seen too much —

Yes, night has thickened in my blood
I tear the amulet away from my breast!

I turn towards what I had not seen
towards what I shall never see

wherever I ascend these heights
where no streams or springs murmur ...

But you I found, you my dove
in the crevice, in the cliff's hiding-place —

And the mountain became a sea, heaving towards
the moon, a space traversed

by oblivion.

R.F.

Sideglance

Iron!
and eyes that perceive ...
Iron!
and a heart that apprehends ...
Iron —
and a yellow, a flame yellow dandelion
which alone weighs against a whole marshalling-yard
on this beam
where world and heart balance,
and which tips the scale ...

R.F.

SONJA ÅKESSON (1926 — 1977)

To be an infant

to be carried on the arms of daddies
as conversational bait for strange ladies

to cause obsessions
to be flung off cliffs

to be choked strangulated varnished
covered with yellow ointment
to be canned and consumed

they puke
(infants do)

they don't want to be laved in yellow ointment
they don't want to be varnished

(infants have to be varnished
all the unsightly cavities
must be varnished over)

infants must be re-modelled

the festival of the infants
is known as Xmas

that's when they burble so happily
over their little porridge bowls
that's when their blue eyes shine so blue
staring away at far away chimneys

then comes the time they aren't infants
they look down on the infants
on the infants' porridge bowls
they cover themselves with yellow ointment
they stare at their varnished knees

they swaddle the infants and varnish them
they sit over their porridge bowls
spreading the stuff on the infants
working it in
into all those awful unseemly cavities

                                                        A.H.

310

BJÖRN JULEN (1927 –)

The inhuman factor

Most of the accidents of our time
can be explained simply
by a reference to
the inhuman factor.
Somewhere backwards-upwards
in the hierarchy we glimpse through the clouds
the driving-belt jaws of the decision-maker.
Opening, closing a powerful
prestige mouth
for Yes or No — and two
paragraph eyes, almost obscured by the vertigo
of staring upwards, blinking their non-seeing
approval; the system works.

The outcome is always the same —
eviction, transferral, layoff,
shutting down the line, asphalting, and other
useful things down there
when our contemporary god of thunder with his goats of power
put the ill-starred principle
of the inhuman factor to work.

With thunder-claps of profitability.

M.A.

STAFFAN LARSSON (1927 –)

Bach the fisherman

Bach the fisherman
measures his fishing luck
in the silvery grey dawn. Farther
ever farther the melody stretches.

He lingers on, lost in his dreams.
— So much greater,
so much deeper ... Who knows
what the bottom hides?
The line, baited with musical notes
sways temptingly in the stream.
Dimly the tangled violin bows of the trees shadow
the silvery waters of the cembalo.

Then the god intervenes. Dangerous
is he who looks inward, the persistent
spy of the deep. — A wind
thins the mists, a shaft of steep
sunlight falls on the river, a bird fugue

rises to the sky.
Then he wakes up, Bach the fisherman,
and returns.

— Spots of sunlight round the bow
as the boat breasts the waves
with rhythmic oar strokes, nearing
the shore. The leaves dance, the day
sings, and the heart ...
Would you believe it, he is humming.

M.A. R.L.

LARS THUNBERG (1928 —)

Under the prism

Far out in gigantic space
where a bluish fire races
through the dark like a windmill
and the thorny bush is still unknown

a hammock of love is suspended
between invisible trees
like an impenetrable eel's net
to our space missiles.

And at its bottom there floats
an immense prism
which the invisible source of light
under the wings of darkness
is kissing incessantly.

M.A.

LARS FORSSELL (1928 —)

The Swedish summer

Do you know the country where the cannon blooms
and spreads its pollen all over the world?
Impregnates wars so that they burst open as scabs,
bleeding calyxes all over the world,
poppies like grenades?

Do you know the country? Do you know that country?
Do you know the country where the cannon blooms?

Her name is Sweden, if you didn't know, located by a lake,
and is mirrored nude in the surface of the water
or in a camera lense. She boasts readily
of her figure, of her buxom forms,
and of her welfare
that is based on cultivated cannons

that are grafted in Bofors, from which the summer wind
spreads destruction all over the world ...
The little country's welfare is based on destruction,
on pus yellow pollen from the cannons
by the shore of Bofors, glistening red
in the sunset all over the world.
That is the way that Sweden's law reads in the heat wave
that death brings bread.

Do you know the country where the cartridges bloom?
The cartridges that are fed in to rifles
with which others kill others
far beyond the lake — oily from herring shoals —
in which Sweden mirrors herself contentedly
far away far from the sound of a harp
in all the golden strings that are tossed over the cliffs
in Bofors ... Do you know the country?

So far far away that the bang
in the ears of those who voluptuously wallow
on the shores of the lake
and who are snapped in Expressen
with innocent-weighted breasts
in the summer, when according to an old tradition
the legionaries took the chance
and all the wars mushroomed and raced ...

Do you know the country where the cannon blooms
Do you know the country? Do you know that country?
Her name is Sweden, located by Bofors
and she basks herself in the sun
while Swedish steel bites abroad
and leaves the jaw marks of bullets
in the skin of others ...

The Swedish skin is being bitten on the thighs and the back
by a summer sun and mosquitoes.
A stranger runs doubled up and howling
while the Swedish sun burns richly.
Your sun of white-hot shrapnel
guarantees mine.

Do you know the country where the cannon blooms?
Do you know the country where the cartridges bloom?
Do you know the country? Do you know that country?
Her name is Sweden.

Expressen is a Stockholm evening tabloid.   *F.F.*

Van Gogh's ear

Van Gogh cuts off his ear
he wraps it in a towel

313

slowly turning red
and sends it
to you

What will you do with this token
of his love, his madness, his sorrow?
Will you scornfully throw it into the fire
or on to the rubbish heap?
Or will you furtively, perhaps with some pride, conceal it
in a little box?

You whispered something into it once
something you yourself have forgotten
but he remembered

It occurs to me
that the ear is still alive
responding
hearing eternally
the light of the cruel grain fields

and the roar of the inexorable sun.

N.J.A.

You say that poetry is dead

You say that poetry is dead
or at least dying
But then you forget, well-fed friend,
that it lives like you
as a neighbour to death
a half-flight down
in the darkness

The bricklayer sings
The carpenter sings
The cashier in the supermarket sings
Cabinet ministers and the opposition
and you and I and the grave-digger

Everyone sings for life
everyone shouts and sings for life
until the fellow a half-flight down
knocks on the ceiling with his cane!

F.F.

INGEMAR LECKIUS (1928 —)

The voyeurs of suffering

On TV we see those who starve. They don't see us.
Their eyes are lost in black space.

The appeals multiply! But we sink deeper down
in the big easy chair, the diving-bell of compassion.

Time has come to a stop for them out there and for us
who are sitting here glued to the peeping-hole of hell.
M.A.

LARS LUNDKVIST (1928 —)

Experience

Long wars often start quietly.
The number of dead is remarkably low
and he who lives in order to survive
can die fairly well-known,
especially in places with clayey soil.

But soon even the value of the dead decreases.
In the blasted cemeteries the corpses are mixed,
head by head, bone by bone.
M.A.

SEBASTIAN LYBECK (1929 —)

It is often true

It is often true
to say:
— I am the grain of sand
—I am close

— Look for me
and you will find me under your shoe
M.A.

No life

The ocean moves over the pebbles of the beach
mortally ill
The sail extinguished, the pennant
dead of drought
A feverish swell
under the dreaming keel

All about us doubles its weight
— the ocean's lead
the iron vomit of the coast
the ashes of the clouds

The eye fails
and the last white spark
dies

In a wordless swell
we, too, are broken down
into what life has lost

M.A.

MAJKEN JOHANSSON (1930 –)

Housecleaning wife

Vacuum heart inhaling,
straightening the corners out.
In a crease of the curtain, happy home misery
making its comments. The flowers are washed, the cat is hushed,
the husband in the easy chair is moved out,
crushed. In case we have guests.

At night by the fire
you suffer all the worries of others
brushing the spots off their clothes
and their clothes off their bodies
and their bodies off their bones
which are scrubbed so clean
that not a trace of decency
could lead them into hypocrisy.

Vacuum heart inhaling
with
swirling delight
the last remainder of bone-meal
from the circle of family friends.

M.A.

LENNART SJÖGREN (1930 –)

The people with bleeding stomachs

The people with bleeding stomachs go down to the water
and vomit up their blood there,
those who have tumors inside their body and outside
try to wash themselves clean,
the people with scars and acne. The people with the soul's eczema.
The people who itch intolerably at night
the people who have lost the light of their eyes
and are groping their way with a constant risk of falling
they go down there
and beg the water for dissolution.
There is sludge all round them
all the dirt they removed by washing
it's like the mouth of a sewer.
There must be one or two who still believe in the possibility
of a new life
the rest just ask for water — ask to become water.

M.A.

316

SIV WIDERBERG (1931 —)

The bedmate

The little spigot of skin
in its hiding place
down there inside
            between the soft fold
right above the slit
tickled in friendly delight
as my fingers found their way
to feel and pet

What luck
that no grown-ups
discovered my game
and made me quit
'cause I would have lost
a loyal bedmate
in the evenings before I fell asleep

                                        V.M.

Stamps

I collected stamps
Papa gave me a big bagful
I didn't collect stamps any more

                                        V.M.

GÖRAN PALM (1931 —)

The megaphone in poetry park

Beautiful words are fine. But make the rhythm firm. Enclose them.
Bad words? Just make the rhythm real soft. Let them glide in.
But nothing clear and direct. Remember, you are writing poetry.
Draw your breath, stop, hold your breath. Poetry is a compressor.
No, not everyday language — imagery. Are you a prose writer?
And for goodness' sakes don't stretch it. Maybe you're breathing
        between the lines?

Remember that you are writing poetry!
You're welcome to make experiments. Bring in something new, as
        Pound says.
The experimental tradition needs to be dusted off at regular intervals.
Your poem looks uncaressed? It revolts you? Well, stroke it the wrong
        way.
You want to think? Well, find a metaphor to hide your thought in.
We have any number of Santa Claus beards in this park.
You want to plead some cause? You'd better write a tract.
And you want to criticize?
You'd better become a columnist.
You're never going to stop? Well, why don't you write a short story or
        an epic poem?

You have an aim, an idea, a philosophy? Very good.
Poetry needs people who want to achieve something.
Only don't forget that by its very nature poetry has no aims.
And you feel that the dress you got is too small?
You feel that you can't "move" in it — is that right?
Did no one tell you that the costume of poetry is always one or two sizes
  too small?
You write too directly. Poetry is the art of being indirect.
You write for an audience. Poetry is the art of disengagement.
And you feel committed? You can't sleep until Algeria is free?
That's even better! Just don't forget to make your feelings impersonal.
Poetry needs people with strong feelings and strong self-control.
Dialogues? Just make sure they're monological.
Address? Only one person at a time (usually yourself).
Afraid of navel gazing? Call yourself Tom and you'll feel better.
And you have nothing to write about? Well, then write about that.
You are suspiciuous of poetry? That's something you can turn into
  excellent poetry.
Who was shouting as if he was writing a play? Lower your voice.
Remember that poetry is closely related to silence.
And you say you want to "use" poetry?
Wait till poetry has used you, then you will know better.
Your poetry is too open. Tighten it with irony and imagery.
But you are not ironical? Try being demoniac, or maybe sonnets.
Don't feel that it's necessary to be complicated.
Simplicity on several levels is just as effective. Like mysticism.
Concretizing is not necessary either, as long as you can *see* the
  abstractions.
Remember: you are writing poetry!
Build yourself an alley and die every cobblestone in your language.
You may choose both the color and the alley freely, quite freely,
as long as you choose well.
The meaning? You are asking for the meaning?
But poetry itself is the aim of poetry, did you not understand that?
Of course you have to identify with your poem,
become a megaphone yourself.
But I don't want any of this!
How's that? How did you get in here?
You must have gone wrong, this is Poetry Park. Get out!

                                                                    M.A.

NENAD ANDREJEVIC (1931 —)

Consolation

I can sing
and I can give someone
a smile.

I know what sin is,
but joy is not
a part of me
and my tramp verse.

                                    M.A.

318

TOMAS TRANSTRÖMER (1931 —)

The half-made heaven

Despair breaks its course.
Anxiety breaks its course.
The vulture breaks its flight.

Dazzling light pours forth —
even the ghosts take a gulp.

Our images, red-painted beasts
in the glacial cave, see day

Everything stares nakedly around.
We walk in the sun by the hundreds.

Each one is a half-open door
that leads to a room for all.

Unfathomable ground under us.

Water glitters between the trees.

The lake is a window into the earth.

                              M.Sw. L.S.

Allegro

I play Haydn after a black day
and feel a simple warmth in my hands.

The keyboard is willing. Mild hammers strike.
The sound is green, lively, tranquil.

The sound says that freedom exists,
that someone does not pay Caesar's tax.

I put my hands in my Haydn-pockets
and pretend to take a cool look at the world.

I hoist the Haydn-flag — it indicates:
"We won't surrender. But want peace."

Music is a glass house on the hillside
where stones fly, stones crash.

And the stones crash straight through glass,
but the house remains whole.

                              M.Sw. L.S.

Nocturne

I drive through a village at night, houses step forward
into the headlamps' stream — they are awake, and are thirsty.
Houses, barns, billboards, driverless vehicles — it is now
they clothe themselves with Life. — The population sleeps:

some in peaceful sleep, others with strained features
as if they were entered in hard training for eternity.
They dare not let go of everything even in deepest sleep.
They rest like lowered barriers while the mystery rides by.

Beyond the village the road runs along between firest trees.
And trees trees tramp in silent concord side by side.
They have a theatrical look, as if seen by firelight.
Every leaf distinct! They follow me all the way home.

I lie down ready for sleep, I see the queerest pictures
and signs that scrawl themselves behind my eyelids
on the dark's wall. In a slot between waking and dream
a very large envelope tries in vain to push itself through.

M.Sw. L.S.

The rocks

I hear the rocks which we threw
fall, glassy clear, through the years. In the valley
the confused acts of the moment
fly screaming from tree-top to tree-top, becoming silent
in thinner air than that of the moment, gliding
like swallows from mountain peak
to mountain peak until they
have reached the farthest plateaus
at the limits of existence. There
all our actions fall
glassy clear
to no bottom
but our own.   **M.A.**

BERTIL PETTERSSON (1932 —)

The curtains

The curtains have blown down
and shrouded me

Reality dissolves in water

Who is able to take away
not only the sins of the world
but the whole world

What nameless birds am I listening to

320

Suddenly life lies still
Here the present ends
Here the past begins

People coming down the drain-pipes
People streaming in the gutters
while the city's remnants of sound melt away

R.F.

In the beginning was the word

In the beginning was the word
and the word became many more

until at this moment
only silence
can bring paradise
from heart to heart

R.F.

LARS GUSTAFSON (1936 —)

The balloon travelers

Look at that tall man over there in the top hat.
He is leaning out, looking toward the west.
It is late morning, a resounding brightness.

The city with its clocks is waiting in the distance.
The points of the towers unwittingly cast blue shadows.
Everything is quite still. Something is about to happen.

At close quarters the balloon is huge, like a giant marrow
it shines and grows in many colors.
And the murmur of the onlookers: a swarm of bumble-bees.

They are shouting and waving to the travelers in the basket
who pretend not to see them, and remain silent about their goal.
They themselves are motionless and ready to start.

The man in the top hat is still looking and looking,
and he raises a tube of shining brass
as if he were looking for clouds or something invisible.

As they rise they will shrink to a small dot
until they reach the highest layers of air, and snow,
whitest snow, cooling and dazzling,

will fill the air they breathe, touch their brows.
In the autumn you can see it fall like frost,
the breath of the heights groping over the fields,

321

and some autumn, when the frost falls early,
you will suddenly remember them and their journey,
and how they are still rising vertiginously higher

through a thinner air than that of winter
with a sound like that of broken glass
from deep forests of brittlest rain,

and how they will rise ever higher through the years
until memory itself sings gently like glass
— and it becomes unbearable, forget me, believe something else!

A pleasure journey, an adventure for the connaisseur.
A gentleman over there in a light jacket and light blue waistcoat
slowly gives the sign with a gloved gesture.

It is free, already rising.
Imperceptibly the cheering recedes.

M.A. R.L.

GÖRAN TUNSTRÖM (1937 —)

Letter from a renegade

Tell my congregation, my treasure,
that I am now going for the life of the moles

because I am tired of your inner life
tired because it always leads to the same thing:

a forest edge in your brow, with trenches
and guns pointing to my secret city

Sure the brethren were fine worshipping purity
while stiffly walking to penance church

But tell them from me that that is their light
an eternal slide on the chute of their value judgments

You suspect me of being one who misses you
On the contrary: I had too much of everything

that was given to many who couldn't choose
And it's not I who am the problem, anyway

In my room you will find buckets
of pictures which I collected with my bag net

But they were not of me, they concerned a light
which I had been ordered to catch

That's why I have to go on a mole trip
although it hurts as much in Sunne as in Athens

in order to learn to see what my eyes are seeing
very close to me, in less spiritual regions

M.A. R.L.

BJÖRN HÅKANSSON (1937 —)

Marx in the U.S.

Here the heat is reserved for those who are already hot
and Venetian blinds for those who always have been able
to screen themselves off from the light when desired.

When desired, turkey is prepared for the well-fed. A feather
is offered to those who have overeaten so that they needn't
eat more before they have emptied themselves by vomiting.

Here everything serves man if he has the right dimensions.
Evrything else is unknown to the producers. They act
on orders from those who have the power to want.

It is the consumers who have the power to want. It is
the shortage that wnats if there are products to describe it.
Products are where the power is and money wields power.

Power is not absent. What happens here happens
nowhere else as in poetry and metaphysics.
Power shines and jingles. You can bite it.

And the sun exists for everything that can reflect light,
for jewelry and treasures, for peacock tails, for bosoms
with nipples, silver-plated as a proof of morality.

But those who freeze are already shadows. Those who are silent are non-
    existent.
A person who is empty without first vomiting is a sponger
on the social system, a shrunken tit that no one wants to see.

Before war comes. Suddnely they become visible. The shortage becomes
    a sun
and the light of the sun gilds their bodies. What perfect dimensions!
Let them describe war for us! Uncle Sam wants YOU, nigger!

Here everything serves freedom, but people have no choice.

F.F.

TORGNY LINDGREN (1938 —)

What it would be like to be Olof Palme

May I inform you:
I have no more visions.

Way back I could say to the home-owners:
your houses are not without foundations.
Dig your basements deeper,
reinforce your hobby rooms!
Your security will increase.

To those who were fettered to wheel chairs:
roll out of your circles!
There are wider circles.
Turn both the wheels, not just one!

To the workers and those who were worn out:
I understand you.
I too have read Marx
and the Statistical Yearbook.

To the immigrants, both the imaginary ones
and the real ones:
Please feel at home!
Try to imagine:
you are at home.

The deserters and the gypsies played in their bowers
under the spreading oaks of the summer vacations.
Wait! I'll soon be there
I, too, with my little bow
and the bowie knife dangling on my shorts.
We're all deserters.
Were all gypsies.

But as I mentioned earlier I now have to inform you:
I have no more visions,
no more summer vacation dreams.
                              (letter draft)

                                            M.A.

GÖRAN SONNEVI (1939 —)

Through the open door

          Just now a small, pregnant cat
     came into the room
     looked at me, went into the kitchen and
     then out again
     What if she gives birth there!
     In her stomach
     a mess of sleeping cat fetuses
     blind, with tousled
     licked hair She is looking
     for a place to give birth
     where no one
     can wash the kittens
     down the toilet

She is not afraid
she is used to people
There is no place here
and no security
Here the thinking head of a man
is trying to sort itself out
A head where
only a small part is active
The head is
almost infinitely large
in relation to the part
A ball of sleeping kittens!
Now came the image
of a very small child
lifting its heavy head
from the first time from the floor
and looking out the door

                                        M.A.

The small remainder in me

The small
remainder in me, that cannot be
reduced   It has
nothing to do
with ego, it is an
outer form, a shell
around a delightful, non-existing
fruit, that grows
on the nervous system's tree
But the remainder, that which is left when even
the fiction ego
is crushed, and the fruit-mass
flows, like water,
transparently, through the body's
limbs
The rhythm in the heart's beat
the frequencies in
the nervous system's cracklying forest
I don't know
it is unknowable
Even if I think I'm speaking
with my voice
it is that that's speaking
Even if I'm silent
Even if I stare in the mirror
at my most dead eyes
it is there
and cannot be reduced
We were together yesterday
You worked within me, with small,
hard movements
You got me so far, as I've never

been
I bit your arms
Breathed quickly, far away
you were
intensively present, and I
have never loved you so

The non-reduceable remainder
worked ever more quickly within me

                                                        B.K.-A.

GUNNAR HARDING (1940 —)

                    Love in the police quarters
                        in the dark the bloodstains
                            on the towel disappear
                                in the dark
                his hands shape
her body. her
                    hands his body
                            he has leather boots
                                & a huge baton
'if we put the light on
        we'd disappear'
                    he whispers
            clings fast
        to the dark. we
                    must say what
                            everyone says
                find the words
                    which won't betray us.now
                        everything is simpler
a car
passes outside the window
                            the headlights
                    wander over the walls
                illuminate the instruments of torture
            the portraits of the generals
                        now she sees
                    that he's dead. his face
                swaddled in white bandages
she begins gently winding off the bandages
                wincing against the strong
                interrogation light
                        and she says:
                                'not only the victims
                                must be identified
                                but also the executioners'
                    she is standing in profile
                        against the window
                    her eyes are filled
                    with tears.   *R.F.*

326

ILSE EDSTRÖM (1941 —)

Illusions

Cruel illusions
got me into
this room
happiness the door said
security was the name of the chair in there
the wallpaper seemed to mean warmth
the windows were dependable
lamps gave the light of fellowship

but one morning
I woke up
the room fell over me
I wanted to get out
couldn't find the door
then I took the chair
and smashed the windows
and jumped out
into the arms of uncertainty

M.A.

HANS EVERT RENE (1941 —)

Robert F. Kennedy

Where life is an approaching wind
and death is a departing wind

as at a twilight or a dawn
where the very light is missing.
As in an expectation
with the unbridled structure
of the world in equipoise.

Suspended in this vacuum
unruled by gravity
where the footsteps had lost their direction
and the struggle its victory.

In the muzzle of the threatening gun
this sudden turn
from the orgy of success
to the shadow of eclipse.

Where death is an approaching wind
and life a departing wind.

M.A.

The swallow

You streak like a flash across the field.
Tensing your wing in inexplicable motion
you rise; touch the sky and turn.
Like the first astronaut.
Fall; skirting the ground in a lightning moment.
Then rising again.
Merely to fall again.
A chance rhythm, innumerable curved lines.
Then you rest your small weight
on the tiny seat of the telephone wire.

                                            M.A.

Awakening

A day approaches.
Hours
with unsoiled minutes
turn over their leaves
rising to the ceiling of dawn
with the unnatural ease
of the seconds.

When the light breaks
I grasp the cup
to drink.
The wine inebriates me a little
and I want to dream a dream
where I could sleep
for ever.

                                M.A. C.R.

JAN MÅRTENSON (1944 —)

To love the President of the United States

To be able to love the President of the United States
I must dress him in grandfather's fur cap
and put the ticking gold watch
in his left vest pocket.
Thumb prints of his brown snuff
would show in the local rag
He would speak the dialect
and not be afraid of comrade Lenin.
If he opens the lid
of his worn suitcase
not one but millions
of men would rise
to take over his post.
To be able to love the President of the United States
he must consist of many
who are not like him.

He would clean the rest rooms
in the early morning factory
and mark the yellow lottery ticket
with a cross
at the entrance lodge.
Through the morning mist
he must grope his way
to the best blueberry patch
and return
with a full bag.
He must have a red mark on his brow
from the sweatband
of his Vega cap
and never be afraid
of a life on equal terms
with the rest of us.
If we are going to be able to love
the President of the United States
he must understand
the language we speak
in my home city of Tidaholm.

M.A.

Shadow play

People say I'm just
a shadow of myself.
But I'd rather be that
than a shadow of someone else.

M.A.

LARS NOREN (1944 —)

The first and last effort

Last night I knew once more
like so many times before
that if I just flapped my arms
even faster up and down
I would be able to fly
    Lord, what a ghastly joke

M.A.

JAQUES WERUP (1945 —)

Icarus still takes wing

Icarus still takes wing
he follows you as the stripes
of fear follow the tiger,
as the alphabet spells
the word Peace for man.

329

His optimistic flight
interrupts your speech
sticks like oblivion
to your babbling tongue, indeed,

whether his wings
were made of goatskin,
web, or bird's plumage
they are part of your body
and all its jerky movements,
everything in its passage
between beast and God, God and beast.

M.A.

YLVA EGGEHORN (1950 —)

Teresa

I'm sitting here calculating the costs
with your face before me
there are furrows in it
since you left the garden at Loreto
life has traveled through you
and left a salty taste on your lips
you are tired
and in your eyes there is a light
which cannot be hidden

on your shoulders you are carrying Christ
crucified
and you know no other way

... suddenly
my headache eases

St. Luke 14:28
St. John 12:25
1 Corinthians 2:2

M.A.

FINLAND — SUOMI

FINLAND

Poetry in the Swedish language

Since time immemorial part of the population of Finland has been Swedish-speaking. In our own day this element constitutes some 8% of the total population, living mostly in the northwest (Ostrobothnia). During the long period of history — from the 12th century until 1809 — when Finland was an integral part of the Swedish realm the literature written in Finland was, of course, part of national Swedish literature.

From 1809 until her independence in 1918 Finland was a Duchy under the Czar of Russia, and the Swedish-speaking population became a minority which had to struggle for the continued existence of its language. J.L. Runeberg, who was Swedish-speaking, became the national poet of the whole country; his national anthem was translated into Finnish, and is sung in Finland to the same tune in both languages (Our Land). The pressure on the Swedish minority was at times very strong, and gave rise to a number of fighting poems expressing a spiritual and moral defense of its language, culture, and identity.

To a nation — or language community — which is struggling for its existence the language becomes its foremost expression, and poetry a prime source of strength, worthy of defending and developing. This is the reason why the Swedish-language literature of Finland — and especially its poetry — is extremely rich, and can, during several epochs, well be compared with contemporary national Swedish literature although its population base in Finland was only about 300,000 persons. The love of home and native country which becomes evident in the Swedish poetry of the 1890s appears in Finland already a decade earlier with Karl A. Tavaststjerna.

In Finland the *fin-de-siècle* poets are also one step ahead of their contemporaries in Sweden: *Arvid Mörne* (1876 — 1946) and *Bertel Gripenberg* (1878 — 1947) had certainly experienced and been influenced by moods of fatigue and paralysis of the will, but commenced their struggle for their native country and their language with a change in the direction of action and optimism. Mörne, who made his debut in 1899, is also the first militant poet of socialism, long before the first ''proletarian'' authors appeared in Sweden.

In national Swedish histories of literature interest has often been

333

focused on the modernism which, mainly through *Edith Södergran* (1892 — 1923), and *Elmer Diktonius* (1896 — 1961) became very influential in the development of poetry in the Swedish language. These poets very soon acquired admirers and followers on both sides of the Gulf of Bothnia. Pär Lagerkvist had written expressionistic poetry earlier in Sweden, but beginning in 1922 *Gunnar Björling* (1887 — 1960) developed a very independent form of expressionism. In the words of Hans Ruin, his quick, suggestive lyrical essences were distilled from "mountains of manuscripts".Nothing like this happened in Sweden until the experimentation of the Forties. Among the other early modernists the sharpest profiles belong to the sensitive and ingenious poet *Rabbe Enckell* (1903 — 1974), in whose poetry "the joy of heightened sense impressions" prevails, and *Henry Parland* (1908 — 1930). While Enckell has been called "the apollinicist of modernism", Parland represents its irony, double-bottomed and self-critical.

Thomas Warburton (1918 —), best known as a superb interpreter of English literature, but also a prominent poet, has called the poetry of Edith Södergran "among the most powerful and liberating poetry ever written in Swedish." Something similar could be said of the poetry of *Solveig von Schoultz* (1907 —), one of the most virtuouse artists of the Swedish language, equally distinguished in her lyrical poetry with its unsentimental love of life, and in her short stories and novels, characterized by a sure sense of style and subtle psychological analyses.

Like Warburton, many other Finnish poets are also critics or professors of literature. Among these are *Ole Torvalds* (1916 —), who made his debut at the outbreak of World War II, and in Finland created poetry which corresponded to the poetry of defense and occupation in the other Nordic countries. *Nils-Börje Stormbom* (1925 —), eminent translator from Finnish and literary critic in Finland's most important Swedish-language newspaper Hufvudstadsbladet, belongs to this group. So does *Bo Carpelan* (1926 —), who received his doctoral degree for a dissertation on the poetry of Björling, and *Lars Hulдén* (1926 —), who is a professor at the University of Helsingfors, and has analyzed older poets such Bellman and Runeberg, mainly from a philological point of view.

In Sweden Carpelan, whose debut took place as early as 1946, has long appeared as the major Finnish poet after his modernistic precursors. In many ways he is a Finnish parallel to the critically analyzing and romantic traits in the Swedish Forties, but with a specially melodic diction somewhat reminiscent of Södergran, which has captured the ear of his audience. In Finland, however, Hulдén is probably the most widely read poet. His poetry is very close to everyday life, with both tender and flirtatious accents — sometimes in the manner of the old ballads, sometimes more like proverbs and wise sayings. A rich selection from the poetic production of Hulдén appeared in 1976 under the title of "Långdansen" ("Dancing hand in hand through the rooms") which further enhanced his popularity.

The most recent Finnish poetry in the Swedish language is many-facetted, and it is perhaps too early to pinpoint dominant tendencies or poets. Some poets have settled in Sweden, e.g. *Ulla Olin* (1920 —) and *Sebastian Lybeck* (1929 —). Among the most talented of those who live in Finland are *Gösta Ågren* (1936 —) and *Claes Andersson* (1937 —). Ågren is a peasant-worker poet who continues the tradition from Mörne,

334

but with a more direct and often rougher language. Andersson is also a critic of society, often subtle and ironic. In his attacks on weaknesses in Finland-Swedish society and conservative social patterns he also throws open windows to Europe and the rest of the world.

Helmer Lång
Helsingborg
Sweden

ARVID MÖRNE (1876 — 1946)

Before a runic stone

A thousand winters' snow blew round the stone.
A thousand springs their verdant leaves returned.
Erect, in all that changes unconcerned,
he stands, a talesman silent and alone.

The writing worn, the spirit mighty stands.
Still seas are thundering and tempests roar
their pride of men who traveled far of yore,
and vanished without trace in Eastern lands.

Shall once, when our millennial and free
defiant viking fleet that sunward raced,
and what we wrought, is ruthlessly effaced
like wakes of dragons on the endless sea,

shall a remembrance then on Swedish strands,
the last reflection of a splendor gone,
tell our adventures on a bauta stone:
''They vanished without trace in Eastern lands''?

M.A.

A boat in the bay

A lonely boat. A lonely man who steers,
and all around — an empty bay.
At the horizon some deserted isle
in solemn mirage. Autumn rules the day.

How paltry seems all human sorrow here,
how vast, how sacred sky and main!
A lonely boat. A lonely man who steers,
with nothing in the world to lose or gain.

M.A. J.H.

337

BERTEL GRIPENBERG (1878 — 1947)

Don Juan

The man who has slept his feverish sleep
in bed with every young maid,
his heart is adrift on a stream so deep
no power can come to his aid.
He left behind with each one of them
his highest and finest for toll,
and never one single woman's home
can hold his unhappy soul.

He pawned all his dreams and the glow of his heart
for hundreds of hands to acquire.
To bite every offered fruit was his art,
to bite with unceasing desire.
He learned no respect for measure and balance,
his yearning embraces all;
and never *one* woman could bring to silence
the many who send him their call.

He drifts down homeless on life's great stream,
the gleam of a myth on his brow,
and hundreds of hearts who wait in a dream
will ask who possess him now.
In vain, in vain — but farther away
from soothing and restful strands,
from coasts with waiting homes in the bay
he drifts toward fantastic lands.

M.A. J.H.

GUNNAR BJÖRLING (1887 — 1960)

I am a cup of longing

I am a cup of longing for all the body's longing
I am a morass where nothing sinks,
I am the style of pointed arches to him who rounded squareness
and earth offers me her prize.

L.F. C.A. M.A.

I set out to find the only word

I set out to find the only word
the only word which is the thousand words did I set out to find
the only word and all contained in all that drifted past in you and me
the only word is the thousand thousand words, and not stopping and not
    flying past.

L.F. C.A. M.A.

Charlie Chaplin

No one's
laugh from his mouth,
the great sorrow.
Look, Missus and the cop hot dog stand kid,
painting crazy eyes
with your feet
packed threefold in a packing-case sent
in the last railroad car
to a place for what will become of us.

L.F. C.A. M.A.

A child playing

A child playing with buttercups
its large head shapeless
like a sunflower.
Steps tottering
as with drunken men.
And he must play with everything, the broom
and the kind voices of the women.

E.W. M.A.

I do not write literature

I do not write literature, I seek my face and fingers,
I came like the shadow of my labor's joy,
I came like the longing for the great poem of life
and carried my poem
like a broken day,
like a day of life that flowed in new forms, rich and whole,
like the murmur of days together,
of people with whom I live.

P.B.

I want to live in a city

I want to live in a city just like it is
with a W.C., electric light, a gas stove
and well-swept streets
a rich man's park at every other corner
and palaces and cafes, with wealth on display in the windows,
and at five marks or two marks rectilinear
glory.
A sea of light and gaudy colors
and faces, destinies
and the light of heaven — irritating my thoughts and a struggle and
      fresh-kindled love
for one at a time

339

and for all, all!
to be like a herb in the spring meadow
to stand like a tree among trees
filling one's place like a brick among the bricks
of the building,
to know that thousands love and are happy and have worries
and that the same beautiful eyes smile tears and burn and suffocate,
    dream, stumble, and are destroyed
but are going to a land for all and to a heroic deed with bright
    perspectives.
— I am happy with the streets and factories of the cities
and there is beauty without and within.
The heavens and the waters remain the same
and the night is not so dark under the lamps round streets and waters.
The emptiness comes alive with the sound of the collected dancing,
    cries, despair, and solidarity with all the well-known things,
and loneliness is a destiny to be borne alone among a thousand eyes,
    and struggling in the teeming crowd
is like walking under the heavy vault of the forest
with the vault of the stars hidden in your heart.
The thundering roar of the cities — all of them!
the like and brother of all
and the struggle for thousands to thousands
and the struggle against all
and finally the eyes, many eyes
known,
not known,
which we carry as in a bowl
which must not be spilled.

                                                        M.A.

EDITH SÖDERGRAN (1892 — 1923)

The land that is not

I long for the land that is not
for all that is, I weary of desiring.
The moon is telling me in silvern runes
of the land that is not,
the land where all our wishes are wondrously fulfilled,
the land where all our shackles fall,
the land where our bleeding forehead cools
in the dew of the moon.
My life was a burning illusion.
But one thing I found and one thing I really gained —
the road to the land that is not.

In the land that is not
there walks my beloved with a glittering crown.
Who is my beloved? The night is dark
and the stars quiver in answer.
Who is my beloved? What is his name?

The heavens arch higher and higher
and a human being is drowned in endless mists
and knows no answer.
But a human being is nothing but certainty.
And it stretches its arms higher than all heavens.
And there comes an answer:
I am the one you love and will always love.

M.A.

The stars are teeming

The stars are rising! The stars are teeming. Wondrous night.
A thousand hands are lifting the veils from the face of the new age.
The new age looks down on the earth: a burning gaze.
Slowly madness runs in the hearts of men.

Golden madness embraces the threshold of men with the passion
     of young vines.
Men open their windows to a new yearning.
Men forget everything on earth to listen to a new voice singing up there.
Every star throws down its penny to the earth with a fearless hand:
     ringing coins!
From every star there emanates a contagion to all creation:
the new disease, the great happiness.

M.A.

The moon

How wonderful and unspeakable
is everything dead:
a dead leaf and a dead person
and the disc of the moon.
And all the flowers know of a secret,
and the forest preserves it.
It is that the circuit of the moon around our earth
is the course of death.
And the moon spins her wonderful web
which flowers love,
and the moon spins her fantastic net
round all that lives.
And the moon's sickle mows the flowers down
in late autumn nights,
and all the flowers wait for the moon's kiss
with endless longing.

E.W. M.A.

The foreign lands

My soul so loves the foreign lands
as if it had no home.

341

Afar stand the great stones
on which my thoughts are resting.
It was a stranger who wrote the wonderful words
on the hard slate that is my soul.
Day and night I lie thinking
of things that never happened.
My thirsty soul did once drink.

M.A.

There is no one in the world who has time

There is no one in the world who has time
but God alone.
And therefore all the flowers come to him
and the last of the flowers,
the Forget-me-not, asks him for higher lustre
in her blue eyes
and the ant asks him for greater strength
to grasp the straw.
And the bees ask him for a strong victorious song
among the purple roses.
And God is there in all connections.
When the old woman chanced to meet her cat at the well
and the cat its mistress
it was a great joy to them both
but greatest of all the joy that God had brought them together
and granted them this wonderful friendship
for fourteen years.

M.A.

The creators

My heart of iron will sing its song.
Force, and force
the sea of mankind,
shape, and shape
the great mass of mankind
to a joy for gods.
Swaying in loose saddles we come,
the unknown, light-hearted, strong.
Will the wind carry us on?
Like a mocking laugh our voices ring from afar, afar ...

M.A. C.E.

EVERT HULDEN (1895 —)

The lumber load

The lumber load swaying between the trees.
Worn forest road glimmering in moonlight.
From the depths of the forest comes the lumber.

The sweat of the horse has frozen to hoar-frost.
Clouds rise from his nostrils
like the steam of a locomotive.
The man sitting on top of the load
claps his frozen boots together.

The winter road winds across frozen moors
through open forest clearings
nearer and nearer to the village.

Cold stars are looking down.
Trees bent with their load of snow.
Blue shadows from trunk to trunk.

Now the glow of a friendly fire
from the first farm in the village.
The lumber load must sled down to the saw-mill
where the half-frozen rapids
sing their song of lonesomeness and night.

M.A. J.T. R.L.

Cot-Ant

Glittering snowdrifts in the cold February sun,
a keen north wind.
Low clouds of fine snow sweeping across the fields.

Cot-Ant tugs at a load of windfalls
which he has stolen somewhere.

He pulls his head down into his neck-marked sheepskin collar
and holds a torn mitt
to his nose against the cold.

With spear and shield the sun stalks
one tree-top farther north every morning.

The smoke rises from the cottage chimneys.

M.A. R.L.

ELMER DIKTONIUS (1896 — 1961)

A child in starlight

There is a child,
a new-born child —
a rosy, new-born child.

The child whimpers —
all children do.
And the mother takes the child to her breast.

343

Then it is quiet.
So is every child.

The roof is not over tight —
not all roofs are.
And the star puts
its silver muzzle through the chink
and steals up to the little one's head.
Stars like children.

And the mother looks up at the star
and understands —
all mothers understand
And presses her frightened baby
to her breast —
but the child sucks quietly in starlight:
all children suck in starlight.

It knows nothing yet about the cross:
no child does.

                                        M.A.

Granite

Petrified my veins,
all the atoms pressed into a rock,
barren, rough;
hot I was,
cold I am,
hardened,
no sun will melt me,
no cold will burst me,
many a drill point cracked against my armor,
there is no lever can lift me,
rock.

Granite.

But I want to rush out,
be a green forest.
I want to flame like northern lights
writhing in lightning paroxysms;
motion I would be,
mortal life of life,
not this contour attitude
between time and eternity.

The spring is weeping at my foot,
the dragon-fly has her seven-hour joy,
but I have but one mask
for all my passions.
It is slow
to live a granite life.

It is slow
to die a granite death.

I rage,
beat my forehead bloody,
tear my heart in agony,
raise my harsh cry:
hot I was,
cold I am,
I want, I want — !
But what avails it
granite.

M.A.

Dostoievski

A city.
An alley.
A beggar.
A whore.
Dark.
Wet.

This scabby mouth!
This ill-kempt hair!
This liquor-babbling voice!
Misery!
Oh — !

Then you come, silently.
You kiss that mouth.
You lay your hand on that hair.
You leave.
Silently.

The voice is stilled.
The sneer dies.
But I scream:
Why all this? —
Tomorrow brings no change.

But all is not unchanged.
There lives a memory of you,
your Christlike look,
your Christlike silence
in us all whom you caressed,
in us all whom you have kissed,
little brother.

M.A.

Was it a poem

Was it a poem I wrote?
I thought I exploded

and flung my shrapnel
at the world.
Of course I want also:
to sow unrest
breed discontent
prick the sluggish to howl —
but most of it was a 'must'.
My holiness:
that I was ablaze.

P.B.

RABBE ENCKELL (1903 — 1974)

In your soul

In your soul no sacred flames are burning.
No pageants wave their torches' gleaming fire,
no swords brandish their sharp edges.

A grey morning with thin mists
and a sunbeam coldly playing with a frog
which croaks her lonely sorrow in the bog
reign in your soul.

And the water that slept in
the white gown of the mist
puts its shimmering arms
along the coasts of the morning.

M.A.

The poverty that came to me

The poverty that came to me
in childhood's quiet years
is the treasure I hoard like a miser.

The slow-moving roads with their wheel-tracks,
the hay steaming on hurdles in the evening sun
and mist over the lake
hide what I scarce know I am missing,
hide my sense of loss itself.

O rich heirloom of poverty!
From the univocal heart of faithfulness
rose the star.
Constancy is its name.

C.E.T.

Spring sits behind a rock

Spring sits behind a rock
with snow in its shade.
He whistles with the stiff blade of grass in his mouth

so shrilly
that the wood-louse asks the ant what it is,
so shrilly
that the mosquitoes over the bog begin to dance!

M.A.

One can't find anything in life

One can't find anything in life
if one can't find the words
which are translucent
with what the spirit has in common with all and everything.
One can find nothing if one is not able to make oneself
a scoop-net which fits all the oceans and all the rivers.
In the connecting words I found a strong thread,
dipped in the wax of eternity — in the connecting words which grow
like the spider's web in the morning light:
its brittleness often tests the spider's patience
and it is beautiful only to him who sees,
but it supports the spider, its creator,
as the world supports God. What does it matter
if much is torn! It matters not!
as long as the thread supports its creator.
I found the waxed thread of eternity in the spider's web and in the
    connecting words,
which, dipped in my heart, did not break
even as it was bleeding its hottest blood.

M.A.

SOLVEIG von SCHOULTZ (1907 —)

The lovers

Round us thunder of universal night
where the hunter walked with resounding heels
and the dog with desolate barks,
where arrows were shooting from unknown planets
and where the black storm drowned all cries.

But we were resting on a bed of stars,
a bed of stars and feared nothing.
And as long as my face breathes its summer on your shoulder,
and as long as your hand rests its repletion on my hip,

as long as we listen inward with hidden eyes,
inward toward each other, no memories or longing,
as long as our smiles glide out together in the dark,
so long we are enclosed in our radiant confidence
and no evil befalls us.

M.A.

These

But these, O God, who are wandering eyes
and homeless smiles and babbling mouths,
these, whose limbs hang like lumps about them,
these bodies, oblivious of their dignity,
these lost ones, God, who remember not themselves,
who with every autumn lean closer to the black earth,
these who are shoveled out of life, manure for the future,
— say that you have a surprise in store for them,
that you are hiding their souls in the cup of your hand,
that you only desire the casket closed and the cage opened
before you gently permit your birds to fly out,
fairer from waiting, to their morning homes.

M.A.

The deaths

Wherever I walk there are only little deaths,
and I am weary of all the deaths.
Last May I died from a friend while the linden scent of the past
flowed like spilt honey in lamenting ruts.
In the city of July, while the rose leaves were falling,
I died from my children until we parted by morning
and my heart was unrecognizable, frozen, the size of a lentil.

Every hour I die from resolutions and memories,
they fill me with a bitter fragrance like rotting hay
while I am slowly, slowly gliding into new deaths.
Every autumn I die from the trees in a helpless farewell,
and each time for ever, I die from my years,
wherever I build a home a secret change takes place,
the water is imperceptibly cooled and the leaves of security grow yellow,
the future creeps like a shadow across the fields,
and while I am losing them I love unspeakably.

M.A.

Three sisters

A woman bent and lifted her child
and hair fell over her face
and inside her bent a little old woman
clear-eyed and dry
with trembling head
for her knitting
and inside her
bent a girl for her doll
with tender hands

three sisters
who would never see each other.

P.B.

348

HENRY PARLAND (1908 — 1930)

Gasoline

I am a great God
and I sell for 20 cents a gallon
and men kill each other
for my sake.

Whizz!
When the fire has kissed me
and the iron quivers with life!
Then
I know
why I lay dreaming
so long in the earth.

E.W. M.A.

EVA WICHMAN (1918 —)

Evening wind

I wake up with the evening
move the threads of the cobweb
put arms through the dead branches of dry trees,
slide over the waters
bend the back of the grass
steal moisture from meadow stalks
and hurry down the road.

Through the curtain meshes I come in
to you who are slumbering
wrapt in the velvet hue of dreams
— and gently, gently
I make you shudder.

M.A.

THOMAS WARBURTON (1918 —)

From: Sixteen hours
For K.

Outside
Waking, I hear
rain swish by on the windows.
Then I fall asleep again.

Vein in the earth
Through the dream wall
seeps a waking thought
like water in sand.

349

Mirror
That face
should be so familiar to one
— that is what one would most like to believe.

Resolve
Light steps.
So this is supposed to be
an uphill road.

Pretending
Reading papers,·
moving papers, writing,
looks like thinking.

Escape
In through the gate,
quickly up the stairs,
shut the door.

Arrival
Then I realize
that I would be outside everything
if you did not exist.

Self-satisfied
The best age:
the day lies open
but begins to close.

Commitment
The theatre-goers
acting like theatre-goers —
that's what the setting requires.

Intermission
Outside our stage
we quite consistently act
outsiders.

M.A

NILS—BÖRJE STORMBOM (1925 —)

We, too, were there

We, too, were there.
We, too, saw some particularly fertile fields
and asked how it was that they were so fertile.
The guide quite correctly informed us that an emperor
had 200 poets buried alive there. Only the heads
appeared above ground. Then he had the field harrowed, turned,
      and ploughed.
Then we went back to the city and enjoyed

many delicious variations of
Peking Duck. After the meal some of us
penned a few exquisite poems. Others expressed their dissatisfaction
that it was hard or almost impossible
to get hold of girls in the new kingdom
even if one paid quite well.

M.A.

BO CARPELAN (1926 —)

The boy who ran through the flowing water

The boy who ran through the flowing water
has disappeared into the mountain. He does not shout any more.
You may see yourself but you can't hear his voice.
And maybe you don't see him either in the summer twilight.
His mother is calling him.
Now all the flowers are brittle with frost.
It is the snow of winter falling on the other side of the mountain
and someone already expecting to see his image engraved in the
    mountain side.
It is the shadow of the unchanged landscape
where the birds of death raise their happy song
reminiscent of his voice.

M.A.

Listen

Listen,
in the silence
there is no silence:
the nails,
the wall.

M.A.

The ocean

The ocean,
a human dimension:
that of drowning.

M.A.

What the evening said

What the evening said,
all that was extinguished close to you,
the leaves that fell, you forgot.
The wind, greater than the birds,
carries you away

351

more easily than the words which say
that it is so.

M.A.

When the summer had precipitated its rain

When the summer had precipitated its rain as leaves
and the leaves too had fallen, and September had come,
I saw a bird sail over my head,
a shadow of me who am living on earth,
foreboding October, wordless, itself a song.

M.A.

Ski-ing trip

I have followed in the footsteps of my destiny,
the snow is drifting across the coarse sand,
you can't see the ice channel, not the years,
nor can the visible be seen, you see yourself,
the emptiness which is you in yourself,
in glimpses, poking your way
between left-over branches and poems
where not even the snow is sufficient for a rosy fire
in your soul at confirmation or in a dark December.

M.A.   J.T.   R.L.

When one drives up to the ninety-six octane pump

When one drives up to the ninety-six octane pump
there is always another car there, dirty, empty,
just standing there, the owner God knows where.
The number plate shows that he's from these parts.
At the self-service pump: nobody.
It's dirty and cold, neon lights here too,
and a deafening rock drill
excavating a hole for a new tank.

As one pays the bill one can also buy
soft candy, cassettes, pornographic magazines, contraceptives
and drive out into the dark landscape
with a full tank, oil changed, and a clear windshield
before anyone from the gang which is loitering outside
has time to grab the door, and, with a face
pale as paper, reeling shout something
which you don't quite get but are afraid of
or get boiling mad about later on
when you are alone on the road with the radio playing
wonderful, clear Vivaldi.

M.A.

LARS HULDEN (1926 —)

Come and be my quilt

Come and be my quilt.
I am the earth which is to be covered with snow.
;lie down softly over me, my snow.
Let your soft mouth meet mine.
Let your breasts be snowdrifts over my heart.
Which will keep it free from frost.
Let the silken insides of your thighs
slide down over the scrubby outsides of my thighs.
And let my good steed borrow your stable.
He has trotted a long, long way
and is standing with his nose to the door.

M.A.

A winter dragon

A winter dragon rolled over the city
His tail was rattling all the roofs
tongues licking in gateways and crevices
kept us in for days on end;
I played the harmonium in the living room
and read stories from the South Sea Islands.

When the dragon had made off
I went out and found
that the jackdaw coffee party had started,

that the big shots seemed unimpressed
in spite of the storm' bucketfuls over their heads,

that
the Polynesians hardly climbed
up their palm trees more elegantly
than the snow
on the windward side
of a Finnish pine.

M.A.

As the mistress of the house

As the mistress of the house gently
pulls her fresh baked bread from the oven
the forest puts forth
its shadow spade toward evening
lifting the hot farm
to cool off in the July night.

M.A.

Although the crow has been lying for hours

Although the crow has been lying for hours
on the road after it was run over and has become
quite flat

because the drivers didn't
take the trouble to swerve
and even aimed at it

the wind has not quite
given up hope
it gently caresses the crow's neck

or what was once a neck
(tiny feathers still wafting a little in the air)
and says with a soft but commanding voice:

Arise, arise!

M.A.

PER—HAKON PÅWALS (1928 —)

Salad-green mistress

I press the pedal with care
someone might bump into me
my salad-green mistress
stops soft as a cat
the light shows red

I look up through the windscreen
the sky is grey, a deep colour
beginning from the nervous system
in a window in a flat
a mummified head
an old person
by a flapping curtain

I see myself
in an anonymous future
the children grown up
and become strangers
my salad-green mistress scrap
and I myself
an old man with
prostate trouble

The lights turn amber
I press the pedal hard
to get there first

P.B.

PETER SANDELIN (1930 —)

There is no safe place here

there is no safe place here
no crossword puzzle where the squares stay put:
white squares change places with black squares
black squares change places with white

and no piano that keeps in tune:
black keys change into white keys
white keys change into black ones

M.A.

CAROLUS REIN (1935 —)

The city bells

The city bells, some rosy,
others golden, the shadow of evening
over seas of dead stone
wandering like a mother's cloud of worry,
the tigers of the earth are playing softly,
the darkness triumphs, before the end of the day
the bronze giants will capture, bind
the heart in its pillar of doom.

M.A. J.T.

GÖSTA ÅGREN (1936 —)

The factory worker

One August night
I was standing in my yard looking at the moon,
looking at the mists which were slowly dissolving,
and I was praying.
I knew that another night of frost this year too
would conquer me.

While I was standing there
the mists were consumed by the night, the moon became ever clearer
in her insistent light, the contours of the forest
appeared more and more inky black,
the setting of a deathly silent drama.

Now I already knew that the frost had won
and I leaned against the corner of my house
cursing and crying.

In the barn I finished a long-hidden

355

bottle of liquor …
All night I told my sorrow to the mare
and she consoled me with her strong presence. But
I knew the old one would soon have to be slaughtered.

That was the night when I became a factory worker.

M.A.

CLAES ANDERSSON (1937 —)

Gladiator

He crawls into his armor, gives gas
and gallops out from the city.

They approach him, cocksure, shiny.
He meets them with dimmed lights.

Zooms in on the vulnerable center. Then rising
in a triumphal arc, higher and higher.

Leaving only his armor to bleed to death
by the roadside.

M.A.

"The penetration of substances through semi-permeable films."

We're pressing against each other
hard harder
my wall hard against yours
hard your wall against mine

When our walls burst the light rushes in
Life rushes out
It's happening to us
It's happening to us in all directions
and at the same time

M.A. R.L.

ROBERT ALFTAN (1940 —)

Portion

my shoes have thick soles
my pants have pockets to clench my fists in
    but there's a button missing here and there
I have strained my brain to black and blue marks
and I have never danced with a rose
with my hot dog I use strong mustard
    and I turn down all eyelashes
I have downed life in the raw
    and without ice cubes

        M.A.

FINLAND

Poetry in the Finnish language

The poetry of Finland has long and deep roots. It has also been consi-
derably more important to the general cultural development of the
country than poetry in most other parts of Europe. The national revival
and the development of the Finnish language happened together with
the growth of Finnish poetry, often even under its inspiration and leader-
ship. In 19th century Finland the central events were not only political,
social, and economic; among them we must include also the publication
of Kalevala in 1835, as well as the contemporary poems of Runeberg.
For more than four hundred years literature in Finland has been
written in two languages, Finnish and Swedish. In administration and
legislation Swedish was long the dominant language. But during the
course of the 19th century the Finnish language began its forward
march, and at the close of the century Finnish had achieved equality with
Swedish as a medium of literary expression. Many of the most important
19th century authors, however, completed their life's work in Swedish,
e.g. *J. L. Runeberg* (1804 — 1877) and *Zachris Topelius* (1818 — 1898),
and even the foremost champion of the Finnish language, *J.V. Snellman*
(1806 — 1881). About 1900 it seemed as if the country was to have two
distinct literatures which would each go their own way; for a few decades
there was a tendency to regard Finno-Swedish literature as a part of the
literature of Sweden, and not of Finland. But after World War II it was
clearly understood that Finno-Swedish literature also belongs to the li-
terary treasure of Finland. Today Finno-Swedish and Finno-Finnish lite-
rature are very close to each other, both as regards style and subject-
matter.

                    *

The Finnish poetry of the early 20th century has its roots in a literary
movement which is often referred to as "national neo-romanticism". As
in several other European countries, the word "neo-romanticism" is
also used in Finland in very much the same sense as "symbolism" —
but in a particularly Finnish version with several elements from the
German *Jugendstil*. The attribute "national" in this connection implies

that poetry sought and found its dominant themes and metaphors in the landscape of the Finnish wilderness. In Finland European symbolism took on clearly national features — not only in literature, but also in music (Jean Sibelius), art (Akseli Gallen-Kallela), and architecture (Eliel Saarinen).

The great poet of national neo-romanticism was *Eino Leino* (1878 — 1926). In his poetry all that was in the air at the time is concentrated: individualism, tragic optimism, nietzscheanism, mysticism, and an expectation of something new which was already waiting behind the door. But he is at the same time — because of the political conflicts of the period — a powerful national poet, a patriot capable of giving expression to the deepest thoughts of the whole nation during the time of Czarist Russian oppression. In his style Leino follows European symbolism; in some of his creations, however, he makes use of the ancient Finnish Kalevala "runic meter". He also had important fellow poets who gave strong lyrical brilliance to the whole epoch: *Otto Manninen* (1872 — 1950), a very talented and many-sided translator, and *V.A. Koskenniemi* (1885 — 1962), who wrote pessimistic philosophical poems on cosmic or classical themes.

The early 20th century was a great period in Finnish literature, both in poetry and in prose.

*

"Open windows to Europe!" cried a new group of authors who appeared on the stage at the beginning of the Twenties, and represented the first literary generation of independent Finland. They adopted the name of *Tulenkantajat* (The Torch Bearers), and renewed poetry in the Finnish language much in the same way that the Swedish-language modernists in Finland had renewed poetry on their side: they wrote free verse, and rejected both fixed rhythms and rhyme; they wanted to modernize Finland without further ado, and criticized old, established national values as anachronisms. At first this group took their stylistic ideals from German expressionism, and also to some extent from the Swedish-language modernists in Finland. By comparison, however, the latter make a much more conscious and critical impression.

In the poetry of the *Tulenkantajat* group there were also elements of decorative exoticism and machine romanticism. Most of the important poets of the time belong to this generation, e.g. *Katri Vala* (1901 — 1944), *Olavi Paavolainen* (1903 — 1964), *P. Mustapää (Martti Haavio, 1899 — 1973), Lauri Viljanen* (1900 —), *Elina Vaara* (1903 — 1980), *Yrjö Jylhä*(1903 — 1956), *Mika Waltari*(1908 — 1980), *Arvi Kivimaa*(1904 —), and many others. Some of them abandoned the central stylistic ideal of the group and chose an individual path of their own, as e.g. *Uuno Kailas* (1901 — 1933), who soon approached a more symbolistic and classical style, and P. Mustapää, who wrote his best poetry after the end of World War II.

But there were other poets who moved farther away from the *Tulenkantajat* group, and who were not able to share the group's somewhat naive optimism and enthusiasm at everything new. The most important of these poets was *Aaro Hellaakoski* (1893 — 1952), who, together with P. Mustapää, was destined to play an important role in the poetry of the Forties, and *Kaarlo Sarkia* (1902 — 1945), the most refined postsymbolist in Finnish poetry, a master of melodic language and complicated rhyme schemes.

360

The poets of the 1930s chose more traditional paths than those of the previous decade, and wrote mainly rhythmically bound and rhymed poetry — e.g. *Saima Harmaja* (1913 — 1937), *Aale Tynni* (1913 —), and *Oiva Paloheimo* (1910 — 1973). But the same decade also saw the birth of a new group of poets, *Kiila* (The Wedge, 1936), which represented the political left and united its social radicalism with the free rhythms of the Twenties. Within this grouping appeared such important poets as *Arvo Turtiainen* (1904 — 1980), *Viljo Kajava* (1909 —), *Elvi Sinervo* (1912 —), and *Jarno Pennanen* (1906 — 1969). They continued to write after World War II, and many of them produced their best work during the Forties and Fifties.

*

The war was a period of great change also in Finnish literature. During the war years many new poets made their debut — e.g. *Eila Kivikk'aho* (1921 —), *Eeva-Liisa Manner* (1921 —), *Sirkka Selja* (1920 —), and *Anja Vammelvuo* (1921 —) — but the real rejuvenation had to wait for a younger generation. Of the older lyrical poets it was above all Aaro Hellaakoski, P. Mustapää, and Viljo Kajava that gave them important impulses. Recent foreign poetry also exercised a strong influence, hitherto relatively unknown in Finland. The prophets of the new generation were T.S. Eliot, Ezra Pound, Franz Kafka, and a few modern Swedish poets. This generation continued the work of the Swedish-language modernists in Finland — but without a very profound knowledge of that work! — and began to write without rhymes and firm rhythms, with powerful, often visual metaphors, and with a new, non-decorative language. Intellectual awareness, rejection of political ideologies, relativism, skepticism, and an effort to create an "unpoetical", precise style were hallmarks of this poetry.

The modernism of the Fifties never organized itself into a uniform group, but one may perhaps nevertheless speak of a "school". Some poets were quite far removed from this — e.g. *Lauri Viita* (1916 — 1965) and *Aila Meriluoto* (1924 —), but there were also poets of the older generation who adopted the new stylistic ideals (Eila Kivikk'aho, Eeva-Liisa Manner). There were poets who combined "old" and "new" elements, such as *Helvi Juvonen* (1919 — 1959), *Marja-Liisa Vartio* (1924 — 1966) or *Kirsi Kunnas* (1924 —), and some who became real pioneers and radical renewers — especially *Paavo Haavikko* (1931 —), the most many-sided and ingenious of them all. In his rich production he has manifested surprising inventive ability and created a very personal style with óriginal touches and original images, which unite with lightning rapidity historical events with today's social realities. *Lasse Heikkilä* (1925 — 1961), who was influenced by the Swedish Forties, and *Tuomas Anhava* (1927 —), who has certain affinities both with Anglo-Saxon poetry and the classical verse of Japan, and Eeva-Liisa Manner, who is probably the most widely read of the modernists of the Fifties. Some of these poets, such as Marja-Liisa Vartio and *Pentti Holappa* (1927 —) have later turned to prose.

*

The most recent Finnish poetry belongs, particularly in style, but also in general, to the wake of the modernism of the Fifties. One may say that *Mirkka Rekola* (1931 —) in some way continues the line of Helvi Juvonen, and that *Jyrki Pellinen* (1940 —) continues the linguistic experimentation of Paavo Haavikko. But there are also important exceptions, e.g. *Väinö Kirstinä* (1936 —), who has taken an interest in dadaism and French surrealism, and *Anselm Hollo* (1934 —), who, after a beginning as a Finnish poet and translator, has become an English-language poet in the U.S.A. The strongest profile among the younger poets is that of *Pentti Saarikoski* (1937 —). Saarikoski started as a precocious wonder child and brilliant translator (he translated i.a. Joyce's Ulysses) which soon opened up a new line in Finnish poetry in the early Sixties with spoken language political poems, using current items from the newspapers and the public debate of the day. Alongside of, and after,his poems, songs, and poems of protest poured forth in Finnish poetry, which during a few short years received many poems against the war in Vietnam, or reports about the oppression and injustice of the capitalist system.

However, toward the end of the Seventies this wave had subsided in favor of gentl'er and more soft-spoken poetry, which again uses motifs from Finnish nature, or takes a more profound interest in man's inner and individual experiences.

Kai Laitinen
Helsinki
Finland

OTTO MANNINEN (1872 — 1950)

The cotton rooter

The cotton grows for others' shirts,
I'm just a rooter, I.
I give the others joy
but inwardly I cry.

How beautiful the russet cloud
in the evening sun.
I used to have faith
but now my faith is gone.

The clouds are clouds, however
they may blush in gold.
Every wish is vain, its happiness
a story quickly told.

(U.M.) (T.S.K.) M.A.

EINO LEINO (1878 — 1926)

A legend of Finland

In days of yore (or so the legends say)
God and St. Peter passing on their way
o'er land and sea, when night was near at hand
touched on the shore of this, our blessed land.

They sat them down upon the sloping ground
where birch trees grow down to the quiet sound.
No sooner there, than Peter, who was wont
to argue, opened with this his taunt:

"O Lord, what land is this we've come upon!
What people rudely poor and bent with brawn!
Soil rocky, rugged with but scanty yields
of mushrooms and poor berries from the fields."

363

But in His quiet strength the Good Lord smiled,
"The land may neither fruitful be, nor mild;
cold and uninviting lies each farm,
but every heart is beautiful and warm."

Thus saying, the Good Lord smiled silently
and lo! a splendor spread o'er all the sea.
The marches dried, the wilderness was cowed
and frozen fields soon yielded to the plow.

God and St. Peter then did take their leave,
but it is said, "If on a summer eve
you sit beneath the birch, you still can see
God's smile move on the water — quietly."

R.I.

V.A. KOSKENNIEMI (1885 — 1962)

Behold, O my soul

Behold, O my soul, the sun's serene elevation
above the roofs and streets of the stony city,
above the lies of the centuries, bringing
all the pain of the coming light.

Behold, O my soul, the bliss of vanishing life!
It lies before you as an immense temple;
under its vaults the silent awe of infinity, the spirit of the master.

Behold, O my soul, in the night itself a light supreme,
in pain itself the peace and quiet of the darkest hours,
in the lies of the centuries, in the lie of life, the whitest, most eternal
    truth!

(U.M.) M.A.

The grave of a small child

Out of the night I came, into the night I traveled, and hardly saw
    the light.
        Of life's day I did not even see the dawn.

They did not want me in the world, and nor did I;
        chance was my beginning, chance my birth.

A strange, incessant rumble passes over my grave,
        hurrying steps, stumbling, rising, and stumbling again.

Wanderer, walking in the day of life, tell me:
    Whose steps are hurrying above me?

(U.M.) M.A.

364

AARO HELLAAKOSKI (1893 — 1952)

The painter

All day long I lived
the landscape,
with thirsty eyes I touched
the hills, the trees,
not till evening did I paint
the birch leaves.

P.B.

Forest moonlight

Under the sleepy branches of the night
there shines a mysterious light —

an enchanted path in the forest gloam
coming from nowhere, not leading home.

My body dissolved in moonbeams,
my shadow fled from me, it seems.

My steps hang loose in the air.
My hand touches emptiness there.

(U.M.) (T.S.K.) M.A.

P. MUSTAPÄÄ (1899 —)

Cornflowers

Tenderhearted?
We tough warriors?
Never!

But still in all, as we crept along,
as through the grain we crept along,
in our helmets, we plucked the flowers,
flowers, yes, cornflowers,
remembering our homes.
In the cornflower petals
shows the home sky blue,
deep blue,
and the fields' black loam,
the fields of home, of home.
When once from this war's agony
home we return, we'll see that sky,
we'll see that sky's deep blue
and the black fields of home.

And when the shrapnel whistles
and fighting is the heaviest
and down the ditch a short way off
your brother hero meets the test,
he falls among the flowers
 blue — — black
so deep
and between the heaven and the black earth
he finds sleep.

R.I.

Folk tale

I am still far away.

I will arrive tomorrow.
Hey, my pack, my laughing pack!
Hey, my friendly walking stick!
Tomorrow we shall arrive.

At a beautiful time.
Just when the old sexton opens the loft of the belfry.
Steam bath, Saturday steam bath.
The music of the round
sounds in the village.

I am still far away.
A mist, a wild wizard's mist
seeks the hollows, mounds, shadows,
groups of aspen trees.

Slippery rocks under foot,
stumps with staring eyes along the roadside.
Welcome to you,
welcome, I am a bridegroom,
the bridegroom of happiness.

And so wildly in love.

R.I.

UUNO KAILAS (1901 — 1933)

The house

My house rose overnight.
Who built it the Lord must name.
Did the black Axeman lend His might
to help in rearing the frame?

My house is cold and drear.
Its windows face the night.

Its chill and hopeless fire
casts a frozen light.

My house stands still and lonely,
no door for friend or guest.
My house has two doors only:
one to dreams — the other to death.

                                        R.I.

Stupid people and smart people

I'm laughing at the sun.
It's laughing too.

It's stupid to laugh at the sun.
Dad and mom and uncle and auntie
never laugh at it.
They're grown-ups, you know.
Grown-ups are smart.
Smart people can't see anything.
Smart people don't understand anything.
Smart people don't know the sun at all.

But I'm stupid
and I laugh at the sun.
You know, sun, I almost think
you're stupid too.
You and I are laughing at the smart ones.

                              (T.S.K.) M.A.

The word

In the beginning was the word.
Nothing else existed.
And it emanated from the Highest.

And the Almighty brought it
far into the primeval night.
Thus were created the earth, the ocean, and man.

And after its work of creation
it returned to the Father.
He always kept it on his lips.

But once in the middle of the night
the serpent, the spirit of deceit,
stole it and took it to the world.

And the creator of the universe —
now it was barren
when man raised it to his lips —

nothing but a clay whistle for children,
nothing but a broken chord,
nothing but a handful of sound under the heavens.

(T.S.K.) M.A.

KAARLO SARKIA (1902 — 1945)

Metamorphosis

You see a dragonfly
above the water on glittering wings
Emerald
its eyes, its body a golden needle.

But there is a slimy puddle —
look, the ugly creature,
muddy, horn-headed,
like a foul little dragon-foetus.

Like an evil dream in the puddle night
it kills and drinks the blood
until one day
it throws off the mask of its ugliness —

and you see a dragonfly
on beautiful, glittering wings.
Emerald
its eyes, its body a golden needle.

(U.M.) (T.S.K.) M.A.

Meeting

The rush and bustle of the street are gone. The heavens,
the deep, singing light came lapping over me.
From the stone's heart the glorious roses put out shoots.
Somewhere far away I left my misery.

Something immortal must have brushed by the black earth.
The song of the heavens possesses me.
Who am I? Longing for what? All forgotten.
In the street your dancing feet I see.

(U.M.) (T.S.K.) M.A.

KATRI VALA (1902 — 1944)

Flowering earth

The earth breathes with purple clusters of lilacs,
with the frost-like flowers of the mountain ash
and the crimson star-clusters of the lime tree.
Blue, white, golden flowers
wave in the meadows like a mad sea.

And the fragrance!
Sweeter than holy incense —
warm and trembling and drunkenly maddening —
the pagan breath of the earth.

Live, live, live!
Live life's high moment madly
with petals open to the utmost.
Live gorgeously flowering,
drunk with the fragrance of flowers and warmth of the sun —
fully, deliriously alive!

What then if death must come!
What if the rainbow glory trembles withered to the earth!

It has flowered once
and the sun has beamed
the great and burning love of heaven
straight to the heart of the flower,
straight to the quivering core of its being.

R.I.

Winter has come

Winter has come again —

If I were young
who knows but I might sing
of the earth's black bowl
filled with fresh flowers,
who knows but that the starry dew
would burnish my song on the dark blue meadow of night.

But frozen are the songs of youth.
My song is poor and weary
like an old woman
whose gnarled hands, blue with cold,
gather brushwood
for the fire of her leaky hut.

I cycle my hunger's orbit
bare and dreary as a prison yard.
My senses and thoughts are rough from work.

Winter has come
to scourge with his sharp whip the children of want.
But the logs blaze brightly
as a beacon fire.

R.I.

Blue flower

Who wanders singing under the palms?
Her breath fills with cool grace
the birds' nests and the flowers' hearts.
Has evening come with lovely footsteps?
Has evening touched with its blue flower
my heart that slept in the sun?

The bird has gone,
behind my hut tinkles a little silver bell,
and from the fallen jug
runs water ringing on the threshold stone.

P.B.

YRJÖ JYLHÄ (1903 — 1956)

Wounded

Stuck the knife into my side
and trembling fled from me.
Soon they'll come running to look
and could reach the attacker
if into the ditch I fall.
So I hold my breath
and lean against a wall.

My own knife. Almost the hand, too,
which took it from my belt
just to play — and thrust it
through my lungs.
The cause full well I know.
Like a rolling avalanche
above our heads I saw it grow.

Too weak to stand up any more.
Already my vision is blurred.
May the night and the dark protect
the one who is fleeing from me.
— Now my wound is bare
and kissing my knife's handle
I mumble the Lord's prayer.

(U.M.) (T.S.K.) M.A.

Wedding dance

Yours is the joy, mine is the sorrow.
I have a funeral, you go to marry.
So give me your hand as a bride
the last time that here I tarry.

I'm treading your wedding dance, but soon
the virgins of death
will take me to dance.
For your happiness' sake I'm leaving you now.
May the blessing of your eyes be mine.

Soon your dancing is over, soon you are old,
but you'll always see the youth that fled.
I go to marry the virgins of death —
yours is the funeral, I go to wed.

(U.M.) (T.S.K.) M.A.

ARVO TURTIAINEN (1904 —)

Spring

Spring jumped up on a branch.
The buds broke with a snap,
their eyes wide open.
Spring sang them a song
and they fell in love with spring.

But what does spring care about buds,
everybody loves the spring.
Spring ran out onto the meadow
and threw a swallow up into the air ...

it rose and rose,
twittering, twittering ...

Spring opened its arms
and like pearls and silver bands
songs flowed from the sky
into the arms of the spring.

(N.B.S.) M.A.

Salin

You work eight hours a day,
you sleep thirteen hours.
You use three hours to eat
and tell bedside stories about women.

When one says to you:
friend,
at least you ought to read something —
you're wasting your life,
you answer:
When you live like this
you have everything to yourself.

Salin, Salin,
is it for your sake
that we should change the world?

(N.B.S.) M.A.

VILJO KAJAVA (1909 —)

I am a guitar

I am a guitar
made from red, warm wood,
I am a wall
on which to smash the guitar.
I am the man
that smashes the guitar.

I am the event
where the guitar's red flame is extinguished,
I am the shape
above the event that momentarily flares up,
I am the silence
after the event
and I vanish there.

P.B.

OIVA PALOHEIMO (1910 —)

August night

The grain slumbers.
Silent are the trees.
Into the night mist rises
a pale sickle moon,
as from the deeps of heaven rises
a pale sickle moon.

A foggy fragrance
hovers over the earth.
The grasses breathe it softly
in their quiet dreams —
like ill, restless children
stirring in their dreams.

The wind sleeps.
Silent are the trees.
A solitary bird glides
across the August night,
as though the Creator's hand
stroked the August night.

The stroke of her wings
is a blessing.
The solitary, far-off bird
traces the bounds of the field,
as the far-off Almighty hand
traces the bounds of all.

The grain bows down.
The slender straws
bend under the golden weight,
a burden hard to bear,
as all things heavily
are a burden here below.

The region slumbers.
Silent are the trees.
On the water's trembling bosom
flickers the curved moon,
as though a harvest throng
sharpened its sickle there.

R.I.

ELVI SINERVO (1912 —)

Autumn day

The height of heaven is immeasurable,
and the cold autumn blue overhead.
The bird's flight goes slowly southward.
O freedom.

Only the wild longing of its farewell cry
is left in my ears
as the strokes of its wings fade into the twilight.
O freedom.

I turn away. The narrow prison circle
is my lot. The rest a dream
buried in snow with the coming of winter.

O freedom.

R.I.

LAURI VIITA (1916 — 1965)

Disease was dancing on the winter road

Disease was dancing on the winter road,
asked me if I had a greeting.
From where, I muttered.
Did you remember to call in at home?

373

I remembered, but I didn't go there.
There was dying there. Who was dying?
Each one died in his turn,
only you are alive.

And now you will be killing me too?
No, I'm not killing you;
who would mourn for you?
When I kill the wife of the house
I strike the husband at the same time,
soon I will give them all their orders.
You serve better
when you are not dead, just whimpering.

(U.M.) (T.S.K.) M.A.

Has the fly been killed yet?

Has the fly been killed yet?

Not yet, good wife.
First one must clean the table,
first the table, then the living-room.

Has the fly been killed yet?

Not yet, good wife.
First one must club the cattle,
knock down the barn.

Has the fly been killed yet?

Not yet, good wife.
First the well must be dry,
first the well, then the lake.

Has the fly been killed yet?

Not yet, good wife.
First one must enter the kingdom of death.
Then one will get good news:
now the fly has been killed.

(U.M.) (T.S.K.) M.A.

Happiness

Narrow path from well to door
grassed over,
before the window
a dried-up apple-tree.
Bag on nail by the door,
a bird's nest there.
When I am dead, when I am dead.
Summer will continue. Summer. *P.B.*

HELVI JUVONEN (1919 — 1959)

Bottom ice

My joy is bottom ice.
It will not melt.
Far beneath a vein of water,
inexhaustible,
the well shines
above my silver ice
clear as glass.

You see my ice.
Do not touch.
The water of the well
is cold.

Look.
You see the features of a human being,
your own
fine features.

                              (B.C.) M.A.

I give

From my heart's treasure
I proudly place in your hand
half of my life's riches.

I give you decades of sleeplessness
empty beyond endurance, and a contempt
which no words suffice to describe.

I give you all the scorched lands,
all the rocks, all the furrows in my cheeks,
the hard road like a wounding knife in my breast.

Too heavy the hand I put in yours.
I gave you all, and yet you tarry here.
Why is the upward slope I face so beautiful?
                              (B.C.) M.A.

EILA KIVIKK'AHO (1921 —)

The song to summer

I sing the summer of the wings.
Like the morning, the wind, the morning wind
blossoms the summer of the wings. Like the storm.
Beyond and above, far off,
opens the summer of the wings.

He who did not courageously follow

375

was
left to the autumn of the wings.
I sing the summer of the wings
when the great plain shrinks, the flight is checked,
when my seeing eye is closed by the autumn of the wings.

I sing the summer of the wings,
though my wing did not grow and carry me
from shy dreams to brave ones,
did not carry me
from the close to the distant,
from hesitation to goal.
Poor, I am broken by the autumn of the wings,
the dull sorrow of the wings.

And still a harvest ripened in the bud of the flight,
the song of summer, the summer of the strong wings.

(S.v.S.) M.A.

Peter

If I offered them something
they would not accept.

With stones they understood Stephen,
with mockery the crown of thorns,
with deaf ears the new message.

I would hear: mad (when the secret was revealed to me)
I would hear: evil (when I found the fountain of mildness)
and : dangerous (when I wanted to help)

I would rather despise myself,
my own pitiful fear.
In my own breast the cock crows,
crows contemptuously: already morning!
Crows contemptuously every morning,
crows as long as I live.

(S.v.S.) M.A.

EEVA-LIISA MANNER (1921 —)

Strontium

Scuttle
your world. Imagination has already done it.
The Venus wave circles like a betrothed scorpion round the globe —
just a sufficiently hot embrace,
and love, death resembling the tail feathers,
will destroy the rest.
The spores are floating through the air,
the cloud grows more intense and returns.
The cup of heaven is already full:

376

                    Nine destructions.
                    Eight terrors.
And the world wanders on
an empty buoy severed from its anchor
deceived, encircled by railroads, exchanged
for dreams whose core was sick,
heavier than lead.
                    No world
could stand a burden of such dreams.
How could a hand which loved flowers
give the world such a gift?

Empty hospitals Empty corridors Empty flues lost echoes
Empty mussels Who had glued his house
Empty leaves Empty glued-on letters
Empty clocks Time has left its home
The hours have moved off
all twelve soundless women
They have covered the windows of heaven and earth
they are watching in silence The houses would weep
if their cleft eyes
had the power to see:

The wires are hanging down over streets and roads,
the words have floated away like rainwater,
rails stick out, a streetcar
full of posters executed on a pole,
a bull pierced with the innocent side open.
Boston has floated off to the Japanese
where Warsaw and Viborg and Vienna
raise their sunset towers
there where my city
raises its peacock color
the streets are changing their patterns
in the streets there are poems like children
born out of the morning, playing with verbs

On the merry meadows
the blue-skirted children are no longer
romping rose-fingered
the confidants of the flowers
On the streets
no red hoops are playing
joy brings no news
the pigeons do not kiss
The trees do not bend
their fragrant burden
the wind cannot remember
purl my well
the shadows of the lovers
are not united
in the alleys of memory and oblivion
no one remembers

A tank has come to a stop in the field
The trench of the buttercup is growing
On the roof of the bunker fog-enveloped grass grows
like a lace to the emptiness

And turned around by the air pressure the radioactive families
stagger, empty bones,
a swollen corpse is swimming in the canal with its feet toward the sea,
the fighter fish has gotten himself a wife for his helmet
and is celebrating his wedding with glittering sides

On the dock lies an exhausted daily paper
with open wings
the ink fading:
Holland ist in Not
Holland gibt's nicht mehr
The corpse has reached its goal
The world has shaken off its illness

The Weltall rises, an enormous bat,
terrible, immeasurable wings,
the armies in its creases, a forest of spears,
fame and honor and religious pestilences.

Welt als Wille und Vorstellung
Die Welt als Wolle die Welt als Hölle und als Verstelltheit
A mammal with a wolf's face A huge squealer
tasted all the diseases collected all odors
spreading itself out
coming to the molten magma

And the stolen planet, disposed of by a lottery
between the great armies as earlier between the gods
divests itself of its beauty for the sake of a blind person.
The playing, dancing, singing animals,
the brilliant fishes and eager birds
are dying.

Barren waste. It is snowing on the mountains. The reeds do not
remember.

On the other side the stars are turning round.

(U.M.) M.A.

At the street corner

At the street corner they are already roasting chestnuts on a grill
if you buy a handful you can also warm up.

A hot chestnut, as if one were eating bread,
it serves as bread to many in this place.
The rattle of the wheels, the cries of the vendors,
the sharp, melodic urging of the donkey driver

as he moves the straw, old bits of sunshine
shaking from the straws along the road a brittle music.

The alley elm trees are brown, the reeds burned,
leaves fall, November news.
It is autumn. A sigh through the forest
from tree to tree; the tenderest are already stripping down.

(U.M.) M.A.

The trees are naked

The trees are naked.
Autumn
drives its misty horses to the river.

The dogs are barking far, far away.
Small carts leave the narrow gate
alone, without drivers, and disappear.

One says, That's how a ghost drives,
if the heart is sleeping under a holly tree.
But the ghosts are just memories.

Night comes early.
Soon it will be winter
deep and cold, like a well.

(U.M.) M.A.

A cup of tea

A shadow passed over me. A bird, a cloud
or the image of my dark desire?
Or something else ...without contours, full of content,
that which cannot be changed and does not come to terms,
that with which I sway to and fro, and in comparison with which
my own will is nothing but longing, brittle as the crust of a wound,
brittle, light as a tea strainer, as the weight of the leaves in the wind.

Will, show your mettle. A cup of tea
in the empty evening of the porch.
I light the lamp. The wick has burned.
I seek support. I ponder in the depth of the forest,
the movements of the night
make me tired.

(U.M.) M.A.

The women thought Christ risen

The women thought Christ risen
was a gardener.
There probably lingered round him the scent of flowers and
	fading leaves.
On his way to the earthen village he also appeared to others,

379

one said: It was he,
another: No, it was a gardener,

and the disciple prayed: "Stay with us,
evening comes fast, and the day is departing."
And he stayed and dined with him and they knew him.

But the gardener returned to the garden
and turned into a tree,
and the tree is no more, only a warm glow,
a very old, very tired glow.

(U.M.) M.A.

AILA MERILUOTO (1924 —)

Stone God

God, I will, I will, I will!
Begging, blaspheming, praying, I will!
Open your gates, open, open —
Open your eyes, Immoveable One!
See! A thousand loving mothers
screaming fling themselves to shelter their children
from crumbling walls and sagging ceilings.
The world is buried in grit and terror —
tears dig a wound into souls,
a deep and bitter lifelong wound ...
Shattering my fists, I will.

Who art Thou? Terror-struck I see Thee:
stony, immoveable head,
proud nostrils with no breath of life,
a stone mouth, two stony hands,
eyes — ah, mercy — not that —
empty and blind eyes like a grave —
Stone God, lacking life —
He is not, He is not the Savior.

I grasp your hands, sister and brother.
Mutely we rise from the ruins.
A desolate world, dark as a well.
Life and death are one and the same —
But still we rise from the ruins,
still we rise, stony power,
in our breasts a stony defiance and rage.
We arise only for the morrow,
mutely we rise, hard-visaged —
Stony-visaged, stony-breasted,
the image of our Stone God.

Long we had faith in a wakening dream.
Night fell with the awakening,
age-long darkness replaced the day,
God raised His stony visage.

But we grew with the darkness
ourselves stone, ourselves night,
on our shoulders truth like a granite block.
Stone God, Thou hast awakened us,
in Thy image Thou hast created us.
Cold we stand, until tomorrow.

R.I.

Wallis

A poem on Rilke's grave

Narrow long glass tipped
against the lips: O this wine;
full honey-gold of evening,
burning the surprised mouth
with Rhone's bitter green, and cooling
towards the sides to mountain ice.
O this trinity that pours forth
the fine bouquet of memory, threefold too:
once, now, never — or not like that,
shyer, wordless, a stranger to the senses.

That which remains, the final sediment,
that was higher, above the valley poetry
and beyond the iridescent colour — separate:
a bare husk on the mountain side,
a poet's grave,
windy, grey.

P.B.

MARJA-LIISA VARTIO (1924 — 1966)

Two moons

This was not water, it was heavier.
Like molten lead the black
was surging
with mounting waves.
And swimming there by my side with me
O white stallion
O snorting nostril
and his bridle glittered as he lifted his head.

The hands opened for a strong push
and the widening circles of the waves
were crowding each other
with sloping arcs.
So we were swimming under two full moons,
one of them purple,
the other silver.
The dull roar of the maelstrom could be heard.

(U.M.) (T.S.K.) M.A.

KIRSI KUNNAS (1924 —)

At my house is a difficult gate

At my house is a difficult gate
too small for the big one,
too big for the small one,
my own size.

In my house is a difficult yard
there were once, there will be
roses yesterday, pricks today
my own times.

Difficult the path to my house
too crooked for the right one,
too straight for the wrong one,
my own kind.

I think you were a chameleon,
I think you knew the sesame-time,
I think you found your own way:
you showed your eyes.

(U.M.) (T.S.K.) M.A. R.L.

The aspen has shed its leaves

The aspen has shed its leaves
to make the silence of the autumn complete.
Don't look at the silent aspen tree
its nakedness is bare, its peace
too naked
like a sacrifice,
arms with no blood, smooth as a young woman's,
     go into your homes and put the rake at the door,

its submission too blind
hard to look at, chilled to see,
colder than its eternal trembling.

Go into your houses and weep
the wind is on its way and the yellow beauty of the birches
will be shaken off
and the roads to the houses will be covered, invisible.

(U.M.) (T.S.K.) M.A

The landscape of love

The tree grew, the rose tree of the dream
and I myself was ground to dust under its roots
and up into the sky rocked the bird
sprung from the ball of my eye
out across the ocean.

(U.M.) (T.S.K.) M.A.

PENTTI HOLAPPA (1927 —)

Anthem to my country

You are red as the blood in the cups,
you are black: the century of despair,
a current in the bog with mud on its heart.

In the high heavens the stars disappear
darkened by the shadow of silence.
The farmer walks with heavy feet.
He knows: tomorrow is the fullness of time.

The homes like fungi in the landscape,
from their basements rises a cry.
The corpses rot in the churchyards
where the slippery moss thrives.

But, you farmer, and you, sick in the basement,
out of defiance like a winged arrow
a song to this country where we were born to anguish,
born to suffer like animals and leave everything,
knowing nothing, blind as beggars,
boil-eaten without brains.

Leaving the power of despair to the morrow
whose heavy dawn is closing in on us:
here's to our native country, here's to this country
which stores our shriveled dreams.

                                        (N.B.S.) M.A.

It's autumn

It's autumn, game time,
the blood-hounds with sensitive noses
streak along the edge of the moor
toward me
and with them banished memories.

At eventide
something is breathing
behind the closed door
and in the yard the grass breaks.
By these signs
I know the late guests,
they know me
and we know fear, it penetrates us.

                              (U.M.) (T.S.K.) M.A.

TUOMAS ANHAVA (1927 —)

Image of wind and trees

Were I a tree the blind earth
would slowly move in my veins.
Through the tree the earth blossoms in strong green
      to be made silvery by the wind
to be given a reddish shimmer by the spring wind,

on the hillsides the trees grow bent like wind
the crests of the forests in the plains, hard seas
bearing birds, echoing song, teeming squirrels:
the tree, tough, hard time, with the chronicle of the thrushes
      on their branches,
with the falcons' fortresses in their crowns,
owl thoughts in its interior, larva commentaries —

the tree, arrested, is a house, a chest, crossed wood, a wooden cross,
man comes and goes a while, comes and goes,
builds, burns; hastens time
and sinks among the roots:
rises with the patient earth in his veins
and the cones open to the wind.

                        (B.C.) M.A.

The stranger

I am a stranger here, I need information
but you speak of the weather,
you write: the trees are blossoming, the wind is resting —
trees are trees, flowers flowers, the wind wind and rest
takes place from nine at night until six in the morning,
and in spite of the fact that men resemble men and women women,
and woman was made to sweep the home, man the street,
I need a map,
who resembles the other, what follows what,
e.g. mothers resemble each other, children resemble each other,
why do the children here follow their mothers:
let the dead bury their dead, and bury those who are
      living alive
The heads, too, resemble each other, and the bodies,
but here the heads are joined to the body,
I must sort them out
so I won't lose my way.

                        (B.C.) M.A.

The conch

It came from beaches I have never seen,
where merely by raising your eye you forget
what exuberance is.

It was lifted from the ocean, it died.
The sluggish, quivering flesh shriveled,
algae and moss settled on it. It is an empty stone,
green and light blue,

but lifted from the sea, the voice of the sea
has eaten itself through the bone and its quivering
will not cease.

So the cold, sluggish flesh dried,
in wonder, without the contortions of pain,
and was removed, and the swaying algae, the moss
became slime, and was removed. Only something
of the voice was left; reality
and the years subsided, and dreams,
the unseen visions of the ocean,
surround the day.

(B.C.) M.A.

At dusk

A tired day looks with bloodshot eyes
over the iron-colored bay.
The green is black.

And the wave sends soundless ripples to the rock,
and the bird swims perfectly safe.
This is the night itself.

(U.M.) M.A.

The distant sounds grow more distant

The distant sounds grow more distant,
the near ones grow more close,
the wind places itself between the trees and the water.
The waves do not approach, do not move away,
the forest grows denser,
the night deepens from place to place into here.

(U.M.) M.A.

LASSE NUMMI (1928 —)

The letter

Roasting hot. Here, in the wall's crevices
the cricket plays.
The heat wave streets lie empty.
The market square silent.
The light dead.
The grass grows over the walls, covering them
with its billows. The heat corrodes
the gravel.

At night the moon shines the walls white,
memories ooze their way up the branches,
the cicada sings
in the shade. Sings what? Sings to whom?
At midnight the doors open: empty houses.
Silent doors.
Crazy shadows escape along the alleys.
The moonlight beats down on the deserted alleys.
Everything was quiet here after you left.

(U.M.) (T.S.K.) M.A.

MIRKKA REKOLA (1931 —)

You set the table

You set the table, now look at your hunger.
Half a loaf of bread, a glass of red wine.
Who could have brought the other half?
Let's be frank about our common meal:
mouthfuls of the same bread, half a glass of wine.
There's no one to look at here. Well, now.
Drink up your image and stop using first names.

M.A.

PAAVO HAAVIKKO (1931 —)

Scribe of life

Scribe of life, inscribe
the golden book.

I am the world's evening song, the cither,
a sculptor in the red marble of dreams,
the world's door-posts are burning,
a tar torch, smoking,
my face, Nero's face, my face is a mask
      if red
the northern forests weep blood,
the riding horses spatter fire over the world,
      if a red, empty
death's-head's mask, with eyes inebriated with molten lead,
and turning away like a mourning woman,
the world is lost
the darkness pierces, O darkness,
      I smile,
the face of the world's bearers crack open in smiles,
the god's, the emperor's, the actor's, Nero's faces
are turned away, I walk away from Cinotria,
shadows, mocking

(B.C.) M.A.

The pines are playing

The pines are playing, raining cones incessantly,
wood chopper's daughter
plain, rough as the mountains
and fertile, listen,
if you never loved, if I never
loved (your bitter word
at our parting), O listen,
cones from the pines are raining
incessantly, plentifully, over you
passionately.

(B.C.) M.A. R.L.

Let cool waters run through your mouth

Let cool waters run through your mouth
and think not of fear,
let cool waters run through your soul
which is filled with lucidity and fear and free
from worry

like limbs
in half-light, in desire and pain

let the water, the air and the elements pour over you
for this is your lot, O soul: death.

(B.C.) M.A. R.L.

From Native soil

When I tell you of the emperor you see him, the emperor, at the centre
    of this winter,
when I tell you of the emperor you see: it is winter, the emperor is alone,
the emperor, this image which becomes visible at dusk,
the emperor, this image,
dusk falls,
there is rubbish on the hillsides, an eagle's nest, the dense dryness of
    the branches,
and the emperor is alone and visible,
he is in his country palace which is cold in the winter,
he is the one you can see most clearly when dusk is falling, and thought,
the bird, the great horned owl, your blind thought sees the emperor
    even in the dark.

I have led you astray and you stand before a winter mountain
and through the branches you are trying to see the emperor who does not
    exist,
when you close your eyes you can see the emperor again in his palace
and the image is clear, the image of this emperor,

387

and I have led you astray, now open your eyes and do not listen to me,
the power of the empire is in your heart, there it is strong,
the empire rises and falls at the winking of an eye,
the empire rises and falls, now,
it falls when your eyes are opened.

(B.C.) M.A.

The Prince speaks

Most respectfully this nation holds on to the wind.
The people are standing at the gateway to Porvoo: Good day.

I said: Good day, my good Finn.
How's the porker? And the hens? And how's the wife?

I have studied to speak to the people in their own tongue,
but no people speaks,

Finnish is no language but a way of sitting at the end of the bench
                with your fur cap over your ears,
antiquated talk of rain and wind, the traditional banging of the fist on
                the table,

Sire, it's a language like that, you can't talk it
it's just a lot of babble without end,
and we're here for the sake of our sins now that March is turning
        to spring,
March is incredibly mild and its turning to spring.

Sire, say that such half-grown speech is fit for a sack,
the prince, if he is a prince, is a prince and poet, eats steak

and makes speeches and rocks his cradle like this, drinking bouillon
and scalding his mouth.

(U.M.) (T.S.K.) M.A.

I hear the rain waking

I hear the rain waking, but I miss the tears, should I hear the sobbing
        break out
I too would cry, I would not be alone.
The dream fades, the lights go on in the quintets, I can see through
        the dark,
the cranes are moving, their cry is a sound which penetrates the night,
they're flying, grey birds over nocturnal waters,
like a look,
Oh my dear,
you lean against the balustrade and see nothing,
you do not see that the birds have fled. The clouds roll out from the dark,
        the rain out of the dark,
the cranes are looking, are listening through the rain, they are flying,

toward the east, they hear the sobbing, the cranes, the royal birds,
and I knew that they know this sorrow.

(U.M.) (T.S.K.) M.A.

The books remain

The books remain when I, a bird, move from the world,
the books, difficult when moving,
are letters without an address, the wind tears at them,
and when the book has been read its leaves are leaves.

(U.M.) (T.S.K.) M.A.

VÄINÖ KIRSTINÄ (1936 —)

A slender throat

A slender throat
and the golden
copper tone of your hair.
And your breasts, the little beasts,
are sleeping.
Suddenly
we are a windmill with eight wings,
open shutters.
Eight shutters closed, one open,
one closed, eight open.
Double that:
two open, sixteen closed.

M.A.

The virgin

the palm of her hand holds a hotel
her arm fell off in the year this or that
and in her eyes one digs gold
her mouth is an abandoned lake
on her shoulders grow a short pine, a dwarf birch

between her breasts not a single city
between the mounds one or two villages have been planted
from between her legs rises the dead straight smoke of a factory
her thighs are a downy mother's face
her toes varnished, red granite

(T.S.K.) M.A.

389

PENTTI SAARIKOSKI (1937 —)

On that beautiful day when there was snow

On that beautiful day when there was snow
on the branches
this fat man begins to be impertinent.
He is Master of Marxism-Leninism.
With his hands crossed on his belly
he reads my verdict.
The sun and the light: I see them
upside down.

M.B.

Let's meet at the flower shop

Let's meet at the flower shop.
Give me your hand and we'll go in
to the wonderful scents.
I will buy you a flower and tell you to go
away from me,
away from being a witness to my sorrows.

M.B.

PENTTI SAARITSA (1941 —)

Theory

Now
it takes off
the landscape becomes a map
the houses shrink
humans
no longer distinguishable
only the wing
    remains close.

G.Dz. R.C.

SUGGESTIONS FOR FURTHER READING
about Scandinavian poetry 1900 — 1975.

The present volume is a panoramic anthology, intended to give a broad overview of developments in the Nordic poetry of this century. Many authors are presented, but they are not presented in depth. After the first orientation given in this book the reader may wish to acquaint himself more thoroughly with one or more of the poets. To assist him in this some suggestions for further reading are given below.

The addresses of the Scandinavian embassies in the United States and Great Britain, and of Scandinavian institutions which are ready to help the interested reader to obtain further information about Scandinavian poetry, are also listed here.

GENERAL

A useful general publication, which regularly prints Scandinavian poems in English translation, is The Scandinavian Review, American-Scandinavian Foundation, 127 East 73 Street, New York City, N.Y., U.S.A.

In the United States Scandinavian books may be obtained from The Swedish Book Nook, 235, East 81 Street, New York City, N.Y., U.S.A.

The musical scores, with guitar accompaniments, as well as the English and original language texts for the poems where the composer is indicated in the Table of Contents, may be found in *Scandinavian Songs and Ballads* (Anglo-American Center, 56500 Mullsjö, Sweden 1953. Fifth ed. 1979).

ICELAND

Icelandic Lyrics. Originals and translations. Ed. by Richard Beck. Reykjavík 1930.

The North American Book of Icelandic Verse. Translated by Watson Kirkconnel. New York 1930.

Icelandic Poems And Stories. Ed. by Richard Beck. New York 1943.

An Anthology of Icelandic Poetry. Ed. by Eiríkur Benedikz. Reykjavík 1950.

20th Century Scandinavian Poetry. Ed. by Martin Allwood. Reykjavík 1950.

Harp of the North. Poems by Einar Benediktsson. Translated by Frederic T. Wood. Charlottesville, Virginia 1955.

An Anthology of Icelandic Literature 1800 — 1950. Ed. by Loftur Bjarnason. Berkeley, California 1961.

An Anthology of Scandinavian Literature. From the Viking period to the twentieth century. Selected and edited by Hallberg Hallmundsson. London and New York 1965.

*Poems of Today.*From twenty-five Icelandic poets. Selected and translated by Alan Boucher. Reykjavík 1970.

Modern Poetry in Translation. Iceland issue. Translations by Sigurdur A. Magnússon. No. 30, 1977. London 1977.

Further information about poetry in Iceland may be obtained from:

The Icelandic Ministry of Culture. Hverfisgata 6, 101 Reykjavík, Iceland.

The Foreign Ministry of Iceland. Hverfisgata 115, 101 Reykjavík, Iceland.

The Cultural Council of Iceland. Skálholtsstíg 12, 101 Reykjavik, Iceland.

The Manuscript Institute of Iceland. Arnagardur, 101 Reykjavik, Iceland.

The Writers' Association of Iceland. Skólavördustíg 12, 101 Reykjavík, Iceland.

— and from the Cultural Attaches at the Embassies of Iceland:

Embassy of Iceland, 1, Eaton Terrace, London S.W.1, England.

Embassy of Iceland, 2022 Connecticut Aveenue, N.W. Washington D.C. 20008, U.S.A.

DENMARK

A Book of Danish Verse. Ed. by S. Foster Damon and Robert Hillyer. American-Scandinavian Foundation, New York 1922.

The Jutland Wind. Ed. by Robert Prescott Keigwin. Blackwell, Oxford, England 1944.

A Second Book of Danish Verse. Ed. by Charles Wharton Stork. American-Scandinavian Foundation, New York 1947.

Danish Writers, Vol. 53, No. 117. "Life and Letters", London 1947.

In Denmark I Was Born. A little book of Danish verse. Ed. by R.P. Keigwin. Copenhagen 1948.

Modern Danish Poems. Ed. by Knud Mogensen and Martin Allwood. Høst & Søn, Copenhagen 1949.

20th Century Scandinavian Poetry. Ed. by Martin Allwood. Gyldendal, Copenhagen 1950.

Scandinavian Songs and Ballads. Ed. by Martin Allwood. Anglo-American Center, Mullsjö, Sweden 1953.

The Penguin Book of Modern Verse Translation. Ed. by George Steiner. Penguin Books, Harmondsworth 1966.

Grooks by Piet Hein. 1 — 4, Doubleday, Garden City, N.Y. 1973.

Five Danish Poets. Translated by Robin Fulton. Lines Review No. 46. M.McDonald, Loan Head, Midlothian 1973.

Selected Poems by Benny Andersen. Princeton University Press, Princeton 1976.

The Late Day. By Ole Sarvig. Curbstone Press, Willimatic, Conn. 1976.

Selected Poems. By Klaus Rifbjerg. Curbstone Press, Willimatic, Conn. 1976.

Tête à Tête - Poems. By Jørgen Gustava Brandt. Curbstone Press, Willimatic, Conn. 1977.

Contemporary Danish Poetry. An anthology. Twayne Publishers, Boston 1977.

Critique of Silence. By Ivan Malinovski. Curbstone Press, Willimatic, Conn. 1977.

Selected Poems by Henrik Nordbrandt. Curbstone Press, Willimatic, Conn. 1978.

God's House. Poems by Henrik Nordbrandt. Curbstone Press, Willimatic, Conn. 1979.

Arctis. Selected Poems by William Heinesen. Thule Press, Scotland 1980.

Rocky Shores: An Anthology of Faroese Poetry. Translated by George Johnston. Wilfion Books, Paisley, Scotland 1981.

Further information about Danish poetry may be obtained from:

The Ministry of Foreign Affairs (Udenrigsministeriet), Asiatisk Plads 2, 1402 Copenhagen K.

The Ministry of Culture (Ministeriet for kulturelle anliggender) Nybrogade 2, 1203 Copenhagen, Denmark

Det Danske Selskab, 2, Kultorvet, 1125 Copenhagen K, Denmark.

The Danish Union of Authors (Dansk Forfatterforening), Nyhavn 21, 1051 Copenhagen K, Denmark.

Rithøvundafelag, Uppi á Horni, 3800 Hoyvik, The Faroe Islands.

Royal Danish Embassy, 3200, Whitehaven Street, N.W. Washington D.C. 20008, U.S.A.

Royal Danish Embassy, 55, Sloane Street, London S.W.1, England.

SAAME POETRY

Norway, Sweden, Finland

Snow flakes (Muottacalmit). Poems by Pedar Jalvi. 1915.
Gathering Storm (Koccam spalli). Poems by Aslak Guttorm. 1940.
The Lapps. By Björn Collinder. New York 1949.
Eleven. Debut 1966.(Elva. Debut 66). Lapp poems translated into Swedish and selected by Lars Bäckström. Stockholm 1966.
The Lapps in Sweden. By Israel Ruong. Svenska Institutet, Stockholm 1967.
About Yoiking (Om .jojkning). By Israel Ruong. Sveriges Radio, Stockholm 1969.
Gida ijat cuov'gadat (The Bright Nights of Spring). Poems by Nils-Aslak Valkeapää. Finland 1974.
Giela Giela (Snaring Language). Poems by Paulus Utsi. Privately publ. Porjus, Sweden 1975.
Jur'dagat ja sanit. Sámi divtat. (Thoughts and Words. Saame poems). Sweden 1975.
Lávlo vizar biello-cizas (Sing, Chirrup, Little Bird). Poems by Nils-Aslak Valkeapää. Kemi, Finland 1976.
Hilla (Glow). Saame poetry and prose translated into Swedish by Bo Lundmark. Almqvist & Wiksell, Stockholm 1978.
Giela Gielain (Snaring with Songs). Poems in Lapp and Swedish by Paulus Utsi. Porjus, Sweden 1980.

Further information about Saame (Lapp) poetry may be obtained from:

The Saame People's College (Samernas Folkhögskola), Jokkmokk, Sweden.
Samefolket (The Saame People). A Saame magazine. Editorial office: Regementsgatan 32, 83135 Östersund, Sweden.

NORWAY

Poems. By Sigbjørn Obstfelder. Blackwell, Oxford, England 1920.
Owls to Athens. Poems by Herman Wildenvey. Ed. by Joseph Ausland-
der. Dodd, Mead and Co., New York 1935.
Anthology of Norwegian Lyrics. Translated by Charles Wharton Stork.
Princeton University Press, Princeton 1942.
The Spirit of Norway. Translated by G.M. Gathorne-Hardy. Royal Nor-
wegian Information Service. London, England 1944.
All That Is Mine Demand. By Nordahl Grieg. Hodder & Stoughton,
London, England 1944.
Televaag. By Sigmund Skard. Royal Information Service. London, Eng-
land 1945.
Modern Norwegian Poems. Ed. Inga Wilhelmsen Allwood. Bonniers,
New York 1949.
20th Century Scandinavian Poetry. Ed. by Martin Allwood. Gyldendal,
Oslo 1950.
A Little Treasury of World Poetry. Ed. by Hubert Creekmore. Charles
Scribner's and Sons, New York 1952.
Scandinavian Songs and Ballads. Ed. by Martin Allwood. Anglo-Ameri-
can Center, Mullsjö, Sweden 1953.
Five Norwegian Poets. Lines Review, Nos. 55—56. Ed. Robin Fulton.
M. McDonald, Lion Head, Midlothian 1976.
*Olav Hauge.*Poems translated by Robin Fulton. Scandinavian Review,
New York 1980.

Further information about Norwegian poetry may be obtained from:

Det Kongelige Utenriksdepartement, 7. Juni Plass 1, Oslo 1, Norway.
Norsk Kulturråd, Rosenkrantzgaten 11, Oslo 1, Norway.
Den norske forfatterforening, Radhusgata 7, Oslo 1, Norway.

Royal Norwegian Embassy, 2720, 34th Street, N.W., Washington D.C.,
U.S.A.
Royal Norwegian Embassy, 25, Belgrave Square , London S.W. 1, Eng-
land.

SWEDEN

Anthology of Swedish Lyrics 1750 — 1925. American-Scandinavian
Foundation, New York 1930.
Modern Swedish Poetry. Ed. Charles D. Locock. H & W. Brown. London
1936.
Arcadia Borealis. Ed. Charles Wharton Stork. University of Minnesota
Press. Minneapolis 1938.
Charcoal-Burner's Ballads and Other Poems. Translated by Caroline
Schleef. The Fine Editions Press, New York 1943.
Modern Swedish Poems. Ed. Martin Allwood. Augustana Book Concern,
Rock Island 1948.
Swedish Songs and Ballads. Ed. by Martin Allwood and Lindsay Lafford.
Bonniers, New York 1950.
20th Century Scandinavian Poetry. Ed. by Martin Allwood. Kooperativa
Förbundet, Stockholm 1950.
A Little Treasury of World Poetry. Ed. by Hubert Creekmore. Charles
Scribner's Sons, New York 1952.
Scandinavian Songs and Ballads. Ed. by Martin Allwood. Anglo-Ameri-
can Center, Mullsjö, Sweden 1953.
Eight Swedish Poets. Ed. and translated by Frederic Fleisher. Cavefors,
Lund, Sweden 1963.
Selected Poems of Gunnar Ekelöf. Translated by Muriel Rukeyser and
Leif Sjöberg. Twayne Publishers, New York 1967.
Micromegas. Swedish issue. University of Iowa, Iowa City 1969.
Three Swedish Poets. Lines Review No. 35. Ed. by Robin Fulton. M. Mc-
Donald, Loan Head, Midlothian 1970.
Selected Poems by Gunnar Ekelöf. Translated by W.H. Auden and Leif
Sjöberg. Penguin Books, Harmondsworth 1971.
Poems. By Hans Evert René. Translated by Charles Richards and Martin
Allwood. Anglo-American Center, Mullsjö, Sweden 1971.
Lotus Lona. Poems by Margareta Lind. Translated by Martin Allwood.
Anglo-American Center, Mullsjö, Sweden 1971.
Poems. By Helge Jedenberg. Translated by Charles Richards and Mar-
tin Allwood. Anglo-American center, Mullsjö, Sweden 1971.
Carvings. Poems by Sten Hagliden. Translated by Charles Richards and
Martin Allwood. Anglo-American Center, Mullsjö, Sweden 1971.
Dialogue With The Unseen. Poems by Helmer V. Nyberg. Translated by
Keth Laycock and Martin Allwood. Anglo-American Center, Mull-
sjö, Sweden 1971.

397

Meeting Ground. Poems by Ulla Olin. Translated by Martin Allwood. Anglo-American Center, Mullsjö, Sweden 1971.

The Gateway of The Senses. Poems by Inga-Britt Ranemark. Translated by Martin Allwood. Anglo-American Center, Mullsjö, Sweden 1971.

Five Swedish Poets. Translated by Robin Fulton. Spirit, Summer 1972. Seton Hall University, South Orange, N.J. 1972.

Lars Gustafsson. Selected Poems. Translated by Robin Fulton. New Rivers Press, New York 1972.

Water Colors. Poems by Maj Larsson. Translated by Martin Allwood. Anglo-American Center, Mullsjö, Sweden 1972.

Unexpected Image. Poems by Lennart Dahl. Translated by Robert Lyng, Martin Allwood, and Gerry Balding. Anglo-American Center, Mullsjö, Sweden 1972.

Windows and Stones. Poems by Tomas Tranströmer. Translated by May Swenson and Leif Sjöberg. University of Pittsburgh Press, Pittsburgh 1972.

Eleven Swedish Poets. International Poetry Forum. Mundus Artium 1973. Pittsburgh 1973.

Bad Words Feel So Good. Poems by Kerstin Thorvall. Translated by Martin Allwood, Robert Lyng, David Bickel, and Charles Richards. Anglo-American Center, Mullsjö, Sweden 1973.

Between The Lines. Poems by Alf Henrikson. Translated by Charles Richards and Martin Allwood. Anglo-American Center, Mullsjö, Sweden 1973.

The Square Moon. Poems by Karl Bolay. Translated by Martin Allwood. Anglo-American Center, Mullsjö, Sweden 1973.

In This Well-Known Season. Poems by Bertil Pettersson. Translated by Robin Fulton. Anglo-American Center, Mullsjö, Sweden, 1973.

They Killed Sitting Bull And Other Poems. By Gunnar Harding. Translated by Robin Fulton. London Magazine Editions, London 1973.

Selected Poems by Tomas Tranströmer. Translated by Robin Fulton. Penguin Books, London 1974.

The Hidden Music. Selected poems by Östen Sjöstrand. Translated by Robin Fulton. Oleander Press, London and New York 1975.

Friends, You Drank Some Darkness. Gunnar Ekelöf, Harry Martinson, and Tomas Tranströmer. Tr. by R. Bly. Beacon, Boston 1975.

Selected Poems by Werner Aspenström. Translated by Robin Fulton. Oasis Books, London 1976.

Who Lives In The Light? Poems by Ingeborg Lagerblad. Translated by Martin Allwood. Eremit-Press, Viken, Sweden 1978.

Further information about Sweden may be obtained from:

The Swedish Institute (Svenska Institutet), Box 7434, S—103 91 Stockholm, Sweden.

The Swedish Union of Authors (Sveriges Författarförbund), Box 5252, 102 45 Stockholm, Sweden.

The Cultural Council of Sweden (Statens Kulturråd), Box 7843, 103 98 Stockholm, Sweden.

Royal Swedish Embassy, Suite 2000, Watergate Six Hundred, 600 New Hampshire Avenue N.W., Washington D.C 200 37, U.S.A.

Royal Swedish Embassy, 23, North Row, London W.1, Great Britain.

FINLAND

Voices From Finland. Ed. by Elli Tompuri. Sanoma. Helsinki 1947.
Modern Swedish Poems. Ed. by Martin Allwood. Augustana Book Concern. Rock Island, U.S.A. 1948.
20th Century Scandinavian Poetry. Ed. by Martin Allwood. Söderströms förlag, Helsinki 1950.
A Little Treasury of World Poetry. Ed. by Hubert Creekmore. Charles Scribner's Sons, New York 1952.
Finnish Literary Reader. Indiana University Publications, Uralic and Altaic Series, Vol. 44. Bloomington, Ind., U.s.a.
Poetry of the Committed Individual. Ed. by John Silkin. Penguin Books, Harmondsworth, England 1973.
Snow in May: An Anthology of Finnish Writing 1945 — 1972. Associated University Presses, Cranbury, N.J. 1980.
The Collected Poems of Edith Södergran. Translated into English by Martin Allwood. Preface by Helmer Lång. The Swedish Book Nook, New York 1980.

Further information about Finnish poetry may be obtained from:

The Ministry of Education (Undervisningsministeriet, Avd. för internationella ärenden), Fredsgatan 4, Helsinki, Finland.
The Finnish Union of Authors (Suomen Kirjailijalitto), Runebergsgatan 32 C 28, Helsinki, Finland.
The Finnish Union of Swedish-speaking Authors (Finlands Svenska Författareförening), Runebergsgatan 32 C 27, Helsingfors, Finland.
The Finnish Literature Information Centre. Hallituskatu 1, Helsinki, Finland.

Embassy of Finland, 1900, 24th Street, N.W., Washington D.C. 20008, U.S.A.
Embassy of Finland, 38, Chesham Place, London S.W.1, England.